SIMPSON·BAY

YACHT · CLUB
MARINA

Airport Road, St. Maarten N.A. • Phone 5995-43378 • Fax 5995-43446

Simpson Bay Yacht Club is designed to satisfy every need of todays yachtsman and sailor. Beyond the neccessities of running fresh water, power, Cable TV, telephone and banking, Simpson Bay Yacht Club offers the protection of Simpson Bay Lagoon and a brand new Shopping Center with Luxurious Condominiums, Restaurants, etc.

VIP CRUISING GUIDE
ST. MAARTEN/ST. MARTIN AREA
TO ANTIGUA & BARBUDA

FORMERLY ST. MAARTEN/ST. MARTIN AREA + ST. KITTS & NEVIS
CRUISING GUIDE

ST. MAARTEN/ST. MARTIN, ANGUILLA
ST. BARTS (ST. BARTHELEMY), SABA, STATIA
ST. KITTS, NEVIS, ANTIGUA & BARBUDA

William J. Eiman, Editor

We are pleased to add Antigua and Barbuda to this Sixth Edition of our Cruising Guide to keep pace with the expanding interests and ambitions of yachtsmen cruising the Leeward Islands. The 100-odd mile area from Anguilla to Antigua includes seven major islands that provide an extraordinary diversity of cruising pleasures and international flavors that have few, if any, equals anywhere in the world. It is ideal for yachtsmen who enjoy exhilarating tradewind cruising in near perfect surroundings.

Since the First Edition of our guide was published in 1980, the islands we cover have experienced many significant changes as they have attracted ever-increasing numbers of sailors and land based vacationers. Keeping up with the rapid growth and development of the area to give yachtsmen reliable, current, comprehensive information so that they can cruise among these wonderful islands in safety and comfort has been a challenge and a pleasure. I do wish to express special thanks to those who have made major contributions to this effort throughout the years: Malcolm Maidwell, Barry Loeckler, Tim Short, Jeannie and Mike Kuich, Martin Court, Jerry Rosen, Ellie Dormoy, Bill Bowers, Hilary Wattley, Colin Pereira, Jim Anderson, Robbie Ferron, Martin Challis, Val Crocker, Don Walsh, LouLou Magras, and Ed DiRomaldo.

This Sixth Edition could not have been completed without the help and enthusiastic support of many individuals. I am particularly indebted to the following people who have provided invaluable information, advice, assistance and special talents:

JOL BYERLEY	**SIMON MANLEY**
ELLIE DORMOY	**IAN MACPHEARSON**
ROB DONALD	**GAY NICHOLS**
JOHN EIMAN	**JULIE NICHOLSON**
GRAFTON	**DAVID SIMMONDS**
DEREK LITTLE	**IAN THRING**
DAN LOVE	**WILLIAM THOMAS**

William J. Eiman
239 Delancey Street
Philadelphia, PA 19106

November, 1992

Opposite page - West Coast of Antigua; *Derek Little photo*

Published by
Virgin Island Plus Yacht Charters, Inc.
239 Delancey Street
Philadelphia, PA 19106
(215) 627-3238

This guide has been prepared to assist charterers, cruising sailors, and others plan safe and pleasant cruising in the waters of St. Maarten/St. Martin, Anguilla, St. Barts, Saba, Statia, St. Kitts, Nevis, Antigua, and Barbuda. It is based on the personal experience and knowledge of many contributors and on information from a wide variety of official and private sources. Although extensive efforts have been made to insure the accuracy of this guide, the Publisher cautions all readers and users that the information contained herein cannot be guaranteed and must be used with caution. **The Publisher makes no warranty, express or implied, of merchantability or fitness for a particular purpose.**

This guide is not a substitute for official charts, Sailing Directions, Pilots, and other publications of governments, nor is it a substitute for the experience, skill, and judgement of the prudent mariner. It is, instead, a supplement to these and must be used in conjunction with them to help insure the safety, comfort, and pleasure of you and your shipmates. This guide is not to be used for navigation.

The Publisher requests information and suggestions for improving this guide. Please address correspondence to Virgin Island Plus Yacht Charters Inc., 239 Delancey Street, Philadelphia, PA 19106.

FOR ADDITIONAL COPIES: Send $17.95 to V.I.P. Yacht Charters, Inc., 239 Delancey St., Philadelphia, PA 19106; include $2.00 for shipping in the U.S.A. or $5.00 for shipping overseas.

ISBN 0-9635048-0-0

Gear.

MOUNT GAY
REFINED
ECLIPSE
BARBADOS
RUM
AS MADE OVER 175 YEARS
ON THE ISLAND OF BARBADOS
WEST INDIES
CHRIST CHURCH
TRADE MARK
PRODUCT OF BARBADOS   40% ALC. BY VOL. | 80 PROOF
BLENDED AND EXPORTED BY
MOUNT GAY DISTILLERIES LIMITED
BRANDONS, ST. MICHAEL · BARBADOS W.I.

SONY

PORTABLE GPS RECEIVER/IPS-360

GPS

G L O B A L   P O S I T I O N I N G   S Y S T E M

SONY

PYXIS

GLOBAL POSITIONING SYSTEM

SONY

POS *:N 35°32'58.2"
JAPAN:E139°32'27.0"

POS   NAV   TRACK   EDIT   SET   MARK

EXTENSION

CLEAR   RECALL   ENTER

PYXIS

TABLE OF CONTENTS

8

NEAR SCRUB ISLAND *Kramer photo*

A Pyramid of Tailor Made Policies

St. Maarten Insurance's commitment to the marine industry in the West Indies is obvious. Major sponsoring of the Maxi Regattas, support for the Sea Rescue Foundation and continuous initiatives for the St. Maarten Junior Sailing School are some of the more visible activities.
It is evident that this same commitment goes towards covering the risks of the marine industry as well. Especially since St. Maarten Insurance joined forces with insurance conglomerate "groupe des mutuelles du mans assurances" in 1991, the company has been able to play a major role in offering quality policies and services, never before available in the West Indies.

Tailor made for you.... if you wish.

A regular hull policy for example, includes a 3 million dollar liability cover ..... for free! Experience, skill and preparation of the skipper and the better quality of tackle on the vessel, are rewarded in our policies. Racing extensions, cruising range options, charter and bare boat options....the list is extensive. And many of our policy holders enjoy No Claim Bonuses!

Just talk to us.....We're good listeners with experienced advice and the best marine policies anywhere.

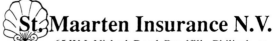

St. Maarten Insurance N.V.

65 W.J. Nisbeth Road, Pondfill - Philipsburg,
St. Maarten - Netherlands Antilles
Tel. (599-5) 26060 • Fax (599-5) 23004

a subsidiary of  **groupe des mutuelles du mans assurances**

ENGLISH HARBOR *Derek Little photo*

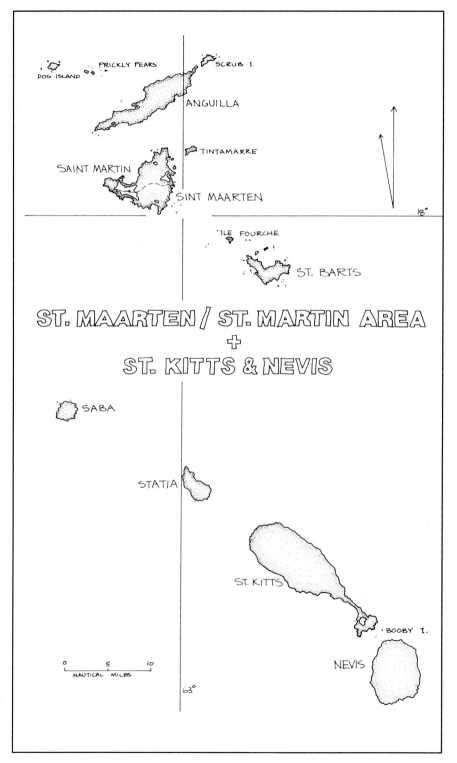

DOG ISLAND · PRICKLY PEARS · SCRUB I.

ANGUILLA

TINTAMARRE

SAINT MARTIN

SINT MAARTEN

18°

ILE FOURCHE

ST. BARTS

ST. MAARTEN / ST. MARTIN AREA
✛
ST. KITTS & NEVIS

SABA

STATIA

ST. KITTS

BOOBY I.

NEVIS

0   5   10
NAUTICAL MILES

63°

INTRODUCTION TO THE ST. MAARTEN/ST. MARTIN AREA

The St. Maarten/St. Martin Area centers around 63° West Longitude and includes ANGUILLA, ST. MAARTEN/ST. MARTIN, ST. BARTS (ST. BARTHELEMY), SABA, and STATIA (ST. EUSTATIUS). Saba and Statia are separated from the others by approximately 30 miles of open sea and a deep trough in the ocean floor where depths are 2400 to 3600 feet and more. To the southwest of Saba is the SABA BANK, a shoal that extends some 30 miles farther to the southwest and about 20 miles in S.E.-to-N.W. direction; small craft are advised to avoid crossing Saba Bank in an easterly direction as extremely uncomfortable, if not dangerous, seas can be encountered there.

Anguilla, St. Maarten/St. Martin, St. Barts and off-lying islands, cays, and rocks lie along the southwest edge of the ANGUILLA BANK that extends 19 miles to the north and 27 miles to the east of Anguilla and about 16 miles to the southeast of St. Barts. Offshore depths throughout the Anguilla Bank vary from approximately 50 to 200 feet or more, and official U.S. and British publications caution that there are reports of considerably less water in places than is charted. However, even in these cases, offshore depths are adequate for the average cruising yacht.

The St. Maarten/St. Martin Area lies roughly 1,500 miles from New York City, some 1,100 miles southeast of Miami, Florida, and approximately 100 miles to the east of the Virgin Islands and 70 miles to the northwest of Antigua. It is reached easily by convenient air service from North and South America, England and Europe and from other major islands in the eastern Caribbean.

SANDY I. & ROAD BAY   *Eiman photo*

WEATHER

We are pleased to provide the following data furnished by the METEOROLOGI-CAL SERVICE OF THE NETHERLANDS ANTILLES:

	Average Wind Direction	Average Wind Speed	Average Air Temp.		Average Max. Air Temp.		Relative Humid-ity	Average Rain-fall	No. of Rainy Days (0.39 in. or more)	Average M.S.L. Pressure	Average Seawater Temp.	
	Degrees	Knots	Degrees		Degrees		%	Inches		Inches	Degrees	
			C	F	C	F					C	F
January	080	10.9	25.0	77.0	28.1	82.6	75.6	2.6	1.1	30.03	25.2	77.4
February	090	10.9	25.1	77.2	28.4	83.1	75.2	1.8	1.0	30.03	24.7	76.5
March	095	11.0	25.4	77.7	28.8	83.8	74.3	1.6	0.9	30.01	24.9	76.8
April	097	11.1	26.1	79.0	29.2	84.6	75.9	2.4	1.3	29.99	25.1	77.2
May	100	10.9	27.0	80.6	30.1	86.2	75.2	3.9	1.9	30.00	26.2	79.2
June	102	11.2	28.0	82.4	30.3	86.5	75.8	3.0	1.5	30.02	26.9	80.4
July	088	10.8	28.0	82.4	31.3	88.3	76.0	3.2	1.8	30.03	27.2	81.0
August	093	11.2	28.1	82.6	31.1	87.8	76.8	4.2	2.5	29.99	27.5	81.5
September	094	9.9	28.0	82.4	30.9	87.6	77.9	5.4	2.8	29.95	27.9	82.2
October	099	9.7	27.6	81.7	30.4	86.7	78.6	4.9	2.8	29.91	27.6	81.7
November	078	9.8	26.8	80.2	29.5	85.1	79.4	5.4	3.4	29.93	27.3	81.7
December	062	10.7	25.7	78.3	28.5	83.3	77.0	3.3	1.8	29.98	26.1	79.0
Mean	**092**	**10.7**	**26.7**	**80.1**	**29.7**	**85.5**	**76.5**	**3.5**	**1.9**	**29.99**	**26.4**	**79.5**

SUMMARY OF CLIMATOLOGICAL DATA FOR SABA, ST. EUSTATIUS, AND ST. MAARTEN
Based on Observations at Juliana Airport, St. Maarten

Please note that the figures in the table represent average conditions only and cannot indicate widely varying conditions that can occur at any time.

The weather in the St. Maarten/St. Martin Area is nearly perfect for sailing year-round and is characterized by pleasantly warm-to-hot temperatures, clear and sunny

I'D RATHER BE SAILING *Eiman photo*

skies, minimal rainfall, and extremely steady easterly trade winds. There are, to be sure, variations from winter to summer and from the rainy season (roughly July through November) to the dry season (about December through June), but conditions are remarkably constant throughout the year, with only relatively minor changes in a climate extremely favorable and pleasant for sailors and vacationers. The worst weather is, of course, associated with hurricanes that come through or close to the area every few years; but the potential for serious trouble for cruising yachtsmen can be minimized because of the seasonality of hurricanes and because of the sophisticated and timely warning and tracking information that is broadcast whenever they are twisting about.

The great steadiness and reliability of the trade winds in the eastern Caribbean help make it one of the finest cruising areas in the world. Although they do vary constantly, they fluctuate within quite narrow limits and follow predictable patterns with great fidelity. In St. Maarten the prevailing wind is between East-Northeast and East-Southeast 80% of the time; in St. Barts the wind is between Northeast and Southeast 90% to 96% of the time!

The average wind speeds shown above show a pattern that is fairly typical throughout much of the eastern Caribbean. Contrary to many subjective reports, the data indicate clearly that fresh-to-strong winds continue during the late spring and summer months. Data from the U.S. National Climate Center and from the West Indies Pilot show that average wind velocities do not fall off in June, July, and August between the Virgins and Martinique. On the other hand, all official sources agree that average wind velocities in the area are lowest in September, October, and November.

Visibility in the St. Maarten/St. Martin Area is rarely less than 10 miles and is often more than 25 miles. Fog is virtually unknown, but haze frequently reduces visibility to about 15 miles. Extremely restricted visibility of 5 miles or less is rare and is usually encountered during very brief rain squalls.

St. Maarten has an average annual rainfall of only 42 inches. On average February, March, and April are the driest months; August through November are the wettest. Even during the rainy season the skies are generally clear and sunny; rain normally comes in short showers or squalls that are followed quickly by complete clearing.

Northern swells are very large waves generated primarily by storms in the North Atlantic between early December and the end of March. Their frequency varies a good deal from year to year; in some winters there will be only a few sets in the entire four month period, but in others they can come in once or twice a month. Although the swells normally pose no great problem at sea, they grow in height in shallow water and can make exposed anchorages and harbors uncomfortable or even untenable. Thus it is wise to be prepared for them, especially in the winter months in anchorages exposed to the east, north, and west.

All islands in the eastern Caribbean from Trinidad to Puerto Rico are subject to hurricanes characterized by counterclockwise rotary winds of 64 knots (74 mph) or more, high storm tides, torrential rains, and extremely restricted visibility; these tropical cyclones generally advance in a westerly or northwesterly direction at speeds of about 10 knots. Approximately 85% of the hurricanes in the islands occur in August, September, and October while the remaining 15% are usually experienced in June, July, and November. Hurricane conditions are experienced on an average of once every 4 to 5 years in St. Maarten/St. Martin; almost every year at least one hurricane occurs within 100 miles of the island. So much for the bad news. The good news is that modern tracking and communications techniques and services are quite efficient and

effective in providing advance information on individual hurricanes so that appropriate preparations can be made. Most yachts head for SIMPSON BAY LAGOON when
hurricanes approach; its landlocked anchorages provide very good protection from
stormy seas. Strangers are advised not to seek refuge in Oyster Pond; it has more yachts
than it can handle safely during hurricanes, and many are forced to seek protection
elsewhere.

It is important to listen to weather broadcasts daily . . . especially during hurricane
season. The following are the most useful broadcast sources of weather information
received in the St. Maarten/St. Martin Area:

AM **895 kHz-VON, Nevis** — Marine Weather 7:45 A.M., 10:45 A.M.,
12:45 P.M.

1000 kHz-WVWI-Radio 1, St. Thomas — Marine Weather 8:30 A.M.
& 5:30 P.M.

1100 kHz-ZDK, Antigua — Marine Weather 6:55 P.M. Weather 8:15
A.M., 9:15 A.M., 11:30 A.M.

FM **94.7 mHz-PJD 1-Gem Radio, St. Maarten** — Marine Weather 8:05
A.M., 6:45 P.M.

VHF Channel 16-SABA RADIO — Broadcasts hurricane advisories and
warnings as appropriate and will provide weather information on request
from 6:00 A.M. to Midnight daily.

COMMUNICATIONS

VHF RADIO is the preferred link among yachts and with many shore stations in the St.
Maarten/St. Martin Area. Channel 16 is only for emergencies and for calling other
stations; when routine contact has been made, switch to another channel to continue;
do not conduct routine business on Channel 16. Channel 12 is for port operations;
Channel 68 is for ship-to-ship and for ship-to-shore; Channel 70 is for ship-to-ship.

SABA RADIO, with its antenna atop Mt. Scenery some 2845 feet above sea level, has
a VHF range of approximately 75 miles and is reported to reach Antigua. It is on the air
from 6:00 A.M. to Midnight daily and provides routine VHF service and communications during all emergencies. Channel 16 is the emergency and call channel; routine
traffic is handled on Channel 26.

Saba Radio can connect you to VHF-equipped yachts you cannot reach directly
and to any telephone in the world. Outgoing calls must be billed to a dependable
account, so it is best to make collect calls. Anyone wishing to call you should phone
Saba Radio (from the U.S.A. direct dial 011-599-46-3402) with the name of your boat;
you have to monitor Channel 16 or call Saba Radio to check for incoming calls.

Quite a few marine services and restaurants monitor Channel 16 and other VHF
Channels; see our St. Maarten/St. Martin Marine Directory for VHF channels and
telephone numbers of marine services.

COMMUNICATIONS SERVICES DOCKSIDE MANAGEMENT at Bobby's Marina in
Philipsburg provides convenient telephone, FAX, and message services for yachtsmen;
the staff can handle any communications problems quickly and efficiently. In St. Barts
overseas calls can be made easily at the Post Office in Gustavia; on other islands similar
service is available at the local offices of the telephone companies.

DIAL DIRECT TELEPHONE service makes calls between the States and the islands simple and easy. You can contact a U.S.A. Dial Direct operator from phones via the following numbers: On Anguilla dial 1-800-872-2881; on Dutch St. Maarten dial 001-800-872-2281. There is a USA Direct phone at Bobby's Marina that connects directly to an AT&T operator in the States.

To phone the islands directly from the U.S. dial the following:

Anguilla	1-809-497 + four local numbers
Dutch St. Maarten	011-599-5 + five local numbers
French St. Martin & St. Barts	011-590 + six local numbers
Saba	011-599-46 + four local numbers
Statia	011-599-38 + four local numbers

EMERGENCY NUMBERS

	Dutch St. Maarten	French St. Martin	Anguilla	St. Barts
Hospital	31111	87.50.07	2551	27.60.35/27.60.00
Ambulance	22111	87.54.14	991	
Police	22222	87.50.04	2333	27.66.66
Gendarmes		87.50.10		27.60.12

CHARTS

The U.S., British, and Dutch governments have improved their charts of the St. Maarten/St. Martin area in recent years. The following are recommended to cruising yachtsmen:

U.S.D.M.A.	25613	Approaches To Anguilla, St. Martin, and St. Barthelemy - 1:75,000 (with details of Philipsburg, St. Maarten - 1:15,000)
	25607	Saba, St. Eustatius, and Saint Christopher - 1:75,000 (with details of Saba - 1:25,000 and of St. Eustastius - 1:15,000)
British Admiralty	2047	Approaches to Anguilla - 1:50,000
	487	St. Christopher to St. Eustatius - 1:50,000
Dutch	2210	Netherlands Antilles - Windward Islands -1:100,000 (Dog Island to St. Kitts & Nevis)

Also recommended are several larger scale government charts that provide more detail on specific ports, anchorages, and areas:

U.S.D.M.A.	25608	Plans of The Leeward Islands - Plans of Marigot Bay, St. Martin; Gustavia, St. Barts; Basseterre, St. Kitts; and Plymouth, Montserrat - 1:15,000 and Approach to Barbuda - 1:75,000
British Admiralty	2079	Plans in Anguilla, St. Martin, and St. Barthelemy - 1:15,000 - Plans of Crocus and Road Bays, Anguilla; Marigot Bay, St. Martin; Great Bay, St. Maarten; and Gustavia, St. Barts
Dutch	2716	Netherlands Antilles - Plans of The Windward Islands - Plans of St. Maarten, St. Eustatius, and Saba - 1:30,000; Philipsburg, St. Maarten - 1:12,500; Oyster Pond, St. Martin - 1:10,000; Oranje Bay, St. Eustatius - 1:15,000; and Fort Bay, Saba - 1:12,500

For interisland passages we recommend **U.S.D.M.A. 25600 Anegada Passage With Adjacent Islands - 1:250,0000 - Virgin Islands to St. Kitts.**

There are several proprietary charts that are practical and helpful. Our own **YACHTSMAN'S PLANNING CHART 63-18** covers Anguilla, St. Maarten/St. Martin, and St. Barts and includes plans of Prickly Pear Cays, Road Bay, Orient Bay, Oyster Pond, Simpson & Marigot Bays, and Gustavia. It is available from V.I.P.Y.C., 239 Delancey St., Philadelphia, PA 19106 (Phone:215-627-3238) for $14.00 and from chandleries and charter fleets in the islands.

Imray-Iolaire publishes three charts of interest: A24 - Leeward Islands - Anguilla, St. Martin, and St. Barthelemy ; A25 - St. Christopher, St. Eustatius, Nevis, Montserrat, & Saba; A-3 - Anguilla to Guadeloupe. They are approximately $18.00 each.

One of the best, most reliable sources for cruising guides, charts, and a variety of nautical books is BLUEWATER BOOKS & CHARTS. 1481 S.E. 17th Street Causeway, Ft. Lauderdale, FL 33316; phone (305) 763-6533. They carry an extensive stock of charts and cruising guides for the entire eastern Caribbean and provide excellent service and fast delivery.

DIRECT DISTANCES

The following approximate distances in nautical miles are provided to assist in planning itineraries. When estimating sailing time between points, allowances should be made for wind direction and strength, tacking, and sea conditions.

	Orient Bay, St.M	Marigot, St.M	Road Bay, Ang.	Gustavia, St.B	Saba	Statia	Basseterre, St.K	Charlestown, Nevis
Philipsburg, St. Maarten	9	12	19	14	28	33	51	59
Orient Bay, St. Martin		9	17.5	15.5	34	38	55.5	64
Marigot, St. Martin			13	23.5	34	41	60	69
Road Bay, Anguilla				28	41	48	67	76
Gustavia, St. Barts					28	27	42.5	51
Saba						17	37	46
Statia							20	29
Basseterre, St. Kitts								11

NAVIGATION AIDS

More government and private buoys, lights and other aids to navigation are appearing each year in the area covered by this Guide. Wherever a system is followed, it is usually the IALA "B" system . . . 'red-right-returning' when entering harbors and black and yellow markers on shoals. Unfortunately, the one word that best describes many of these aids is UNRELIABLE; some lights are weak and very hard to see, and some go out from time to time; charted buoys and spars can move from their designated positions and occasionally disappear completely. Thus, it is good to treat all navigation aids with great caution and skepticism.

RESCUE AT SEA

Antillean Sea Rescue Foundation (ASRF) is a volunteer search and rescue service founded in St. Maarten in 1982 to assist mariners in serious emergencies. It operates a high speed search and rescue vessel from its base at Bobby's Marina in Philipsburg. A.S.R.F. CAN BE CONTACTED IN EMERGENCIES THROUGH SABA RADIO ON VHF CHANNEL 16.

SECURITY

In the larger, more popular islands in the Caribbean theft is probably no more and no less of a problem than it is in the States, but unfortunately it is a fact of life today. A few simple precautions will minimize the risk of having money or valuables stolen: Lock your boat whenever you leave it unattended for a significant period of time. Do not leave money or valuables exposed or unattended in public places.....including beaches. Outboards should be locked to dinghies, and dinghies should be locked to docks and piers and at night should be locked to your boat.

RUBBISH

There are rubbish/trash/garbage receptacles at convenient locations in towns and major harbors throughout the islands in the St. Maarten/St. Martin Area. To protect marine life and the environment and to make the waters and the shores pleasant and attractive for those who follow you, please be sure to bag your rubbish and deposit it in the receptacles provided. Never throw any plastic items overboard, and never throw anything overboard in anchorages. Please.

CURRENCIES

U.S. dollars are used widely on all islands in the St. Maarten/St. Martin area and are accepted by just about everyone cruising sailors will come in contact with. U.S. travelers' checks are similarly acceptable. But the Eastern Caribbean Dollar (E.C. $) is the official currency on Anguilla; francs are official on St. Barthelemy (St. Barts) and in French St. Martin; guilders (or florins) are the official currency in Dutch St. Maarten, on Saba, and Statia. It is important to be sure what currency is used when you pay for anything, as mix-ups can be very expensive and embarrassing. The approximate exchange rates are as follows:

Dutch St. Maarten, Saba & Statia: $1.00 U.S. = 1.77 guilders; 1 guilder = $0.57 U.S.

French St. Martin & St. Barts: $1.00 U.S. = 6 francs; 1 franc = $0.17 U.S.

Anguilla: $1.00 U.S. = $2.65 E.C.; $1.00 E.C. = $0.38 U.S.

HOLIDAYS

Be sure to check holiday schedules carefully when planning to visit the islands; practically all shops, restaurants, services, and businesses close completely during these celebrations.

Dutch St. Maarten, Saba, and Statia	French St. Martin and St. Barthelemy	Anguilla
New Year's Day	New Year's Day	New Year's Day
Good Friday	Mardi Gras	Constitution/Freedom
Easter Sunday	Mi-Careme (Mid-Lent)	Day (April 1)
Queen's Birthday	Ash Wednesday	Anguilla Day (May 30)
(April 30)	Easter Monday	Whit Monday
Labour Day (May 1)	Ascension Day	Queen's Birthday (2nd
Ascension Day	Pentecost Monday	Sat. in June)
Whit Monday	Schoelcher Day (June 21)	August Mon. & Thurs.
All Saints' Day	Bastille Day (July 14)	(1st Mon. & Thurs.
St. Maarten Day (Nov. 11)	Festival of St. Barthelemy	in Aug)
Kingdom Day (Dec. 15)	Aug. 24 + 2 days	Separation Day (Dec. 19)
Christmas Day	Armistice Day (Nov. 11)	Christmas Day
Boxing Day (Dec. 26)	Christmas Day	Boxing Day (Dec. 26)

BROADCAST RADIO

AM and FM radio stations heard in the St. Maarten/St. Martin Area can provide interesting insights into life in the islands through their news, music, and feature programming. For Caribbean flavor it is hard to beat the traditional calypso, steel band, and reggae music, but gospel, rock, golden oldies, and contemporary music is aired regularly. The guide below will help you tune in stations that come through loud and clear most of the time.

AM STATIONS - kHz

555	825	895	1000	1030	1100	1300	1410	1505
ZIV	Paradise	VON	WVWI	WOSO	ZDK	PJD2	PJF1	
St.K	Nevis	Nevis	St.Thomas	San Juan	Antigua	ST.M	St.M	Anguilla

FM STATIONS - mHz

93.9	94.7	95.3	98.0	99.2	102.7	104.7	105.3
PJF1	PJD1	RSM	RSB	LFRO	PJD3	Carib	ZJF
St.M	St.M	St.M	St.B	St.M	St.M	St.M	Anguilla
			(French)	(French)		(French)	

MISCELLANY

PACKING Travel light; you won't need many clothes afloat, and a few informal things will do nicely for shopping, sightseeing, and dining ashore. It is a good idea to include clothes and necessities for your first few days in your carry on luggage so you will be sure to have them when you need them.

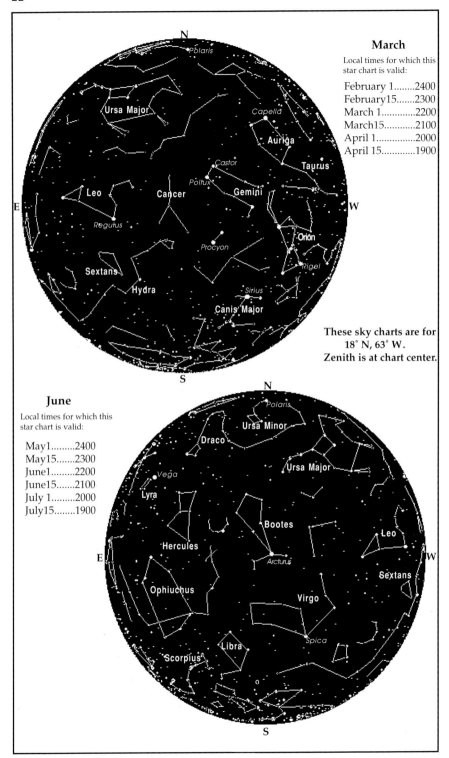

March

Local times for which this star chart is valid:

February 1........2400
February15.......2300
March 1..............2200
March15.............2100
April 1................2000
April 15..............1900

These sky charts are for
18° N, 63° W.
Zenith is at chart center.

June

Local times for which this star chart is valid:

May1.........2400
May15.......2300
June1.........2200
June15.......2100
July 1.........2000
July15........1900

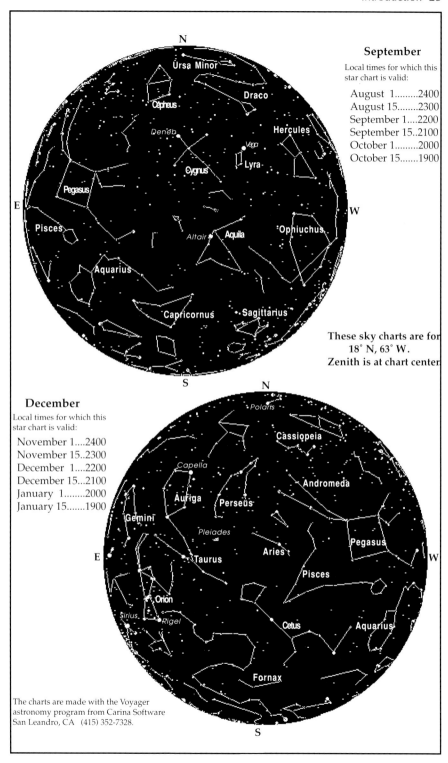

September

Local times for which this
star chart is valid:

August 1.........2400
August 15........2300
September 1....2200
September 15..2100
October 1.........2000
October 15.......1900

These sky charts are for
18° N, 63° W.
Zenith is at chart center.

December

Local times for which this
star chart is valid:

November 1....2400
November 15..2300
December 1....2200
December 15...2100
January 1........2000
January 15.......1900

The charts are made with the Voyager
astronomy program from Carina Software
San Leandro, CA (415) 352-7328.

SUNBURN Be extremely careful about sunburn; the sun is very, very strong and can fry pale northern skin to a crisp if it is not protected. Long sleeve shirts, long trousers, hats, and non-gooey sun block products are essential.

LOCAL CLOTHING CUSTOMS Bathing suits and minimal coverage beach wear are not appropriate in towns and in commercial or shopping areas. Islanders dress modestly and conservatively in public places; it is best to follow suit.

PHOTOGRAPHY Please be thoughtful when using your camera, especialy when photographing people. There aren't many at home who enjoy having their pictures taken by strangers, and feelings and reactions are pretty much the same in the islands. It is best to ask permission before taking pictures of people.

INTERISLAND TRAVEL If you wish to visit islands more quickly, Windward Island Airways has excellent service with two or three round trip flights daily among St. Maarten, Anguilla, St. Barts, and Saba. The flights are spectacular! Ferries connect St. Martin and Anguilla and St. Martin and St. Barts; commercial catamarans make daily round trips between Philipsburg and St. Barts. The best place for information, reservations, and tickets is IRISH TRAVEL in Simpson Bay.

RUNNING Runners are welcome to join the Road Runners Club every Wednesday at 5:15 P.M. and at 6:45 A.M. on Sundays for fun runs that start in the main parking lot of Pelican Resort & Casino on Simpson Bay.

BEACHES AND PRIVATE PROPERTY By law, all beaches on islands in the St. Maarten/St. Martin Area are public property and thus can be used and enjoyed by all. But the land behind the beaches is usually private property; please respect the rights of the owners and do NOT trespass. The abuse of private property by yachtsmen is, we believe, a major reason that yachts are not permitted to anchor in Rendezvous Bay on Anguilla.

FISH POISONING Ciguatera, the fish poisoning that is a problem throughout the tropics, is present in the St. Maarten/St. Martin Area. A cumulative, intestinal disorder that results from eating toxic fish, it is usually characterized by cramps and nausea that sometimes last for weeks. Toxicity occurs primarily in reef fish but only those from certain reefs; shell fish are not affected. If you fish, check your catch with local fishermen and tell them where you caught your fish; they can usually tell what is safe to eat and what is not.

OVEREXPOSURE Although topless swimming and sunbathing are becoming more common in St. Maarten/St. Martin and St. Barts, and St. Martin has one 'official' nudist beach, partial or complete nudity is definitely against the law in Anguilla. And complete nudity is illegal in St. Barts. Be careful.

DRUGS The possession, sale, and use of narcotics and other mind-altering drugs including marijuana (except alcohol, tobacco, and coffee) are illegal in the St. Maarten/St. Martin Area. The drug problem is considered very serious business by officials; offenders are subject to very heavy penalties, including confiscations of their vessels as appropriate.

JOY BATHS To help stretch/conserve the limited water supply on boats, charter captains have long recommended Joy baths to their guests. Joy lathers very well and rinses off quickly and completely in salt water and does a great, refreshing job. But don't drip it on the deck; it is very slippery and thus dangerous.

SNORKELING

Snorkeling is the simplest, easiest, and most convenient way for good swimmers to explore and enjoy the enchanting and exciting underwater world in the Caribbean. With a snorkel tube, a mask that fits your face snugly, and a pair of flippers you can spend incredible hours swimming over and around shallow reefs and along shores where varieties of hard and soft corals and fascinating and colorful reef fish abound. Before starting out, first timers should spend a few minutes in shallow water off a sandy beach getting used to mask and snorkel and learning how to get rid of water that invariably gets inside both. Once you are comfortable with the equipment, you are all set to go.

A few cautions: Do not snorkel alone; be aware of currents so you are not carried some place you do not want to be; do not harass fish, lobster, or other living creatures; do not poke into dark holes or crevices; do not wear bright, shiny objects; do not touch any coral, plants, fish, lobster, turtles, etc.; stay well away from sea urchins....the black balls covered with long, sharp spines that stick out in all directions ready to stick into you (even through your flippers).

It is best to snorkel at midday when the sun overhead gives the best light under the water, but we suggest wearing a T shirts to prevent sunburn. And don't be shocked if you see snorkelers spit in their masks and wash them out before putting them on; this is a time-honored way to prevent masks from fogging up and spoiling the view!

Dive shops (i.e. SCUBA diving shops) normally carry paperback books with comprehensive illustrations of reef fish and corals to help identify what you see under water. The very best for fish is "Reef Fish Identification" by Paul Humann; 288 fantastic pages of brilliant photos and very practical information on hundreds of beautiful reef fish seen in Florida, the Bahamas, and the Caribbean; $29.95 + $3.50 shipping from New World Publications, 1861 Cornell Rd., Jacksonville, FL 322078.

To get you started on identifying fish, we have included here photographs of a number that are very common in the shallow reefs St. Maarten/St. Martin Area. Joan Curtis Borque of SEA SABA DIVE CENTER provided all these remarkable photos except the shot of the yellowtail snapper that was taken by Nancy Ferguson of Kailua-Kona, Hawaii.

FOUREYE BUTTERFLYFISH

SQUIRRELFISH & ROCK BEAUTY

BLUE TANG

DOCTOR FISH

YELLOWTAIL SNAPPER

SERGEANT MAJOR

STOPLIGHT PARROTFISH SUPERMALE

STOPLIGHT PARROTFISH ADULT

BLUEHEAD WRASSE SUPERMALE

FAIRY BASSLET

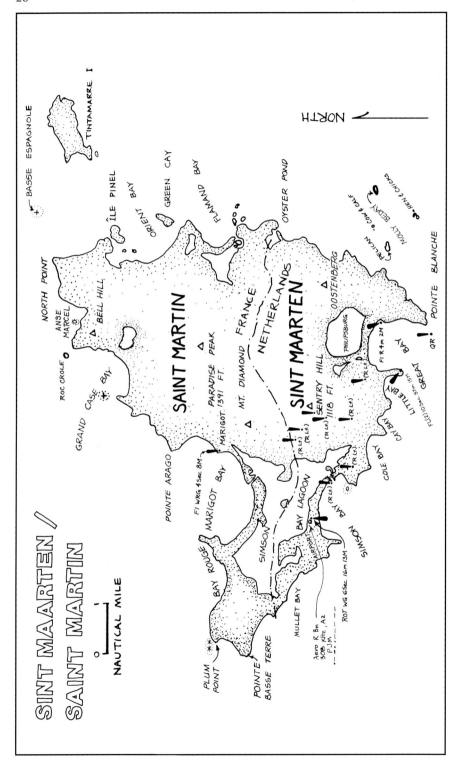

SINT MAARTEN/SAINT MARTIN

CHARTS: U.S. DMA 25600, 25608, 25613
British 130, 955, 2079
Dutch 2110 & 2716
French 6090
YACHTSMAN'S PLANNING CHART 63-18
Imray Iolaire A24

Everyone who travels to St. Maarten/St. Martin, hub of the northern Leeward Islands, hears the same tale: Over three hundred years ago—the date is usually put at 1648—a Dutchman and a Frenchman started walking around the island from its western shore, the Dutchman going south and the Frenchman heading north. When the two met on the east coast, a line was drawn through the land with each country thenceforth having jurisdiction over its segment of the spoils. The result, whatever the truth behind this charming legend, is that St. Maarten/St. Martin is the smallest self-contained land mass ruled by two sovereign nations. The Frenchman, so the story goes, walked faster than the Dutchman. Of the 37 square miles on the island, the French govern 21 and the Dutch 16, but since most people agree that the Dutch real estate is more valuable, neither side need feel cheated.

Located approximately 150 miles east of Puerto Rico, this friendly island has a series of high peaks running from north to south, with Paradise Peak on the French side the highest at about 1,300 feet. It has become a major destination for Caribbean vacationers, thanks to far-sighted plans to encourage tourism that were developed by visiting contractors from Curacao in 1959 and pushed forward by enlightened

GREAT BAY - PHILIPSBURG   *Derek Little photo*

FAST FREIGHT - PHILIPSBURG   *Eiman photo*

governments in the last three decades. Efficient, direct daily air service from New York (3 1/2-4 hours), Miami (2 1/2-3 hours), San Juan, St. Thomas, St. Croix, and Antigua, and direct flights from Europe make Queen Juliana Airport a convenient and well connected gateway for visitors intent on enjoying the pleasures of St. Maarten/St. Martin and neighboring islands as well.

According to another legend, the island was named by Columbus in 1493 when he sailed past it . . . but did not land . . . on the holy day of St. Martin of Tours. The Spanish, English, Dutch, and French have all held sway over St. Maarten/St. Martin at various times when salt, tobacco, sugar, indigo, and trading and military bases attracted European interests. By the mid-seventeenth century the Dutch and French had established settlements, and once each realized that the other was there to stay, they reached an agreement to share the island in peace and friendship.

For more than 300 years now the Dutch with their capital in Philipsburg and the French with theirs in Marigot have lived together harmoniously while preserving national customs and characteristics and maintaining an entirely open border. Dutch Sint Maarten allies itself with nearby Saba and St. Eustatia (Statia) in the Netherlands Antilles, while French Saint Martin is governed directly from Guadeloupe but, like others in the French West Indies, also sends representatives to the parent government in Paris.

Since the opening of Little Bay Hotel on the Dutch side in 1955, the tourist business has grown by leaps and bounds until it now provides the main economic activity for the island and its 32,000 residents. In addition to the superb trade wind climate, there is much to attract the visitor. Beach and water activities abound on dozens of beautiful beaches (some are topless, one is topless and bottomless), and in and under the crystal, turquoise waters of the Caribbean. Airlines, multihulls, and high speed ferrys connect St. Maarten/St. Martin with neighboring islands providing a selection of wonderful day trips. Rental cars, taxis with government established rates, sightseeing buses, and commuter buses make getting around the island simple and convenient. Entrance formalities for tourists are routine and straightforward; U.S. visitors need only a passport (valid or outdated) and a return air ticket; visas and vaccination certificates are not required.

Island shopping delights visitors in both Philipsburg and Marigot. The inviting shops are widely recognized for their varied and attractive merchandise offered at free port prices. They provide some of the most alluring shopping opportunities in the entire Caribbean. Whether you are interested in exquisite jewelry, beautiful crystal and porcelain, tempting linens, seductive perfumes and cosmetics, and superb watches, or in fashions by Pierre Cardin, Missoni, La Roche, Armani, Kenzo, Valentino, Gucci, Yamamoto, and island designers, or cameras, Caribbean art, electronic equipment, and duty free wines and spirits, you will surely be pleased. Shops are supposedly open 8 A.M. to Noon and 2 P.M. to 6 P.M. Mondays through Saturdays and for a few hours on Sundays and holidays when cruise ships are in port, but our experience is that most do not open until 9:00 A.M. Virtually all shops are CLOSED tight on Sundays. Visitors should remember that bathing suits and vast areas of exposed skin are not appropriate in the towns or in public places generally.

St. Maarten/St. Martin is one of the most popular vacation islands in the Caribbean with over a million visitors each year, and its economy continues to grow rapidly. Hotels, condominiums, time share resorts, shops, and restaurants are being built everywhere at a great rate with no end in sight. This dynamic growth has produced some significant problems that have strained the local governments severely. On the

Dutch side the government is under great pressure from Holland to improve its operations.

The island has become a major yachting center. Bareboat charter companies offer more than 200 yachts for cruising the area from Anguilla to Antigua. A wide range of skilled maintenance and repair services as well as marine supplies and equipment are available. The St. Maarten Heineken Regatta in February has become one of the premier racing events in the Caribbean; cruising and charter boats are welcome, and handicaps are arranged with ease. In May the St. Maarten Annual Laser Championship takes place, while June sees the Caribbean Offshore Race to St. Kitts/Nevis and back. For information on the racing scene, contact Robbie Ferron at Robbie Ferron's Budget Marine or Ian Thring at Dockside Management at Bobby's Marina.

APPROACHES In normal visibility the peaks of St. Maarten/St. Martin or the glow of its lights can be seen easily from great distances, and all significant off-lying islands, cays, and dangers are shown on charts of the area. With the exception of SPANISH ROCK and TINTAMARRE off the northeast coast and MOLLY BEDAY and HEN AND CHICKS off the southeast coast, a mile off the shore will clear all hazards to cruising yachts. PROSELYTE REEF lies approximately one and a half miles south of GREAT BAY; it has 16 feet of water over it and is reported to break in heavy weather; a light was placed on it a few years back, but it was promptly washed away and has not been replaced.

At night St. Maarten/St. Martin should not be approached from north to northwest of Anguilla. The lights on both islands can be very confusing; they can make it difficult to spot and avoid the islands and reefs off Anguilla. In darknes it is best and safest to approach St. Maarten/St. Martin from the west, southwest, or south.

GREAT BAY-PHILIPSBURG

GREAT BAY-PHILIPSBURG is the port of entry and principal harbor for Dutch Sint Maarten and is the anchorage for cruise ships, charter yachts, cruising yachts, day charter boats, ferries, and trading sloops. About a mile wide and a mile in depth, Great Bay is bounded on the east by the high ground and cliffs of POINTE BLANCHE, on the north by PHILIPSBURG and a lovely beach that stretches across the entire head of the harbor, and on the west by WEST POINT on which are the ruins of Fort Amsterdam. Inland to the west of the town is 709-foot FORT HILL with the remains of Fort William. The harbor is wide open to the south and provides good anchorage for yachts in normal trade wind weather. When the wind swings to the south or west of south and builds up swells, or when large northern swells wrap around the island, Great Bay can be rough and at times dangerous. In those conditions, head for Simpson Bay or Marigot. The old advice still holds: When Philipsburg is rough, Marigot will be calm and visa versa.

The most conspicuous landmarks in Philipsburg include the eight-story Sea Palace, the red roof of the St. Martin of Tours Catholic Church, and the white, four-story buildings of Holland House Beach Hotel complex. In the center of town is the small town pier that is reserved for loading and unloading passengers and cargo; on the back side there is a dinghy landing where dinghies should be secured with security cables or chains. Great Bay Marina and Bobby's Marina are in the northeast part of the bay. A large commercial pier extends to the southwest near the tip of Pointe Blanche.

APPROACHES • PROSELYTE REEF is about a mile and a half south of WEST POINTE. It has 16 feet of water over it and can break in heavy weather.

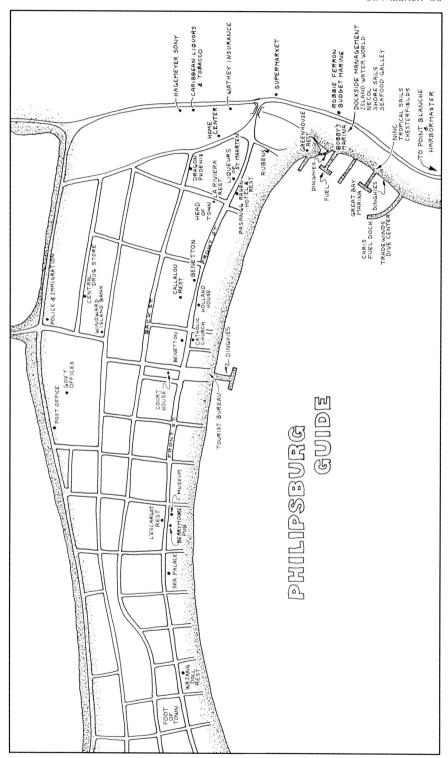

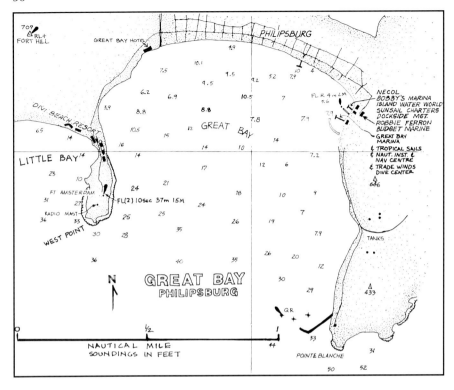

- Avoid the mooring buoys in COLE BAY and the fish pot markers along the southwest coast.

- Give POINTE BLANCHE a wide berth; the seas close in can be rough and confused.

- Do not pass between the commercial pier on Pointe Blanche and the dolphins to the west and north of it; mooring cables frequently there can ruin your whole day.

- A bar with 7-to-10 foot depths extends across much of Great Bay generally on a line from the highest of the two hills on the east side of the Bay to the northwest shore. There are two 6-to 7-foot shoals on the eastern end about 300 to 400 yards off the land, and a 4-foot spot has been reported about three quarters of the way over to the northwest shore.

- Shoaling is reported in the northwest part of Great Bay.

Hurricane Hugo in September, 1989 caused shifting and additional shoaling in Great Bay, so it is best for strangers to proceed with caution. In mid-1990 we checked two good approaches to the anchorage area off the marinas that had least depths of 7 feet. The first was straight up the east side of the bay from the westernmost dolphin off the commercial pier to the end of the curved breakwater at GREAT BAY MARINA; no problem. The second was up the west side of the bay close to WEST POINT up to the Divi Beach Resort buildings on the low ground behind West Point and from there directly over to BOBBY'S MARINA. At the outer end of West Point some 200 yards off to the east we found 25 feet of water. To the north the bottom came up gradually to 16 feet off the Divi Beach Resort. From there to Bobby's depths were generally 8 to 12 feet with a few 7 foot spots.

ANCHORING Yachts drawing 8 feet or more must anchor on the sea side of the bar, but for others the most popular anchorage is in the northeast part of Great Bay where there is good protection from easterly trades and where facilities, supplies, and services for yachts and yachtsmen are close at hand. The calmest water is usually found south of Great Bay Marina in close to the eastern shore. Be alert for the possibility of large swells coming in from the south...especially in winter. Do not anchor in the approach to the small pier in the center of town; keep it clear for commercial traffic. Dinghies can be secured at the town pier and, better still, at either of the two marinas; security cables or chains are advised in all locations. We understand that a few unattended yachts have been broken into at night in Great Bay in 1992; the thieves apparently took money

38

and jewelry that could be easily converted to cash; when you go ashore at night, lock your boat and take your money and small valuables with you.

CLEARANCE Skippers of arriving and departing vessels should clear in and out with Immigration officials. The Harbormaster, Mr. Sunny Hoo (pronounced HOE), advises that arriving skippers should clear in and have passports stamped at the Immigration Office in the new Police Station at the back of town to the east of the main government office building. He also says departing skippers should obtain outbound clearance at the Harbormaster's office on Pointe Blanche and then clear out at Immigration at the Police Station. The Harbormaster's office monitors VHF Channel 12 at all times. The Clearance situation changes from time to time, so don't be surprised if you encounter new requirements or procedures.

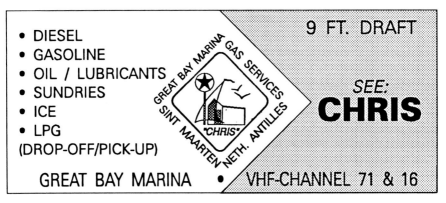

GREAT BAY-NORTHEAST PART   *Derek Little photo*

SERVICES GREAT BAY MARINA is distinguished by its long, curved sea wall extending well beyond its T dock and by its 2-story, cream colored building with reddish roofs. There is 9 feet of water at the FUEL DOCK on the end of the sea wall where CHRIS supplies gasoline, diesel, oil, water, ice, and propane fills; he monitors VHF Ch. 16 & 71. TRADEWINDS DIVE CENTER, also on the sea wall, provides certified instruction, dive trips, equipment sales, and rentals. The slips are filled with catamarans that make daily trips to St. Barts, charter, and private yachts, so there is rarely dockage available for transients, but you are welcome to use its dinghy dock, rest rooms, telephone service, and trash disposal bins. Avis car rentals are available. NAUTICAL INSTRUMENT & NAVIGATION CENTRE has an excellent stock of charts, cruising guides, and nautical books and sells compasses, navigation equipment, and watermakers. TROPICAL SAILS operates a discount chandlery (marine hardware and supplies, paints, rope, batteries, fiberglass supplies, special order service, etc.) as well as a commissary with a good selection of canned and frozen food, meats, grocery items, fresh bread and croissants, sodas, beer, wine, and liquor plus ice cubes. CHESTERFIELD'S RESTAURANT, a long-time favorite of the sailing crowd, overlooks the harbor and is open for breakfast, lunch, and dinner; you'll enjoy the American and seafood entrees in a great setting; happy hour is 5:00 - 6:30 P.M., and Wednesday, Friday, and Saturday evenings are enhanced by live music. MATTHEW AIMABLE, Manager of Leeward Island Yacht Charters, is a very capable and helpful man who will repair anything on your boat or will direct you to a reliable expert who will; if you have any problems with your engine, gear, or equipment, Matthew is a good man to see. GBM monitors VHF Channel 69.

Two hundred yards further north is BOBBY'S MARINA AND BOATYARD, the oldest marina in St. Maarten and the leading full service yard between Antigua and the

THE MARINA BOATYARD IN PHILIPSBURG

BOBBY'S MARINA N.V.

ST. MAARTEN, N.A.

Phone:
22366

FAX:
25442

VHF:
CH 16

P.O.
Box 383

Philipsburg
St. Maarten

Netherlands
Antilles

LARGEST IN THE CARIBBEAN
90 TON TRAVEL LIFT
Expert Services:

- MECHANICAL
- ELECTRICAL
- FIBERGLASS
- ANTI-FOULING
- "AWLGRIP" PAINTING
- WELDING & FABRICATION
- CABINET & JOINERY SHOP

Plus: Tug & Barge Service/Dredging/Marina Construction

HOME OF:
"Dockside Management"
"The Seafood Galley and Raw Bar"
"The Greenhouse Restaurant and Bar"
"Island Waterworld"   "The Bread Basket"
"Necol"   "Shore Sails"   "Sunsail Charters"
Charter Boat Center for Day or Term Outings
All walking distance to shops and restaurants in Philipsburg

Virgin Islands. It is protected from incoming swells and surge by a stone breakwater with a flashing red light, visible for 2 miles, at its end. Bobby's monitors VHF Channel I6. Its facilities include a 90-ton Travel Lift, shops for mechanical, electrical, welding and metal fabrication, fiberglass, and joinery work as well as Awlgrip refinishing. The busy dock at Bobby's is full of fishing boats, SUNSAIL'S charter yachts, the day trip yacht GABRIELLE, and a variety of sail and power boats; transient dockage is seldom available. Gas, diesel, water and block ice are available at the end of the dock where the depth is 10 feet. Visitors can use the dinghy dock, showers, heads, trash bins, and USA Direct phone. NECOL provides expert service and sales for marine electronics, Magellan navigation products, refrigeration, and watermakers. DOCKSIDE MANAGEMENT is a communication and marine support service par excellence handling everything from phone, FAX, copy services to propane fills, laundry, car rentals, cellular phone rentals; they monitor VHF Ch 69. SHORE SAILS makes new sails and repairs old ones, does all sorts of canvas work, and sells and services furling systems. SUNSAIL CHARTERS (formerly BYS) services its bareboat fleet there under the expert direction of Ian McPhearson. ISLAND WATER WORLD operates a chandlery at Bobby's with a full range of yacht supplies and equipment, fittings, paint, and parts.The Bread Basket is a limited stock shop that has case lots of beer and sodas, bread, canned goods, liquor, and a few household items. Completing the facilities is the SEAFOOD GALLEY AND RAW BAR, a very attractive waterfront restaurant that has wonderful local seafood as well as imported delights such as soft shell crab, Maine lobster, oysters, clams, Alaskan king crab, etc.

Within minutes of the marinas are a number of other facilities and services of particular interest to cruising sailors. Across the road from Bobby's is ROBBIE FERRON'S BUDGET MARINE, an absolutely first rate chandlery with extensive stocks of everything and anything you may want for your boat from cotter pins, fuses and zincs to anchors, safety gear, engines, and inflatables; HARKEN hardware and furling systems are sold and serviced; special order items are flown in from Miami in a few days. Robbie is very active in the local sailing/racing scene and is always ready to help with any problem you may have. On the ground floor underneath Budget Marine is Renewed Dry Cleaners & Laundry that has same day service for ship's laundry. Sang's Supermarket is a few steps away towards the town. Along the road beyond Sang's you will find CARIBBEAN LIQUORS & TOBACCO where you can get very good buys on liquor (BACARDI RUM is featured), French & California wines, cigarettes, and Cuban and Dutch cigars. Nearby WATHEY INSURANCE will protect you against all marine risks and HEGERMEYER will help you find yourself with the impressive portable SONY GPS.

A ten minute taxi ride from the marinas will take you to RADIO HOLLAND CARIBBEAN on the far side of the salt pond behind Philipsburg where an excellent selection of marine communication, navigation, and other electronic gear is available together with expert, reliable repair service for all things electronic. Nearby on Illidge Road NAPA AUTO PARTS has a great inventory of batteries, belts, filters, tools, oil, etc. for marine use. A bit further out on the main road is the largest supermarket on the Dutch side . . . FOOD CENTER; it stocks everything imaginable for your galley and bar—fresh, frozen, baked, bagged, canned, bottled, and boxed . . . meats, poultry, cold cuts, cookies, cheeses, canned goods, fresh bread, ice cream, fruit, & vegetables. It's all there for heavy duty shopping in one convenient location.

For a comprehensive list of specialized yacht services everywhere on the island see the St. Maarten/St. Martin Marine Directory at the end of this chapter.

RESTAURANTS The popularity of CHESTERFIELD'S RESTAURANT at Great Bay Marina and SEAFOOD GALLEY at Bobby's is well deserved; location, atmosphere, and food are great. Just across the little bridge beyond Bobby's is the GREENHOUSE where the menu is Caribbean/American and the action lively; the contemporary music is unending, and the crowd loves it; pool and dancing. More modest in all respects is Rubens on the small road past the Greenhouse that runs from the beach to Front Street; neat, clean and inexpensive. Our favorite economy restaurant is the Dragon Phoenix Chinese Restaurant on Back Street at the head of town; the food is very good indeed, and you'll love the prices. Admiral's Quarters is a new waterfront restaurant at the head of Front Street; we have not tried it but understand it is expensive. A few steps down Front Street is the PASANGGRAHAN that started decades ago as the official government guest house; today it is a most attractive hotel, bar, and restaurant filled with the

The ~~*~~ Royal Inn Bar & Restaurant

Pasanggrahan

BREAKFAST • LUNCH • DINNER
HAPPY HOUR DAILY 5-6:30 P.M.
FRONT STREET, PHILIPSBURG   RESERVATIONS: 23588

charm of the old Caribbean; luncheons and dinners offer seafood, Island, Continental, and American selections that are wonderful. LA RIVIERA is a lovely French restaurant a few steps off Front Street where the service is friendly and the dinners are done with a wonderful, light touch. In the center of town the Callaloo is a popular spot with an American/West Indian menu at reasonable prices. On the beach near the town dock San Marco is a top notch Italian restaurant with prices to match but well worth it. Down towards the foot of town L'Escargot has a very good French menu; across the street BERRYMORE'S PUB features fish and chips, ribs, chicken, and other hearty pub fare. Further along Wajang Doll serves tempting Indonesian food, some mild and some very hot, and continues to earn good reviews.

SHOPPING St. Maarten is widely known as one of the leading duty-free shopping centers in the entire Caribbean. Under pressure from shopkeepers a new, attractive brick surface has replaced to old dusty, dirty, cracked pavement making the entire area much more attractive. Wooden bowls and statues, straw hats, T shirts, resort fashions, cameras, perfumes, T shirts, olde maps, high fashions, crystal, watches, T shirts, boom boxes, china, silverwear, fine linens, T shirts, island furniture, wine, cigars, cigarettes, TVs, tape recorders, and T shirts are all there in profusion. Specialties you won't find at home are the six different LIQUEURS Of SINT MAARTEN; they are available across Front Street from Pasanggrahan and should not be missed. Check prices of planned purchases at home before you leave so you will know how good the prices on Front Street are. If you are into really serious shopping, you can buy a time share, a condo, a building lot, or a vacation home. If you need any help from a bank, stroll over to WINDWARD ISLAND BANK across from the main Government Building on the street behind Back Street. Just around the corner from Windward Island Bank is CENTRAL DRUG STORE with everything from prescription drugs and proprietaries to cosmetics,

perfumes and sun tan products . . . anything you would ever hope to find in an excellent drug store.

DEPARTING GREAT BAY-PHILIPSBURG

The recommended course from Philipsburg to MARIGOT or ANGUILLA is westaround along the southwest coast of St. Maarten/St. Martin in the lee of the island. It is shorter and involves less beating and fewer potential hazards than heading up the east coast. When departing Great Bay to the west or southwest, be alert for PROSELYTE REEF approximately one and a half miles south of West Point. Otherwise you can coast along half a mile off shore and clear all hazards except fish pot markers.

When sailing east from Great Bay for ST. BARTHELEMY (ST. BARTS), OYSTER POND, ORIENT BAY, or TINTAMARRE, do not go between the dolphins and the large commercial pier. And give POINTE BLANCHE a wide berth to avoid back winds and turbulent air from the high ground on the point and the rough seas close to it. Normally, seas will be confused, and winds will be unusually strong until you are well away from the land.

If headed towards St. Barts, remain on the port tack until you are near the GROUPERS; then go over to the starboard tack to avoid being set by the stronger, contrary currents. Tack again to pass close to ILE FOURCHE and proceed on into GUSTAVIA.

If bound up the east coast of St. Maarten/St. Martin remain on the port tack until you can clear MOLLY BEDAY and lay TINTAMARRE, keeping well off the shore and HEN AND CHICKS, PELICAN, and COW AND CALF. The east coast is a dead lee shore

EARLY MORNING IN PHILIPSBURG   *Eiman photo*

with many coral reefs and heavy seas that can cause grief for any who venture too close in. Unless you plan to enter OYSTER POND, stay east of the line between Molly Beday and the east end of Tintamarre until you are north of FLAMMAND BAY, and you will be in good water.

SOUTHWESTERN COAST-GREAT BAY TO SIMPSON BAY

LITTLE BAY is the first bay to the west of Great Bay. At the eastern end of the beautiful beach is the Divi Little Bay Beach Resort which ushered in the era of tourism in St. Maarten when it opened its doors in 1955. To the west is the Belaire Hotel. Little Bay is a good daytime anchorage, but because it is open to the south and rather rolly, it is not recommended as an overnight anchorage. There is good holding in sand; the bottom shoals gradually up to the beach with depths of 11 to 12 feet approximately 70 yards off the shore. The water is calmest in the eastern side. There are no obstructions

but be alert for fish pot markers, water skiers, jet skiers, and windsurfers in this pleasant bay.

To the west of Little Bay is CAY BAY with a nice white sand beach, gradually shoaling bottom, and rocky outcroppings extending 70 to 100 yards from the shore. It is a nice daytime anchorage with good snorkeling on both the east and west ends of the beach. It is even more exposed than Little Bay and more rolly, so it should not be considered as an overnight anchorage.

Next along the southwest coast is COLE BAY. Even thought the beach is fine, its appeal is limited by the industrial character of the area. Behind the beach is the Dutch desalinization plant, another plant that generates both electricity and considerable noise, and oil storage tanks for virtually all the fuel coming to the Dutch side of the island. Cole Bay is littered with large and small mooring buoys for oil tankers and other commercial vessels; they are especially troublesome at night as they are not lighted.

LAY BAY is to the northwest of Cole Bay and is separated from it by a point dominated by a conspicuous cluster of low, white buildings with red tile roofs. Stand off this point 1/2 mile to avoid a shoal that is reported to have a depth of only 10 feet. Sail right on by Lay Bay and its coral studded, rocky and sandy coast. The Bay is exposed and has a constant surge and is no place to anchor day or night.

Also keep off PELICAN POINT at the northwest end of Lay Bay by 500 yards or more to clear a 7-foot shoal and two patches of coral to the west and southwest of the Point. Also give PELICAN CAYS a similar wide berth to avoid shoals and scattered coral heads with only 5 to 6 feet of water over them. A breakwater has been built from the shore out towards Pelican Cays; do not attempt to pass in between this breakwater and the Cays; you'll never make it.

SIMPSON BAY AND LAGOON   *Derek Little photo*

SIMPSON BAY AND SIMPSON BAY LAGOON

SIMPSON BAY is a large bay open to the south with a shoreline extending almost two miles from GREAT POINT on the west to PELICAN POINT on the east. A long, lovely, uncrowded beach extends across the northern shore and down the eastern shore to the large silos marking the entrance to SIMPSON BAY LAGOON. The beach to the south of this entrance is backed by the massive new Royal Palm Beach Club, an open piece of land, and The Atrium, a new high rise building. Pelican Point is covered by Pelican Resort and Casino, St. Maarten's first and most popular time share development. Simpson Bay is a good anchorage in normal trade wind weather except on the infrequent occasions when swells roll in making it uncomfortable. Planes using nearby Princess Juliana Airport are noisy, but the traffic is not heavy enough to make it much of a problem.

SIMPSON BAY LAGOON is an excellent land-locked harbor approximately 3 miles long and 2 miles wide that straddles the boundary between Dutch St. Maarten and French St. Martin. It is a popular mooring site for island-based yachts and live-aboards and provides very good protection from hurricanes. Hundreds of yachts and commercial vessels rode out Hurricane Hugo in the Lagoon in September, 1989 with relatively little serious damage reported. Long-awaited improvements in the bridge across the entrance from Simpson Bay created a surge of development of resorts, restaurants, shops, and services for yachtsmen that have made the Lagoon a major yachting center. In the southern part of the Lagoon, known as COLE BAY, depths are 4 to 5 feet. North of Snoopy Island there are several very shallow spots to avoid, and to the north and east of MT. FORTUNE depths are 5 feet or less everywhere except in the dredged channel into Port La Royale. In 1992 a 15 to 16 foot channel was dredged through the entrance under the bridge and on to PORT DE PLAISANCE; channels with 9 to 10 foot depths extend from Port De Plaisance to SIMPSON BAY YACHT CLUB and

to ISLAND WATER WORLD. Depths throughout the rest of the Lagoon are generally 7 to 20 feet, but the possibility of isolated shoals cannot be ruled out, and strangers should proceed with caution.

APPROACH See comments above under DEPARTING GREAT BAY-PHILIPSBURG and SOUTHWESTERN COAST-GREAT BAY TO SIMPSON BAY. When approaching from the northwest, give MAHO BAY a wide berth to avoid trouble with aircraft landing at the airport.

ENTERING The entrance to SIMPSON BAY is straightforward; depths across the mouth range from 17 feet off Great Point to 16 feet off Pelican Cays with 24 feet or more in between. The bottom shoals gradually up to the shores and to the bar with 2 to 3 feet over it approximately 70 yards off the beach south of the entrance to the Lagoon. Avoid the sunken barge 250 to 350 yards to the northeast of Pelican Cays on a line between the center of the Cays and the entrance to Simpson Bay Lagoon; it is marked by a reflecting buoy placed by Ian McPhearson of Sunsail Charters.

The entrance to SIMPSON BAY LAGOON is easily recognized by the large storage silos on its north side and by the huge Royal Palm Beach Club building on the

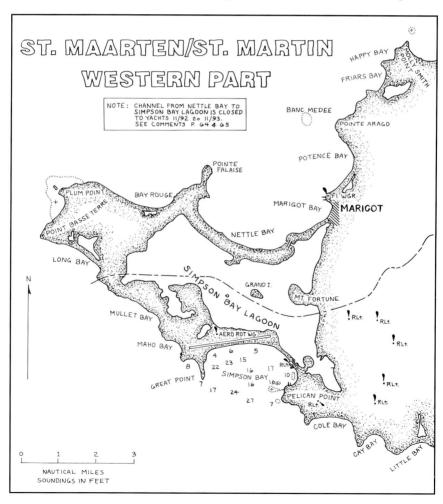

52

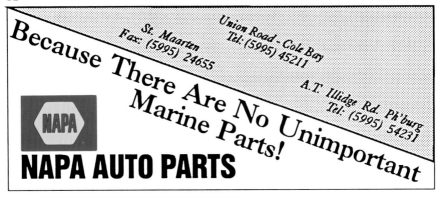
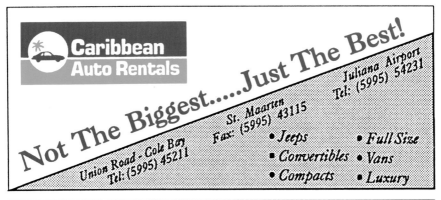
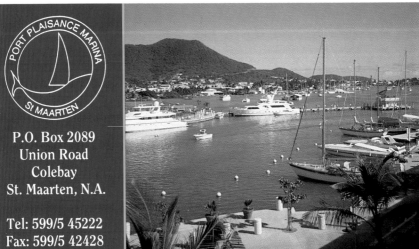

south and by the great, praying mantis arms of the drawbridge. Least depth in the cut is 16 feet, and currents in both directions can be strong. Do not attempt to sail through; use your motor or get a tow. The Harbormaster advises that the bridge opens daily at 6:00 A.M. and 5:30 P.M. when vessels are on the spot ready to go. We understand it also opens occasionally at 11:00 A.M.; contact the marinas at Port De Plaisance (Ch 67) or Simpson Bay Yacht Club (Ch 16) for current information. Outbound traffic has the right of way. Rumors have it that an Immigration office will be opened sometime near the bridge to handle clearance matters and that fees are being considered for all who enter and/or leave the Lagoon, but don't hold your breath for either one. We understand that plans are in the works to develop Snoopy Island as a tourist-oriented 'Fishing Village', and a bridge from Port De Plaisance is rumored . . . ugh!

ANCHORAGES/DOCKING The most protected and convenient anchorage in Simpson Bay is to the southeast between Pelican Cays and the entrance to the Lagoon. Anchor in sand off the bar some 70 yards off the beach but do not block traffic moving into and out of the Lagoon. To land on the beach, dinghy around the southern end of the bar in a good 5 feet of water. The docks at Pelican Resort are primarily for boats serving the Resort; dinghies should not be left there.

In Simpson Bay Lagoon most yachts anchor off the eastern shore between Snoopy Island and Mt. Fortune taking care to avoid the few, isolated shoals there and allowing plenty of room for traffic entering and leaving the Lagoon and for planes taking off from the airport. The holding is good, and all shore facilities are easily accessible by dinghy. Yachts that draw 4 feet or less can anchor in Cole Bay south of Snoopy Island. Marinas at PORT DE PLAISANCE(Ch 67), SIMPSON BAY YACHT CLUB(Ch 16), and ISLAND WATER WORLD (Ch 74) have full service slips; 15 feet can be carried into Port De Plaisance, 10 feet to Simpson Bay Y.C., and 9 feet into Island Water World. Dinghy

ENTRANCE TO SIMPSON BAY LAGOON *Derek Little photo*

landings are available at Port De Plaisance, Island Water World, Lagoon Marina, the BOATHOUSE RESTAURANT, and at the marina-in-the-making at La Palapa. If you land your dinghy on Snoopy Island or along the shore north of the bridge, someone should keep an eye on it.

SERVICES Around Simpson Bay Lagoon there is a very complete selection of suppliers and services to handle virtually any yacht problems. Most are along the eastern shore: ISLAND WATER WORLD (marine hardware, equipment, cordage, rigging supplies, paint, varnish, electronics, electrical supplies, dealers for Evinrude outboards, Avon inflatables, Boston Whaler, Jabsco, Perkins, Yanmar, U.S. charts, and cruising guides) is the oldest chandlery in St. Maarten; fuel, water, showers, and boat care are available; its large crane can lift your boat and set it on the hard, be it mono or multihull.

FKG RIGGING & MARINE FABRICATION(Ch 70) is behind Island Water World; it stocks rigging wire and fittings, roller reefing gear, propellers, and Mariner stoves; FKG has an excellent rigging repair and fabrication service and does all types of metal work in its machine shop; the crew can help with any problem your boat has. ST. MAARTEN SAILS is at the back of the Island Water World building on the second floor; under the friendly and expert guidance of Robert Guilders, it is widely known for its extensive experience and high quality Gowen and Doyle sails, sail repair, and all types of canvas work.

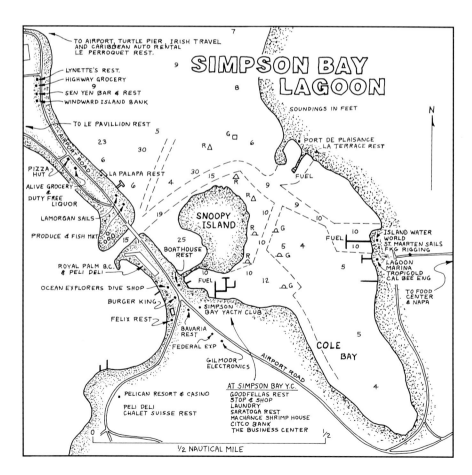

Just to the south of ISLAND WATER WORLD is the Lagoon Marina (water, electricity, laundry, showers, ice, storage lockers, and office services), Calbee Engineering (marine engine repairs and machine shop and yacht repair), and Tropicold (refrigeration, air conditioning, diesel engine, generator, and pump sales, repairs, and service). Next door Soloms Marina can haul power boats up to 35' to 40' LOA.

Along the western shore of the Lagoon north of the bridge LA MORGAN SAILS (Ch 9) will make or repair sails, sail covers, Biminis, etc. and do any type of canvas work; they have foam and fabric for settees and sell and service Profurl systems at their waterfront loft. At Simpson Bay Y.C. THE BUSINESS CENTER provides efficient telephone, fax, mailing, and shipping services. Further south towards town Gilmoor Electronics has Standard Communications equipment and services all sorts of electronic gear. IRISH TRAVEL on Airport Road arranges local tours and trips; visit them for a tour of the island or fabulous round trip flights to Saba, Statia, or St. Kitts. CARIBBEAN AUTO RENTAL and NAPA AUTO PARTS are located on Union Road about half a mile behind Island Water World.

ASHORE Pelican Watersports at Pelican Resort offers windsurfers, parasailing, Sunfish, power boats, and dive trips. Runners are invited to join the Road Runners Club Wednesdays at 5:15 P.M. and Sundays at 6:45 A.M. for fun runs that start at the Resort's parking lot. Ocean Explorers Dive Shop across the road from the Boathouse Restaurant has dive trips and dive gear for sale and rent. Golf enthusiasts who can't stay away from the greens should head for Mullet Bay Golf Club that is now open to the public; rental clubs are available. High rollers may want to head for the action at the Casino at Pelican Resort.

VHF Ch 16

ON SIMPSON BAY LAGOON NEAR THE AIRPORT

Breakfast, Lunch, Dinner

Happy Hour

Dinghy Dock   **Ice**   **Yacht Storage**

For provisioning check out the open air fish market between the bridge and La Morgan Sails and--further out towards the airport-- Alive Grocery, Duty Free Liquor Shop, and Highway Grocery. WINDWARD ISLAND BANK has a branch near the Highway Grocery. Stop & Shop at Simpson Bay Y.C. has a few grocery items, sodas, & beer, and PELI DELI at both Royal Palm B.C. and Pelican Resort stocks cold cuts, milk, pastries, french bread, ice cream, and, of course, deli sandwiches.

For heavy duty provisioning head for the new FOOD CENTER supermarket on Union Road behind Island Water World.

RESTAURANTS in the Simpson Bay & Lagoon area are many and diverse; we have included a number of the most popular in our sketch chart. For French cuisine that is really memorable (and expensive) Le Perroquet near the Airport and La Terrace at Port De Plaisnace are outstanding and worth the investment. At the modest end of the price range GOODFELLAS at Simpson Bay Y.C. has great pizzas and light fare, and the fast food places along Airport Road serve their usuals at low prices. In the mid-range we favor the great barbecues and seafood at the TURTLE PIER & BAR near the Airport (happy hour 6:00 to 7:00 P.M.); the tasty French fare at Le Pavillion on the north shore of Simpson Bay; the BECK'S BEER, schnitzel, and dumplings at BAVARIA RESTAURANT; the seafood, steaks, and live music at THE BOATHOUSE; and the super shrimp at Ma Chance. The restaurant at La Palapa is new to us; it has a dinghy dock and looks to be worth checking out.

NAVIGATION NOTE There is an aero radio beacon at Princess Juliana Airport . . . station PJM (● — — ● ● — — — — —) that operates on 308 kilohertz with 1,200 watts of power. Also at the Airport is a light described on government charts

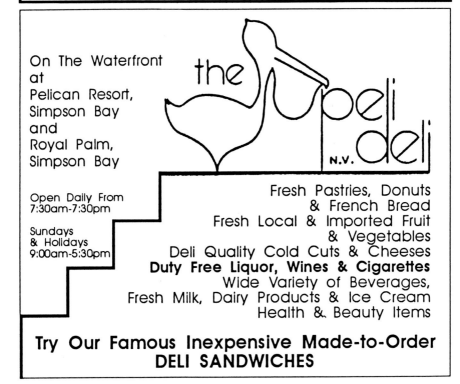

as "Alternate Flashing White\Green"; it is actually a rotating white and green light that is turned off after the last scheduled flight arrives . . . usually 9:00 P.M. May through November and l0:30 P.M. December through April!!!!

SOUTHWESTERN COAST-SIMPSON BAY TO POINTE BASSE TERRE

From Simpson Bay to the westernmost tip of the island at POINTE BASSE TERRE the coast of St. Maarten/St. Martin presents a dazzling array of beautiful and inviting beaches, impressive cliffs and caves, and fabled beach hotels. There are a few places for daytime anchoring, but they are inclined to roll a bit. Just beyond Great Point is BURGEUX BAY (exposed, rolly, and full of coral heads), the delightful Caravanserai Hotel, and clear and lovely MAHO BAY; all vessels are advised not to anchor there and to keep at least half a mile off the beach in Maho Bay to avoid interfering with aircraft landing at the airport.

To the northwest of Maho Bay is the monolithic Maho Beach Hotel & Casino, followed by the widely dispersed Mullet Bay Resort. The facilities of Mullet Bay Resort include a golf course (now open to the public), tennis courts, casino, restaurants, a complete selection of watersports, and the Towers. It is possible to anchor 100 yards off Mullet Bay beach, but the holding ground is poor, and it is a rolly spot where someone should stay on board to look after the boat. The northwestern end of the beach is marked by a star-shaped luxury condominium building trimmed in dark brown and by the neighboring Cupecoy Beach Resort and Treasure Island Hotel.

Beyond Mullet Bay to the northwest is CUPECOY BEACH with its series of coves backed by interesting sandstone cliffs and caves in layers of pinks, yellows, and

ochres...all topped off by a very congested group of holiday homes and condos. The caves are good for exploration and the beachcombing is interesting, but the anchorage is exposed and rolly and is recommended only for daytime stops. Cupecoy Beach terminates on the northwest in a prominent point that divides Dutch Sint Maarten from French Saint Martin.

The point also separates Cupecoy from LONG BAY BEACH (or simply LONG BEACH) and celebrity-studded and ultra-attractive La Samanna Hotel with its Moorish style architect and white condominiums. The best anchorage (daytime only) is in about 9 feet of uneasy water just off La Samanna which, understandably, does NOT really welcome visiting yachtsmen ashore even though the law does allow anyone to land and use the beach. Long Beach is very, very long and very, very lovely.

To avoid problems at Pointe Basse Terre, resist the urge to cut in close to shore; it is better to stay at least 300 yards off, because depths of 10 to 12 feet extend out approximately 200 yards, and large swells can make corner cutting more than merely uncomfortable.

NORTHERN COAST-POINTE BASSE TERRE TO MARIGOT

The beach between Pointe Basse Terre and PLUM POINT is known as PLUM or PRUNE BEACH, depending on which chart you use; but either way it is a pretty beach that is slightly steep for landing. In settled weather it is a reasonably good daytime anchorage, but you will have to pick your way carefully in among the shallow patches; the best anchorage is in the northeast part of the bay.

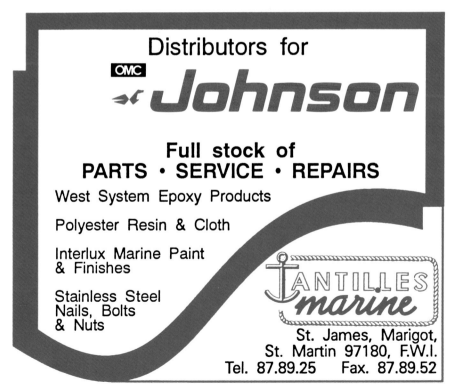

MARKET DAY IN MARIGOT *Eiman photo*

PLUM POINTE has two off-lying rocks awash and shoal water extending 100 yards or more to the northwest, so a wide berth . . . 300 yards or so . . . is advisable. Those sailing to MARIGOT or to BLOWING POINT on ANGUILLA in the usual easterly trades are advised to make a series of shorter tacks along the north coast of St. Martin. Beyond mid-point in the Channel the westerly current is usually a bit stronger and the waves are higher than on the St. Martin side. Tacking to the east you will pass the CLIFF OF THE BIRDS (FALAISE DES OISEAUX), topped by attractive homes, before coming to BAY ROUGE with its beautiful, inviting beach. The holding ground in Bay Rouge is good in clear sand, and the best anchorage is off the eastern end of the beach in 12 to 14 feet of water. Be sure your anchor is well set, especially if the beach is a lee shore. Just beyond the eastern end of the beach are two minute coves with caves, arches, and rocks of tremendously varying colors . . . a great place to explore cautiously by dinghy. Bay Rouge is a wonderful daytime stop in settled conditions.

Near POINTE FALAISE behind BAY OF CAILLES you'll see the bell tower of La Belle Creole, a luxury hotel complex in the form of a Mediterranean village. Started in 1960, construction was halted before completion by financial difficulties, and this unique project stood lifeless like a ghost town for three decades! With the problems finally solved, La Belle Creole was completed and opened at last in 1987.

MARIGOT

If you have only heard about French flair, style, elan, and joie de vivre, MARIGOT is a good place to experience them all and more; the town is delightfully French and French/Caribbean and full of laid back charm and chic excitement. It is the main port, commercial and political capital of St. Martin . . . a magnet that attracts an incredible assortment of pleasure seekers and those who only too willing to oblige them. The shops, boutiques, restaurants, the people, and lovely old buildings are marvelous. Activity in Marigot changes a good deal with the seasons. Winter is the high season and busy time; in the late spring and summer the visitors thin out, and many shopkeepers close up and go on vacation themselves so parts of the town seem almost deserted . . . and that can be nice too.

Marigot Harbor is in the large bay between POINTE FALAISE on the west and POINTE ARAGO on the northeast; the bay is open to the north and west and consists of NETTLE BAY off the southern shore, MARIGOT BAY in the middle, and POTENCE BAY on the northeast. The center of the town is just south of the point and 200-foot hill that separate Marigot Bay and Potence Bay; the ruins of Fort St. Louis atop the hill are most impressive when bathed in light after dark; the commercial and ferry piers and the Port Authority office are at the base of the hill along with a 35-foot white tower with a flashing WRG light that is difficult-to-impossible to see against the lights of the town.

The French government has done an impressive job of planning and managing the explosive growth in Marigot. Much of the charm and delightful feeling of the traditional French West Indies remains, and compatible new shops, hotels, and restaurants, etc. add greatly to the enjoyment of both visitors and local citizens. Sailors will be particularly impressed with the wonderful new landfill in the center of town that has created greatly improved landing facilities for dinghies and local fishing boats.

In 1992 we received several reports that many unattended yachts in the harbor were broken into by thieves who stole money and valuable personal possessions . . . presumably to buy drugs. This problem apparently has continued for many months.

Until security is drastically improved, we must recommend that yachts should not be left unattended at night in Marigot.

APPROACHES From the west a quarter mile off the shore clears all hazards from Plum Pointe to Pointe Falaise. Similarly, from the east a quarter mile off will keep you in good water from MOLLY SMITH POINTE at the western end of GRANDE CASE BAY to Pointe Arago. BANC MEDEE, about 700 yards west of Pte. Arago, shoals to 15 feet, but otherwise depths over to Pte. Falaise are 20 to 25 feet. Approaching the town the bottom is somewhat irregular but generally comes up to 8 to 10 feet well off the shore.

ANCHORAGE For the best protection and greatest convenience anchor in as close to Marigot as your draft will permit; we anchored 200 yards off the new waterfront landfill in mid-1990 in 7 feet with no problem. When the harbor is full, yachts anchor all the way down to Morne Rond in settled conditions. Nobody anchors in Potence Bay probably because of the commercial shipping there and the noise from the desalinization and power plants. But up towards Pte. Arago there are two small beaches that look like quiet spots to spend the night. The anchorage off Marigot has good holding in sand and grass and provides fine protection in all weather except when the wind is from the north or northwest or when infrequent northern swells come in. Again, when it is uncomfortable in Marigot, head for Philipsburg, and visa versa. Dinghies can be left along the new landfill in the center of town; security wires and locks are, as always, advised. There is a dinghy dock in Port La Royale Marina, but it is a long trip around from the anchorage off the town and hardly seems worth the effort.

CLEARANCE The Port Authority office behind the commercial and ferry piers handles clearance matters simply and easily from 7:00 A.M. to 5:00 P.M. Mondays through Fridays and from 7:00 A.M. until noon on Saturdays. Crewed charter yacht captains are

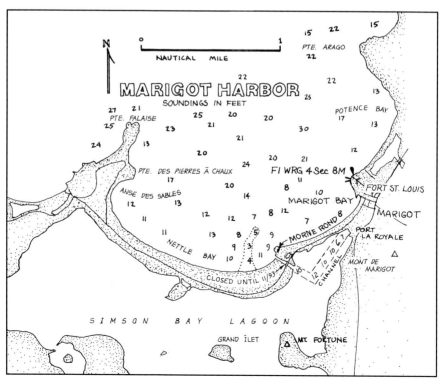

64

cautioned that French cabotage law prohibits foreign vessels from chartering between French ports without a special license; violators can be subject to severe penalties.

SERVICES Near the bridge over the channel leading into the Lagoon MERCURY MARINE CENTER (Ch 72) sells and services Mercury outboards and maintains an extensive stock of parts and some chandlery items. Nearby in the Sandy Ground-Nettle Bay area SGP (Ch 12) hauls boats up to 20 tons and 7 foot draft; Sailen makes and repairs sails; Diesel Marine Services (Ch 7) specializes in Perkins engines and repairs all diesels; Egreteau Marine Services (Ch 77) carries inflatables and furling systems; and Electronic Center (Ch 10) provides sales and service for electronics and navigation equipment.

Inside the Lagoon at St. James near Port La Royale ANTILLES MARINE distributes and repairs JOHNSON OUTBOARDS and carries a wide assortment of Johnson parts as well as fiberglass products, paint and varnish, etc.

Port La Royale is Marigot's marina and the home of CARAIBES SPORT BOATS - CSB - where you can rent/charter 13' to 46' sail or power boats by the day or week; it is great for anyone eager to water ski or take a fast run to Tintamarre or to Anguilla for a quick trip to Sandy Island, Little Bay, or Prickly Pears. It is also home for the bareboats of Sunsail and Dynamique. The limited dock space is always jammed full, and only water and ice are available. There is a dinghy dock, but otherwise there isn't much to attract transient yachts. The marina is surrounded by a great array of restaurants, shops, and boutiques that are all very accessible by land.

The usual approach to Port La Royale through the channel into Simpson Bay Lagoon from Nettle Bay near Morne Rond will be closed to yachts from November,

MARIGOT *Derek Little photo*

1992 to November, 1993 because of construction of a new opening bridge over the channel. Dinghies may still be able to pass through, but that is not certain at press time. During construction yachts can get into and out of Port La Royale from the Dutch side via Simpson Bay and Simpson Bay Lagoon and a new 3 meter (9.8 ft) channel dredged from between MT. FORTUNE and GRAND ISLAND over to the 'regular' channel into Port La Royale. We have not been able to learn how this new channel will be marked, but presumably suitable markers will be placed in due time. The situation is somewhat uncertain as we go to press in November, 1992; for the latest information contact one of the charter fleets or marinas.

In the Port La Royale complex La Case Bernard repairs outboards. In town across from the Hotel De Ville (town hall) Team No. 1 has an assortment of cruising guides and charts, dive equipment, and fishing tackle. On Rue D'Anguille Shoreline Marine distributes Yamaha outboards and stocks some marine hardware and accessories. Up in the Potence Bay area Carib Diesel/Danish Burt repairs diesel and gas engines, transmissions, shafts, alternators, starters, etc.

Provisioning in Marigot is out of this world. If your taste runs to tempting cheeses, wonderful pates, fresh produce, meats, and French canned fruits, vegetables, bread, butter, and wine, etc. head for the new MAMMOUTH SUPERMARKET (pronounced Ma-Moot) a few steps to the north on the main road to Grande Case; the selection of foodstuffs will amaze you, as will the housewares, clothing, etc.,etc. On a smaller scale but also impressive is the K-Dis Supermarket on Rue Charles De Gaulle near the Town Hall. The bakery (boulangerie/patisserie) on Rue De La Liberte across from the Palais De Justice and the Post Office is our favorite for wonderful breads, croissants, mouth-

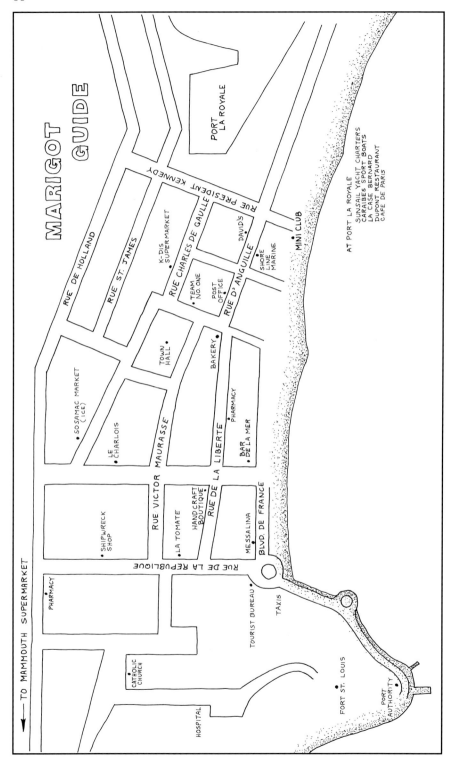

watering pastries and snacks; enjoy them all at the shaded tables along the sidewalk. For those who appreciate the finer things in life CHAMPAGNE on Rue Kennedy offers an impressive selection of vintage wines, fine digestifs and apcritifs, caviar, and delicious smoked salmon.

The most colorful, exciting, and interesting provisioning by far is done at the open air market on the waterfront Mondays through Saturdays starting at about 6:00 A.M.; Saturdays are the biggest and best Market Days with the greatest selections of locally grown fruits and vegetables, fresh fish, conch, meat, spices, T-shirts, jewelry, and audio tapes. Go early and take your own shopping bags as the vendors do not supply them. The Saturday market is the major social and shopping event of the week . . . .a wonderful slice of traditional West Indian life that should not be missed.

RESTAURANTS Marigot is well known . . . and rightfully so . . . for the variety and excellence of its restaurants; the quality of the cuisine and service is generally high, and frequently the prices as well. Restaurants such as La Maison Sur La Port, L'Aventure, La Vie En Rose, Messalina, and Jean DuPont, La Calanque, and Le Poisson D'Or generally serve elegant lunches and dinners at elegant prices; Messalina is especially noteworthy. Great, more realistically priced favorites among yachtsmen are the Mini Club and David's along Rue D'Anguille. The dining terrace at the Mini Club is like a tree house among swaying palms overlooking the harbor; the wonderful menu features French and seafood delights; buffets on Wednesday and Saturday nights are memorable with dozens of selections including beef, pork, fish, lobster, cheeses, salads, pastries, and wines all at a reasonable prix fixe with a nice guitar playing in the background. David's is a lively spot that reflects the English heritage of its yachtsmen-owners; Beef Wellington is featured along with steaks, seafood, and conch fritters; happy hours, entertainment and sing-alongs are part of the warm and friendly atmosphere. Cas Anny

MARIGOT MARKET *Eiman photo*

68

is a modest spot for good Creole food at modest prices. Le Charlois has earned very favorable comments for its delicious and reasonable roast beef, steak, etc. We like the menu and entertainment at Cafe De Paris at Port La Royale as well as the al fresco dining overlooking the action along the marina. A special find is La Pailotte just before the bridge over the cut into the Lagoon; the French West Indian atmosphere and menu features grills, lobster, and fish; it is right on the water so you can come and go by dinghy and enjoy romantic views. And for pizza, hamburgers, and more in a chic atmosphere with live music lots of activity at night in season try the popular Le Bar De La Mer just back of the open air market on the waterfront. And those are just a few highlights.

SHOPPING From Rue De La Republique to Port La Royale Marigot is filled with shops presenting merchandise that is stylish, dazzling, colorful, amusing, impressive, revealing, touching, delightful, interesting, laughable, exciting, practical, outrageous, and beautiful . . . things to slip into, things to use, things to slather over your body, things to play with, things to look at, things to slip out of, things to smell, things on strings, things to hide behind, things to remember. Along Rue De La Republique and Rue De LA Liberte the shops are often among or actually in beautiful, old West Indian houses with balconies and lovely ornamental iron work. On Rue Charles De Gaulle and in Port La Royale they are all in smart, state-of-the-art facilities. Shopkeepers prefer to appeal more on quality, originality, style, and allure than on bargain basement pricing.

English: How much is it? French: C'est combien? (or SAY COMB BIEHNN?) English: In dollars? French: En dollars? (or AHHN DOLAAARZE) English: Ah, inexpensive. French: Ah, bon marche (or AHHH, BOHNN MAR SHAY) ENGLISH: That's too expensive! French: C'est tros cher! (or SAY TROW SHARE!) Bonne chance alors!

MARIGOT TO GRANDE CASE

The coast is clear for cruising yachts between Marigot and MOLLY SMITH POINT at the western end of Grande Case Bay; just stay a few hundred yards off. To the north of the industrial area and long beach in Potence Bay there are two small, isolated beaches that look attractive; they might be worth investigating. To the northeast of Pointe Arago is FRIAR'S BAY; all is peaceful and quiet along this 150-yard beach, which is usually deserted because access from the road is difficult. The house above the south end of the beach used to belong to Senator Brooke from Massachusetts. The water is normally calm and protection is good except when the wind or swells come in from the north or northwest. The bottom shoals gradually, and 6 feet of water can be found about 20 yards off the beach. Hopefully, the land behind the beach here will not be covered with hotels and condos for a while so this attractive, uncrowded anchorage can remain unspoiled for a few more years

HAPPY BAY is between Friar's Bay and MOLLY SMITH POINT. Exposed more to the north, the beach there is slightly steep. There is good holding ground in sand in 9 feet approximately 20 yards off. The best anchorage is in the northeast end where there is less surge, but stay clear of the rock outcroppings at both extremities. Happy Bay is the site of the Happy Beach Hotel consisting of about a dozen buildings . . . rooms, villas, and other facilities for guests. A nice spot for a lunch stop and a swim.

GRANDE CASE

GRAND CASE is the second town in French St. Martin. For ten years we have described it as an attractive fishing village that is even more charming when viewed from close range ashore. There may still be some fishing going on, but today it is basically a restaurant village where there are over twenty establishments serving tasteful Creole or French food in attractive settings at prices that are generally . . . but not always . . . more reasonable than found in Marigot.

READY FOR THE CLEAN, SWEET WIND   *Eiman photo*

APPROACHES There is one special hazard for cruising yachts in the approaches to Grande Case: a small, dangerous reef with depths of 4 to 6 feet off MOLLY SMITH POINTE. It is not named in charts and guides, but we will christen it MOLLY SMITH REEF. The location of MOLLY SMITH REEF is described as follows:

- Approximately 200 to 300 yards off Molly Smith Pointe to the northeast
- Just to the northwest of the line between Molly Smith Pointe and ROC CROLE
- Bearings from the reef are approximately 57° magnetic to Roc Crole and approximately 112° magnetic to the large pier in Grande Case

The safest approach from the west is to pass outside Molly Smith Reef to the north and east and then head in towards the town pier. There are a few rocks off Molly Smith Pointe and a shoal that extends out 50 to 75 yards so passing between the Pointe and the Reef could be dicey.

If approaching Grande Case from the east, do not pass between Roc Crole and Bell Pointe where winds and currents are uncertain. Stand off Roc Crole by 100 yards or more and swing around to the west of it. In settled weather there is good snorkeling around Roc Crole; approach with care from the west and anchor to the south of the rock. Alternately, you can anchor off Grande Case and dinghy out.

ANCHORING The bottom in Grande Case Bay shoals gradually and evenly to depths of 6 to 8 feet some 50 yards off the shore. Anchor in fair-to- good holding in sand and grass anywhere you like; the best protection and calmest water is usually between the town pier and the Grande Case Beach Hotel to the northeast. Dinghies can be secured to the dinghy dock beside the large pier; don't forget the security wire and lock.

ASHORE Limited provisions can be bought at Self Service Shopping Center and Tony's Meat and Vegetable Market. The excellent Grande Case Pharmacy has pharmaceuticals, cosmetics, sun tan products, film, etc.

GRANDE CASE *Derek Little photo*

For tasty food, fast and cheap, try the road stands behind the main pier for barbecue chicken, fish, ribs and lots of smoke, but it's great. To the west of the center of town Club South has burgers, fish, onion rings, french fries, etc. From there it is all up and up and up in ambiance, quality, and price. Of the fine restaurants Panoramique at the Grande Case Beach Club has the most dazzling view and a good menu with realistic prices. Newcomer Cha Cha Cha features Creole food at relatively modest prices. Sebastino is definitely different with its fine Northern Italian cuisine. Towards the western end of town is our favorite for a memorable evening Rainbow Cafe (superb contemporary cuisine, delightful ambience, quite expensive); reservations necessary. Along the main street just let your eyes be your guide; menus are posted outside most restaurants. You can hardly have a bad or mediocre lunch or dinner anywhere in Grande Case. If you are a Bogart fan, you might enjoy the 40s atmosphere and decor at the new Key Largo that offers a mixture of Italian, French, and West Indian delights.

GRANDE CASE TO NORTH POINTE

From Grande Case Bay to North Pointe a quarter mile off the shore and rocks clears all hazards. As mentioned, snorkeling around ROC CROLE is good, but do not pass through between Roc Crole and Bell Pointe where fluky winds and currents can cause problems. Off the bulge in the coast near North Pointe breakers often extend a few hundred yards off the shore; give them a wide berth.

DUCK BEACH

Marcel Rock lies some 3/4 of a mile east of Roc Crole; it is about 15 feet high and divides ANSE MARCEL to the east from DUCK BEACH to the west. A shallow reef

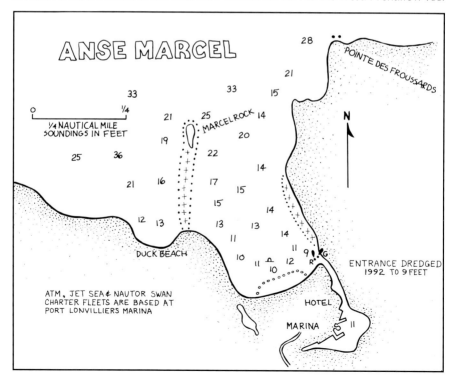

Free and Easy...

...that's our style. Whatever your vacation date, we offer sun spangled cruises in the ultimate crusing locations. Choose from our fleet of 200 specially designed sailing boats crafted to suit your seagoing skills. Our philosophy is one of comfort and freedom.

ATM *yachts*

Crewed and bareboat yacht cruises

CARIBBEAN ISLANDS: Martinique, Saint-Martin, Guadeloupe • GRENADINES • TAHITI

ANSE MARCEL AND DUCK BEACH   *Eiman photo*

extends south from Marcel Rock to the land. Although this reef is terrible for keels, it is excellent for snorkeling with interesting coral and lots and lots of colorful fish.

Duck Beach is a lovely, small beach that is usually uncrowded and peaceful. Head straight in to the beach keeping 200 yards off Rock Marcel and the reef behind it. There is 30 feet of water west of the Rock and 12 feet 100 yards off the beach with no problems in between. In settled conditions it is a fine daytime anchorage for enjoying the beach and the snorkeling in peace and quiet.

ANSE MARCEL

ANSE MARCEL provides fine protection in all conditions except when the wind swings around to the north. Behind the beautiful beach at its head lie the expanding facilities of Le Meridien Habitation that include guest accommodations, restaurants,

PORT LONVILLIERS   *Eiman photo*

Skipper one of our yachts and see why we never call it "bareboating."

Take the helm and capture the tropical adventure of your dreams. Sail with Jet Sea, on your own or with our friendly crew, and anything wonderful is possible. All aboard the newest, most luxurious sailing fleet serving the Caribbean. At your command are such world-class performance yachts as Henri Wauquiez and Kirie. Each of our 135 yachts is fully equipped and impeccably serviced. Only Jet Sea yachts are complete with auto pilot, Sat-Nav and spinnakers as standards. Never "bare." Any Caribbean itinerary is available including one-way destinations: cruise the islands of your choice from the Virgins to the Grenadines. While paradise on earth may not have a specific address...it does have a telephone number: 1-800-262-JETC.

THE FINEST YACHT CHARTER VACATIONS IN THE CARIBBEAN

JET SEA

1650 S.E. 17th Street, Suite 204, Ft. Lauderdale, FL 33316
Call Jon A. Lind (305) 467-0528, FAX (305) 467-6661

pools, shops, a fitness center, a helicopter pad, and the Port Lonvilliers Marina; another marina on the western side of Anse Marcel is in the talking/rumor stage. The colored roofs of the buildings . . . a few are bright red . . . make identification from the sea easy.

ENTERING AND ANCHORING The shoal shown on U.S. and Dutch charts smack in the middle of Anse Marcel does not exist. The only dangers are the coral extending out about 150 yards from the eastern shore, the reef south of Marcel Rock, and the jet and water skiers zooming around and around from morning till night, especially in season. The calmest anchorage is well up on the eastern side of the bay, but don't block the entrance to the marina. Backwinds curl over the hills to the east, so you'll need a stern anchor to keep you from swinging around. Be sure your anchors set well in the grass covered bottom.

The entrance to Port Lonvilliers Marina is in the southeast corner and is marked by red and green lights and buoys (red-right-returning). The channel has been dredged to a least depth of 9 feet. It is wide enough for only one boat, but a passing bulge has been provided half way along. It is a good idea to check with the Dock Master on VHF Ch. 16 about traffic before you start in. Depth in the lagoon is 11 feet; gas, diesel, water, ice, showers, laundry, rental cars, telephones, and fax service are available; there are transient slips although they are usually booked solidly in season. Lonvilliers Yachting is a small chandlery, and the Superette carries basic provisions. The Dock Master can arrange for help with mechanical, electronic, and other problems. ATM YACHTS, NAUTOR'S SWAN, and JET SEA base their impressive bareboat fleets at Port Lonvilliers.

ASHORE The attractive public facilities of the Le Meridien Habitation complex are available for your pleasure. A few shops carry souvenirs, art work, resort wear, etc. Restaurants range from Le Barbecue on the beach and La Belle France to the haute

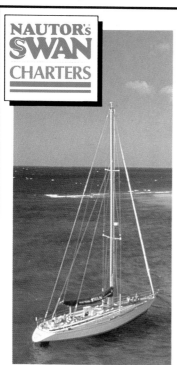

76

cuisine haute on the hill and a new Italian restaurant to open in late 1992. High flyers will go wild over helicopter flights that can be arranged, but they may gasp at the cost. In the French tradition, half the fun is often people watching; the crowd is attractive, enthusiastic, and active.

EAST COAST OF ST. MARTIN/ST. MAARTEN

The east coast of St. Martin/St. Maarten is a usually a dead lee shore; most of it is covered with coastal reefs and breakers. Stand well off it at all times unless you are entering ORIENT BAY or OYSTER POND, and before you do enter either of these bays, make sure you are absolutely certain of your position so you won't go up on the reefs as a dozen or so yachts have in recent years. Give wide berths to MOLLEY BEDAY, COW AND CALF, PELICAN, and HEN AND CHICKENS off the southern end of the east coast and be especially careful to avoid the shoal extending to the east of Molly Beday.

SPANISH ROCK (BASSE ESPAGNOLE) is a small, dangerous reef that lies approximately 3/4 of a mile off to the north and east of North Pointe. It is just north of the line between the northernmost extremity of St. Martin and the north end of TINTAMARRE ISLAND. The bearing from Spanish Rock to the southwest tip of Tintamarre is approximately 144° magnetic. The bearing from it to the flat top of OOSENBERG PEAK, the isolated and highest hill on the eastern side of St. Maarten, is approximately 210° magnetic. Spanish Rock juts up to within 7 feet of the surface in one or possibly two spots and breaks in heavy weather. It sits on a fairly large shoal that has depths of 20 to 22 feet; water around this shoal is 50 to 60 feet deep. The positions of Spanish Rock shown on charts are APPROXIMATE and should be treated with great caution. We understand that Spanish Rock is an excellent dive site for experienced, open sea

divers.

The safest way to pass Spanish Rock is to sail well to the east of it way over towards Tintamarre to avoid the chance of going up on the shore reefs off North Pointe and extending south from it to ILE PINEL. If you do go between Spanish Rock and North Pointe, stay 1/2 mile off North Pointe; at all times keep a safe distance off the lee shore of St. Martin.

TINTAMARRE ISLAND, known locally as FLAT ISLAND, is a popular daytime anchorage and in settled conditions can be a good spot to spend the night if there are no bothersome swells running. Privately owned and uninhabited except for scores of goats, lizards, and a few tortoises, Tintamarre is about a mile and a half long, half a mile wide, and 125 feet high. The most popular anchorage is off the beautiful beach in the bay on the west side of the island; the beach has a few tall, isolated cedar trees behind it and is bounded by low outcroppings of rocks on the south and by cliffs 50 to 60 feet high on the north. Shore reefs extend out from the point at the north end of the beach. The bottom falls off rather rapidly with 10 to 12 feet of water over clear sand about 35 yards off; farther off the bottom is covered with grass. This is a thoroughly enjoyable anchorage in settled weather with the wind from the east, especially if you are not upset by topless bathing and sunning. If you anchor in really close, be on the lookout for wind shifts and use a second anchor if you stay overnight. Day trip boats and occasionally cruise ships anchor off Tintamarre and increase the beach population dramatically. There is pleasant but modest snorkeling off the rocks and the remains of the concrete pier at the south end of the beach. One story has it that the Germans established a small operating base on Tintamarre during World War II to service submarines operating in the Caribbean; this small pier was supposed to have been used in refueling the subs.

TINTAMARRE I.   *Eiman photo*

Behind the beach are the overgrown remains of an airstrip, pieces of old aircraft here and there, a few ancient buildings, and some sort of an animal compound towards the middle of the island. M. Remy de Haenen of St. Barts is reported to have established a base for planes here in the late 40s and 50s, but nobody seems to know if the remaining bits and pieces come from his aircraft or others. According to the caretaker/watchman visitors are not permitted beyond the beach; their presence disturbs the goats and makes them more uncooperative at round-up time. In addition, there has been trouble with people stealing the goats, and that is another reason for visiting yachtsmen to stay on the beach and not venture inland.

The best snorkeling is in the bay on the northwest side of Tintamarre where there is good protection when the wind is from the south of east. It has no beach, but the rugged cliffs along the shore give it a wonderfully wild feeling. The bottom is grass with large areas of clear sand, and depths of 10 to 12 feet are found 100 to 150 yards off the shore. In closer there are numerous patches of coral that come up to within a few feet of the surface and provide excellent snorkeling. Pick your way in carefully and anchor where you won't swing onto the coral even if the wind shifts. Or, better still, anchor off the western beach and dinghy around to enjoy the snorkeling.

100 yards of so off the southwest tip of Tintamarre is a very small, gravelly island and a very shallow, tricky dinghy and outboard entrance into the lagoon behind the reef that lies 200 to 300 yards off the southern shore. Once through this narrow passage, an outboard can be used cautiously but be alert for patches of coral near the surface. The caretaker and workmen enter the lagoon in their outboards and anchor in its eastern end. Snorkeling along the inside of the western end of the reef is disappointing; we have found lots of dead coral and routine to dull scenery. Exploring the eastern end of the lagoon by dinghy would be great sport; you might find some wonderful snorkeling.

ORIENT BAY

ORIENT BAY is a large open bay facing slightly north of east with an entrance approximately three-quarters of a mile wide between ILE PINEL on the north and GREEN CAY (CAYE VERT) on the south. It is a wonderful place to visit; the beaches are picturesque to spectacular; the snorkeling is modest to wonderful; and there are opportunities to beachcomb, windsurf, dine ashore, enjoy St. Martin's only official nudist beach, and relax and unwind.

IT IS EXTREMELY IMPORTANT TO KNOW YOUR POSITION ACCURATELY BEFORE YOU ENTER ORIENT BAY AND TO ENTER ONLY BETWEEN ILE PINEL AND GREEN CAY. There are small, dangerous openings between Ile Pinel and the mainland to the northwest of it and between Green Cay and the land south of it. DO NOT ATTEMPT TO ENTER VIA THESE SMALL OPENINGS.

APPROACHES AND ENTERING

In normal conditions entering Orient Bay is straightforward as long as you avoid the shoals, reefs, and breakers that extend out from Ile Pinel and Green Cay. The good water is generally in the middle of the large entrance between these two islands, and usually you can run right in without difficulty. As the wind freshens and the seas build up, the breakers around Pinel and Green Cay get bigger and bigger and extend farther and farther out from the shore and thus reduce the usable entrance area. The directions

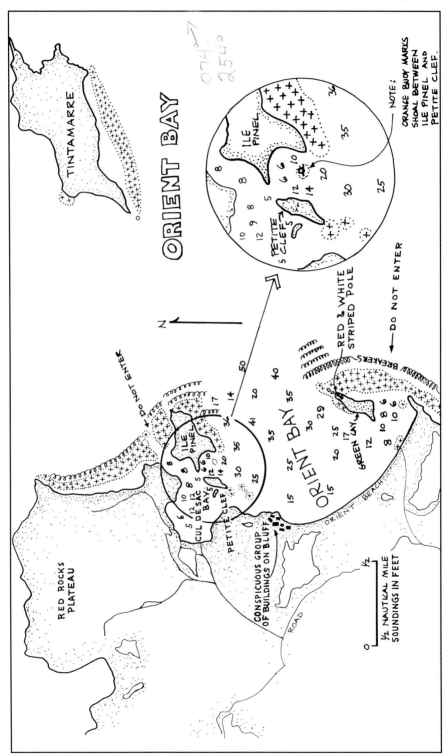

Opposite page Orient Bay; *Derek Little photo*

below are intended to help you enter Orient Bay in average-to-fresh conditions when you know your position accurately and when you can see and identify the significant landmarks. Whenever you cannot avoid breakers or high seas that could cause problems for your boat, your crew, or your dinghy, do not enter Orient Bay; come back another day.

FROM THE NORTH:
- Stand well off the lee shore and reefs from North Pointe to Ile Pinel and avoid Spanish Rock as noted above.

- Stay off Ile Pinel a half mile to the east to avoid shallow water where breakers can build up in heavy weather.

- Proceed south past Ile Pinel until the conspicuous group of buildings at the northern end of the long beach in Orient Bay bears 290° magnetic. (See our sketch chart and photo).

- If the course is free of breakers, turn onto 290° magnetic and proceed on in. If there are breakers ahead on 290° magnetic, do not attempt to enter.

FROM THE SOUTH
- Stand well off the lee shore on St. Maarten/St. Martin and avoid the islands and rocks off the southern part of the coast as noted earlier.

- Identify Green Cay and the small opening to the south that separates it from the mainland of St. Martin.

  You may see boats anchored in this opening; they are on the far side of the dangerous reefs across the entire opening. Identifying Green Cay can be quite difficult because it matches and blends in with the western shore of Orient Bay behind it.

- Proceed north until you can identify positively the red-and-white pole at the northern end of Green Cay.

- Continue past the reefs and breakers off Green Cay until the conspicuous cluster of buildings at the northern end of the beach on the western shore of Orient Bay bears 290° magnetic. (See our sketch chart and photo.)

- If there are no breakers on the course, turn onto 290° magnetic and proceed on in. If there are breakers ahead on 290° magnetic, do not attempt to enter.

ILE PINEL

Ile Pinel is a classic tropic paradise complete with a magnificent white beach, sparkling clear water, swaying palm trees, and a comfortable and secure anchorage. When hordes from cruise ships or day trippers are brought out from Cul De Sac Bay in small boats, the beach is crowded, but peace and quiet return when they all leave late in the afternoon.

ENTERING AND ANCHORING Once inside Orient Bay head for the middle of PETITE CLEF on 325° magnetic and line it up with the westernmost peak in the high ground of Red Rocks. Turn onto a course of 005° heading towards the western end of the foliage on the sand spit on Pinel. Avoid the 3- to 4-foot shoal between the tip of Pinel and Petite

Eiman photo

NOTE CONSPICUOUS GROUP OF BUILDINGS ON BLUFF NORTH OF BEACH

WESTERN SHORE ORIENT BAY

ILE PINEL AND ANCHORAGE   *Eiman photo*

Clef that is marked by a private buoy; there is 10 feet of water between the shoal and Ile Pinel and 10 - 12 feet between it and Petite Cleff. Once past the shoal anchor in 6 to 9 feet in sand and grass; use a stern anchor if the wind is expected to shift.

Don't even think about anchoring in Cul De Sac Bay to the northwest of Petite Clef. The water there is 6 to 12 feet deep, but getting to it is difficult-to-hazardous. There is 5 feet of water at most between the sand spit on Ile Pinel and Petite Clef that will stop all but very shoal draft boats. The narrow passage to the northwest of Pinel has some dangerous coral heads at its outer extremity and a small, wave-swept entrance; thus this passage should be avoided.

PLEASURES Ile Pinel is a wonderful island to explore; take your shoes and camera for the easy hike up to the tops of the hills where the views are exhilarating. Try the beach on the north side for shelling and the one on the southeast for snorkeling behind the reefs. The snorkeling is good off the southern tip of Pinel and around the rocks and reefs south of Petite Cleff. You can buy snacks and refreshments or rent windsurfers and jet skis at the shacks along the beach; ultralight plane rides are sometimes available.

For more extensive exploration ashore, dinghy over to the small dock on the far shore of Cul De Sac Bay; the road behind it leads past local homes, huge French resorts, and DREW'S DELI. Drew's is a real find and a personal favorite of ours. Open daily for lunch and dinner except Friday nights and all day Saturdays. Drew serves great deli-style lunches with island overtones and seafood/steak/burger dinners. There is are barbecue dinners on Sundays and special 3 course dinners Thursdays at very attractive prices.

GREEN CAY (CAYE VERTE)

At the southern end of Orient Bay there is a second small paradise anchorage off Green Cay, the epitome of a windswept, deserted tropical isle complete with nesting pelicans that come swooping in at day's end. Green Cay and the reefs to the south of it provide good protection from the seas rolling in from the east. The area nearby is alive with all sorts of colorful diversions.

APPROACH AND ANCHORING There are no obstructions in the southern part of Orient Bay except the reefs that extend about 150 yards off the west coast of Green Cay. Most boats anchor between Green Cay and the beach to the south and southwest where the depth varies from 7 to 11 feet, and the water is the clearest, most beautiful turquoise to be seen anywhere. Interestingly, we have found 7 to 8 feet of water half way between Green Cay and the beach and a few feet more further on towards the beach. In any event, feel your way in cautiously and anchor in suitable depth wherever you find the best combination of quiet water and cooling breezes; if swells curl around Green Cay, you may want to put out a stern anchor. Deeper draft boats, of course, should not go south of Green Cay, and indeed some . . . both deep and average draft boats . . . prefer to anchor in the lee of Green Cay some 200 yards or more off the shore.

ASHORE The beautiful beach that stretches two miles along the western shore of Orient Bay is breathtaking, and, as almost everybody knows, it is St. Martin's only official nude, naturalist, or clothes-optional beach, as you prefer. The southeastern part of the beach is by far the most active and can be crowded on weekends and holidays. The attractive naturalist CLUB ORIENT hotel, bar and restaurant are there; you are welcome for luncheon, cocktails, or dinner; clothes are optional for one and all. The Club also has a good watersports operation that rents windsurfers and Hobie Cats and runs snorkel trips.

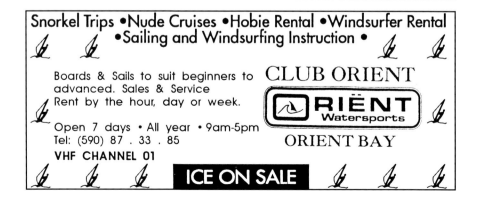

GREEN CAY *Eiman photo*

Nearby is a collection of modest buildings (i.e. beach shacks) that caters to bathers arriving by car or bus; they sell chicken, burgers, fries, ribs, beer, soft drinks, beachwear, jewelry, T shirts, souvenirs, and trinkets. It is strange to see the local entrepreneurs selling chicken legs and beer to tourists with sun hats, sun glasses, and suntanned bottoms! Before you rush ashore, be advised that there is a bit of coral awash near the beach shacks just where you want to land; be careful . . . the coral could damage your dinghy and cut your feet.

Further along the beach to the northwest the new Bikini Beach (Ch 70) sports red beach umbrellas, the Kon Tiki restaurant, and watersports. And beyond that Wikiki Beach is another new restaurant-cum-watersports operation. It is uncertain whether all this development will add to or decrease the pleasures of the nude beach; we'll just have to wait and see . . .

The snorkeling along the west side of Green Cay is very, very good indeed . . . perhaps the best to be found in St. Martin. In the protection of Green Cay the reefs are covered with interesting hard and soft corals and many varieties of colorful reef fish all along the coast and among the reefs to the north.

ORIENT BAY TO OYSTER POND

A mile south of Green Cay, FLAMAND BAY has an inviting, long crescent beach and an assortment of resort hotels, but it is definitely a NO-NO. The narrow entrance through the reefs that extend across the entire Bay is reported to have a bad, unmarked coral patch in it and is no place for strangers. The coast from Flamand to OYSTER POND is filled with shore rocks and reefs; give them a wide berth.

OYSTER POND

OYSTER POND lies a mile south of Flamand Bay and about 3-1/2 miles north of Pointe Blanche. It is a completely land locked anchorage that has long been considered one of the best hurricane holes in the Caribbean. CAPTAIN OLIVER'S MARINA, HOTEL AND RESTAURANT have stimulated much of the recent popularity of the Pond and its growth as a yachting center. There are so many boats based there . . . including the charter fleets of SUN YACHT CHARTERS, Omega, and The Moorings . . . that many have to seek protected harbors elsewhere during hurricanes. Thus, cruising yachts are advised NOT to take refuge in Oyster Pond during hurricanes.

APPROACHES AND ENTERING Stand well off the east coast/lee shore of St. Maarten/ St. Martin until you identify Oyster Pond and the spars marking its entrance channel. The most conspicuous landmarks are the extensive, multicolored cottages of the beachfront hotel (with changing ownership) north of MONT DU FEIF, the Oyster Pond Yacht Club complex that covers almost all of BABIT POINT, and Dawn Beach Hotel just to the south of Oyster Pond.

From offshore the bay outside Oyster Pond often appears to be almost completely filled with breakers, and so it can be. But there is a good, deep, well marked, dog-leg channel that leads safely into the Pond in all but the heaviest weather; it is marked by red and green/black spars (red-right-returning). The spar markers are maintained by Captain Oliver's Marina (see our sketch chart); their positions may change from time to time. An orange sea buoy is reported to be outside the spars, but we have never seen it in place. The entrance is down wind and passes through breakers close to a lee shore, so there is little room for error. In heavy weather or high seas we recommend having a qualified, local pilot on board while entering or leaving Oyster Pond. If you have any doubts or questions, or if you need assistance, contact Captain Oliver's Marina on VHF Ch. 16 or 67 before entering.

- Enter only in reasonable conditions when you can see the channel markers. Morning and midday are best; the afternoon sun reflecting off the water can make it very difficult to see the markers.

OYSTER POND   *Eiman photo*

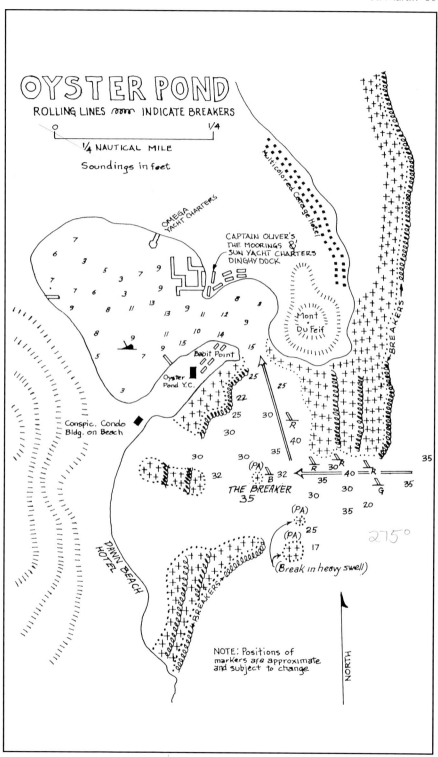

OYSTER POND

ROLLING LINES 〰 INDICATE BREAKERS

0 ————————————— 1/4

¼ NAUTICAL MILE

Soundings in feet

Omega Yacht Charters

Multicolored Cottage Hotel

CAPTAIN OLIVER'S
THE MOORINGS &
SUN YACHT CHARTERS
DINGHY DOCK

Mont Du Feif

BREAKERS

Babit Point

Oyster Pond Y.C.

Conspic. Condo Bldg. on Beach

R

(PA)
B 32
THE BREAKER
35

R
R
G

(PA) 25

(PA) 17
(Break in heavy swell)

DAWN BEACH HOTEL

BREAKERS

275°

NOTE: Positions of markers are approximate and subject to change.

NORTH

Here's to you!

It's your vacation...and at Sun Yacht Charters, we'll do everything in our power to make it the best one ever.

"Everyone we met treated us as if we were their most important customer and would go to any lengths to make sure our needs were met."
–David Netting, Springfield, Pennsylvania

We put 14 years of charter experience and local knowledge at your disposal. We'll guide you to just the kind of sailing you want.

"From the telephone planning sessions to the chart briefing, the staff was courteous and helpful. Their experienced knowledge of the island made for a perfect itinerary and a wonderful first charter in Antigua."
–Chris and Becky Joyce, Gorham, Maine

Exceptional yachts, fast and responsive, impeccably maintained, luxurious below. At your command.

"Your Centurion 40 is a superb sail craft, beautifully maintained and equipped."
–John Temple, Albuquerque, New Mexico

Feeling adventurous? Make a one-way passage through the Leeward Islands — with no drop-off fee.

Arriving late? We'll pick you up at the airport...anytime.

Want to take it easy the first day? We'll provide a complimentary skipper to your first anchorage.

"Thanks for giving us a wonderful time in the Caribbean."
–Denise and George Semke, Garden City, New York

You're welcome!

Call **Sun Yacht Charters** today and start planning your best-ever vacation.
We'll help with special rates for hotels and airfare, too.

800.772.3500 U.S. and Canada

36 Elm Street, Camden, Maine 04843
207.236.9611 Elsewhere   207.236.3972 Fax

Sun Yacht Charters
ST. MARTIN • ANTIGUA • TORTOLA • TAHITI

We Outshine The Rest.

CARNIVAL IN PHILIPSBURG   *Derek Little photo*

- Proceed between the outer markers heading for the black spar marking THE BREAKER reef; approximate bearing is 283° magnetic. Depths are 30 feet and more.

- Before reaching the black spar off The Breaker, turn to starboard and head in the channel to the entrance between Babit Point and Mont Du Feif; approximate bearing is 355° magnetic. Depths are 25 to 30 feet.

- It is important to stay in the marked channel when entering or leaving Oyster Pond. If you leave the channel to cut a corner, you may live to regret it.

ANCHORING Once inside Oyster Pond, feel your way along cautiously and avoid the wreck with mast sticking up in the southern part and the 3-foot shoal off Captain Oliver's Marina. The water is murky, and so you can't see the bottom. Anchor where you will according to your draft, but do not block the entrance channel. The holding is good in mud and sand.

SERVICES Gas and diesel, water, ice, showers, trash bins, telephones, taxis, and a fairly good selection of provisions are available at the Captain Oliver Marina. Gas and diesel are reported to be available at the dock of the Oyster Pond Yacht Club. The Moorings will help out with outboard and diesel repairs and parts.

ASHORE Oyster Pond Yacht Club was the only building at Oyster Pond in 1973 when we first sailed in. Its expanded facilities now cover most of Point Babit and include a highly regarded (and expensive) restaurant as well as a dock with fuel and rental windsurfers, cats, etc. Next came Dawn Beach Hotel at the far end of the beach south of Oyster Pond. This wonderful beach with good snorkeling and a snack bar has long been a favorite with local citizens and visitors alike.

CAPTAIN OLIVER'S HOTEL, RESTAURANT AND MARINA are the work of Parisian Olivier Lange who has been a leading force behind much of the development around Oyster Pond. Monsieur Lange takes pains to insure that his restaurant has the same culinary and service standards that established the reputation of his Parisian restaurant Le Mors aux Dents; luncheons and dinners overlooking the harbor are wonderful. Marina monitors VHF Ch. 16 and 67.

The most popular gathering spot for the sailing crowd is Ryan's DINGHY DOCK where the gams start with morning coffee, build over his tasty sandwiches, snacks, and lunch fare, and end in the spirited happy hour from 5:00 to 7:00 P.M. Ryan knows everything that is going on in the area, and his warm and friendly hospitality makes sure everyone has a wonderful time.

ST. MAARTEN/ST. MARTIN MARINE DIRECTORY

	Telephone	VHF Channel
BOATYARDS/HAULOUT		
Bobby's Marina Boatyard, Philipsburg	22366	16
Island Water World, Simpson Bay Lagoon	45310/45278	74
SPG Marine, Nettle Bay	877477	12
CHARTS/BOOKS		
Island Water World, Simpson Bay Lagoon	45310/45278	74
Bobby's Marina	22675	
Nautical Inst. & Navigation Centre, Great Bay Marina	23605	
Port Lonvilliers, Anse Marcel	873194	16
Robbie Ferron's Budget Marine, Philipsburg	22068	68
Team No. 1, Marigot	875827	
DIVE SHOPS & DIVE SERVICES		
Ocean Explorers, Simpson Bay	45252	16
Maho Watersports, Maho Bay	54387	
Pelican Watersports, Simpson Bay	42503	
Team No. 1, Marigot	875827	
Tradewinds Dive Center, Great Bay Marina	54387	

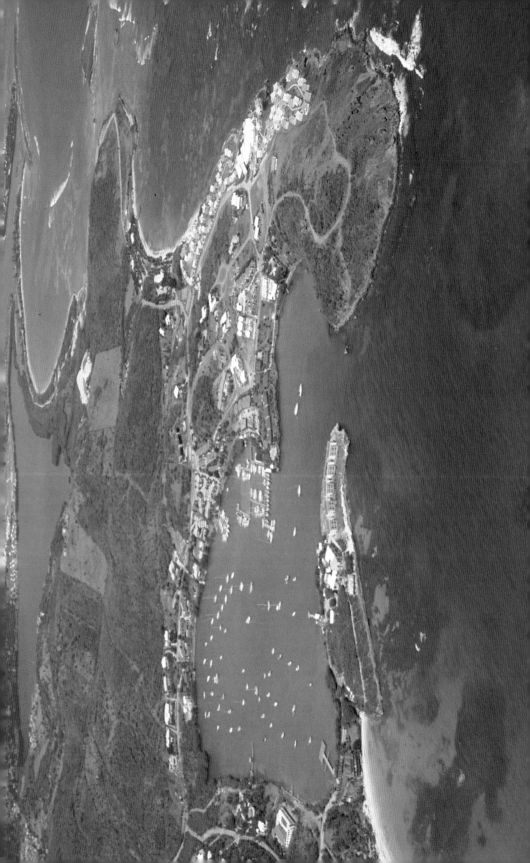

CHANDLERIES/MARINE SUPPLIES & EQUIPMENT

Antilles Marine, St. James, Marigot	878925	
Island Water World, Simpson Bay Lagoon	45310/45278	74
Bobby's Marina	22675	
Lonvilliers Yachting, Anse Marcel	873878	
Robbie Ferron's Budget Marine, Philipsburg	22068	68
Shoreline Marine, Marigot	875313	
SPG Marine, Nettle Bay	877477	
Team No. 1, Marigot	875827	
Tropical Sails, Great Bay Marina	22842	

DINGHIES/INFLATABLES

Egreteau Marine Service, Sandy Ground, Marigot	872392	77
Robbie Ferron's Budget Marine, Philipsburg	22068	68
Island Water World, Simpson Bay Lagoon	45310/45278	74
Bobby's Marina	22675	

ELECTRICAL SUPPLIES & REPAIRS

Carib Diesel, Potence Bay	872006	
Necol, Bobby's Marina - Repairs	23571	
Robbie Ferron's Budget Marine, Philipsburg - Supplies	22068	68
Island Water World, Simpson Bay Lagoon - Supplies	45310/45278	74
Bobby's Marina - Supplies	22675	
Tropical Sails, Great Bay Marina - Supplies	22842	
Tropicold, Simpson Bay Lagoon - Repairs	42648	

ELECTRONIC EQUIPMENT & REPAIRS

Electronic Center, Sandy Ground, Marigot - Equip. & Repairs	875470	10
Gilmoor Electronics, The Corner, Simpson Bay - Equip. & Repairs	42551	
Island Water World, Simpson Bay Lagoon - Equipment	45310/45278	74
Bobby's Marina - Equipment	22675	
Nautical Inst. & Navigation Centre, Great Bay Marina - Equipment	23605	
Necol, Bobby's Marina - Equipment & Repairs	23571	
Radio Holland Caribbean, Philipsburg - Equip. & Repairs	25414/22589	
Unitek Electronics, Philipsburg - Repairs	70225	

HARDWARE

Promart Home Center, Philipsburg

MACHINE SHOPS/METAL FABRICATION

Bobby's Marina Boatyard, Philipsburg	22366	16
Carib Diesel, Potence Bay	872006	
F.K.G. Rigging, Simpson Bay Lagoon	42171	70

MARINAS

Bobby's Marina, Philipsburg	22366	16
Captain Oliver's Marina, Oyster Pond	873000	16 & 67
Great Bay Marina, Philipsburg	22167	
Island Water World, Simpson Bay Lagoon	45310/45278	74
Lagoon Marina, Simpson Bay Lagoon	45210	
Oyster Pond Yacht Club, Oyster Pond		
Port De Plaisance, Simpson Bay Lagoon	45222	67
Port La Royale, Marigot		
Port Lonvilliers, Anse Marcel	873194	16
Simpson Bay Yacht Club, Simpson Bay	43346 16	

Opposite page — Oyster Pond; *Derek Little photo*

MARINE ENGINE REPAIRS/PARTS

Matthew Aimable, Great Bay Marina	22167	
Bobby's Marina Boatyard, Philipsburg	22366	16
Calbee Engineering, Lagoon Marina 45210		
Carib Diesel, Potence Bay	872006	
Diesel Marine Service, Nettle Bay, Marigot	875345	71
Diesel Outfitters, Cole Bay	42320	
NAPA Auto Parts, Philipsburg	23595	
Martin Bateaux, Mt. Vernon	873172	

OUTBOARD ENGINES - SALES & SERVICE

Antilles Marine, St. James, Marigot - Johnson	878925	
Robbie Ferron's Budget Marine, Philipsburg - Mercury	22068	68
Island Water World, Simpson Bay Lagoon - Evinrude	45310/45278	74
Bobby's Marina - Evinrude	22675	
Marshalls Motors, Cole Bay Corner - Mariner, Suzuki	45294	
Mercury Marine Center, Marigot - Mercury	878632	72
Shoreline Marine, Marigot - Yamaha	875313	

PROPANE GAS

Dockside Management, Bobby's Marina	24096	76
Great Bay Marina Fuel Dock		71
Macro Sales, Philipsburg	23050/23073	

RADIO SALES & SERVICE

Gilmoor Electronics, The Corner, Simpson Bay - Sales & Service	42551	
Island Water World, Simpson Bay Lagoon - Sales	45310/45278	74
Bobby's Marina - Sales	22675	
Necol, Bobby's Marina - Sales & Service	23571	
Radio Holland, Philipsburg - Sales & Service	25414/22589	
Radio Shack, Philipsburg	28310	

REFRIGERATION SALES & SERVICE

Necol, Bobby's Marina - Sales & Service	23571	
Tropicold, Simpson Bay Lagoon - Sales & Service	42648	

RESCUE

Antillean Sea Rescue Foundation, Bobby's Marina	Saba Radio	16

RIGGING

F.K.G. Rigging, Simpson Bay Lagoon - Fabrication & Repairs	42171	16
Island Water World, Simpson Bay Lagoon - Supplies	45310/45278	74
Bobby's Marina - Supplies	22675	

SAILMAKERS/CANVAS WORK

La Morgan Sailmakers, Simpson Bay Lagoon	43319	9
St. Maarten (Gowen/Doyle) Sails, Simpson Bay Lagoon	45231	
Sailen, Nettle Bay, Marigot	875372	
Shore Sails, Bobby's Marina	23571	

SALVAGE/TOWING

Bobby's Marina Boatyard	22366	16
J & J Marine Salvage, Tug St. Ven	43248	16

YACHT MAINTENANCE & REPAIR

Matthew Aimable, Great Bay Marina	22167	
Bobby's Marina Boatyard, Phnilipsburg	22366	16
F.K.G. Rigging, Simpson Bay Lagoon	42171	70

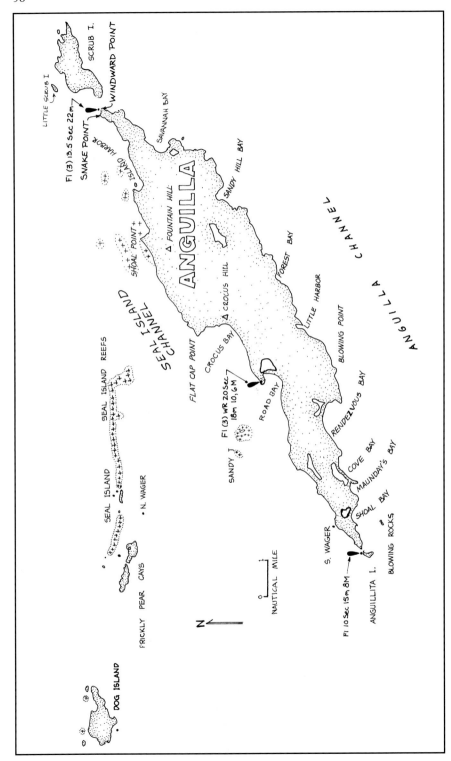

ANGUILLA

CHARTS: U.S. DMA 25600, 25613

British 130, 955, 2047, 2079

Dutch 2110

YACHTSMAN'S PLANNING CHART 63-18

Imray-Iolaire A24

Anguilla reminds one of the saying that less is better; its short supply of congested streets, blaring horns, nightclubs, neon signs, tourist traps, pollution, shopping centers, and pushing crowds help make it one of the truly tranquil havens in the Caribbean. One of the least developed islands in the Caribbean, Anguilla boasts glorious miles of turquoise bays, intriguing coral gardens, and endless, uncrowded, creamy beaches. But perhaps Anguilla's most significant asset is her 7,000 people . . . friendly, helpful, soft-spoken, and proud land owners who traditionally have lived by fishing, farming, lobstering and working the salt ponds.

Northernmost of the Leeward Islands, Anguilla lies five miles north of St. Maarten/ St. Martin. It is one of those rare flat, low, coral islands in the Caribbean and is 16 miles long, 3 miles wide, and 213 feet high. From the peak of CROCUS HILL one has a sweeping view of Dog Island, Prickly Pear Cays and Sandy Island to the west, beautiful cliffs falling off to the sandy beach of Crocus Bay below, and the sloping shelf of all Anguilla as it inclines gently to the southern shore.

Columbus sailed past in 1493 and dubbed the island "eel"—Anguilla in Spanish, perhaps after its wriggling shape in the sea. Details of colonization were left to the British who established a government of sorts in the 1750's. In a move made for the convenience of Foreign Office bureaucrats, the British forced Anguilla under the political control of St. Kitts in 1822. For the next 145 years the Anguillans objected to this senseless arrangement and made repeated requests for return to direct administration from London.

Their requests became more urgent in 1958 when the egotistical, domineering, and ruthless Robert Bradshaw was elected Premier of St.Kitts/Nevis/Anguilla. Bradshaw, miffed because Anguilla did not support him the polls, vowed to "turn Anguilla into a desert." Under the heel of Bradshaw Anguilla in 1965 had no central electricity, no telephone system, no water system, less that 1-1/2 miles of paved road, and a one room schoolhouse for 350 children!

When the British announced, incredibly, that Anguilla's subjection to St. Kitts would become permanent in a new Associated State in 1967, the angry Anguillans shot up the Police Station (manned by St. Kittians), the Customs Building, and the home of a local Bradshaw supporter; they sent a boatload of men to St. Kitts to kidnap Bradshaw; and in July they issued a Declaration of Independence. Bradshaw circulated reports that Anguilla was in the grip of armed gunmen and the Mafia. And so it went from bad to worse.

After two more years of fumbling and bungling, the British sent two frigates, 315 Red Devil paratroopers, helicopters, and support ships in March, 1969 to invade the island and rid it of undesirables...i.e. the Mafia. The troops stormed ashore at 5:15 A.M. to be greeted by the press and barrages of flash bulbs; most of the Anguillans were, of course, fast asleep. The war actually went quite well: There were no casualties; the only shot fired was fired at reporters; no Mafia types were found; and the Brits announced that Anguillans would not be forced to return to an administration they did not want . . . i.e. St. Kitts. The mouse had roared and twisted the tail of the British Lion; the war was over, and the Anguillans got what they always wanted.

The colorful Anguillan boat races held on Easter Monday, Anguilla Day (May 30), and during the annual August Carnival generate tremendous excitement. Far more popular than cricket matches, these races are fiercely competitive events for the beautiful boats with butterfly sails that have evolved from generations of racing. Races usually start with the boats lined up on the beach headed down wind, fully rigged with sails set. The crews push their boats off, jump aboard, sail around a marker boat off shore far to leeward, and usually beat back to the finish flag off the beach where the race began. The rules are few: the first boat to round the leeward mark, sail back and grab the flag is the winner. In close races the struggle for the flag can be sensational. The big races attract large and enthusiastic crowds; interest and high-stakes betting are incredible!

In 1980 there were no luxury hotels on Anguilla and only a few scattered restaurants catering to visitors. But change has been rapid and dramatic as word of its dazzling beaches, its lovely people, its tranquility, and its near-perfect vacation climate spread. Today there are over 500 rooms for visitors with many in super luxury hotels charging $400 to $600 per day for a double room. The island is sprinkled with a growing assortment of wonderful restaurants including ROY'S PLACE, Lucy's Harbor View, THE SHIP'S GALLEY, RIVIERA, The Fish Trap, THE BARREL STAY, JOHONNO'S, and HIBERNIA. Rental cars, taxis, day sails, SCUBA, snorkel trips, and island tours are readily available.

APPROACHING ANGUILLA

In daylight with good visibility approaching Anguilla poses no unusual problems for the sailor aware of the surrounding islands, rocks, and reefs shown on the charts; alert skippers should have no problem avoiding these hazards. But at night it is quite a different story when the low profiles of Anguilla and its surrounding islands and reefs together with the glow of the lights from St. Maarten/St. Martin can cause serious misjudgments of distances. This danger is especially great for strangers approaching from the north, northwest, and west. Do not rely on the flashing lights at Road Bay and on Anguillita when you are far offshore; they are useful only when you are within a few miles of the coast. The flashing light on Windward Point is helpful to vessels approaching Anguilla from the east.

CLEARANCE, CRUISING PERMITS, & ANCHORING RESTRICTIONS

All who arrive in Anguilla by sea are required to clear in promptly with Customs and Immigration at either BLOWING POINT or SANDY GROUND in ROAD BAY. Customs and Immigration office hours in Blowing Point are 7:00 A.M to Midnight daily; at Sandy Ground in Road Bay they are 8:30 A.M. to Noon Mondays through Saturdays and 1:00 to 4:00 P.M. Mondays through Fridays, but be alert for changes! Passports or I.D.s with photographs, ship's papers, and crew lists are required for clearance.

Foreign yachts cruising in Anguillan waters are required to have Cruising Permits. These Permits are available at Customs Offices and are valid daily from Midnight to Midnight. There is no charge for Cruising Permits for private (i.e. non-charter) yachts, but charter yachts must pay for them. The cost varies with the registered tonnage and the time spent cruising outside the harbors at Bowing Point and Road Bay. Regulations in 1992 specify the following rates (U.S. $ figures are based on the rate $1.00 E.C. = 38 ¢ U. S.):

	Up to 5 tons Registered tonnage		5 to 20 tons Registered tonnage		Over 20 tons Registered tonnage	
	EC$	U.S.$	EC$	U.S.$	EC$	U.S.$
1 Day	$ 25	$ 9.51	$ 100	$ 38.02	$ 150	$ 57.03
1 Week	$ 150	$ 57.03	$ 600	$ 228.14	$ 900	$ 342.21
1 Month	$ 500	$190.11	$1,900	$ 722.43	$2,850	$1,083.65
3 Months	$1,250	$475.29	$5,400	$2,053.23	$8,100	$3,079.85

These charges may seem high, but they are similar to the 8% Anguilla tax on hotel rooms and hotel taxes on other popular islands. Fortunately, they help prevent overcrowding of popular beaches and anchorages.

ANCHORING RESTRICTIONS As the number of yachts cruising Anguillan waters has increased dramatically, so has concern over the damage to coral from anchors. This concern is cited as the principal reason for establishing the following LEGAL RESTRICTIONS ON ANCHORING:

Yachts are not permitted to anchor in Rendezvous Bay.

Yachts are not permitted to anchor in Little Bay.

Yachts visiting SANDY ISLAND, PRICKLY PEAR CAYS, and DOG ISLAND are permitted to anchor ONLY in designated anchoring areas.

A few buoys mark some of the restricted and designated anchorage areas. The government has been planning for years to review (and presumably revise) cruising permit charges and anchoring restrictions and to put down mooring buoys as other islands have to help protect the underwater environment. By late 1992 no changes have been made, and there is no sign of any mooring buoys. The situation may be fluid, so it would be a good idea to check one of the charter fleets for the latest information before heading to Anguilla.

Anchoring restrictions are repeated in the pages that follow, and the restricted areas and designated anchoring areas for yachts are included in the appropriate sketch charts.

NUDITY In keeping with the islanders' traditional and conservative values, public nudity is forbidden by law in Anguilla. And there is a law on the books whereby anyone who violates the law against public nudity can be picked up, jailed, and tried in the nude. Buffs beware; don't get pinched!

SOUTHERN COAST — BLOWING POINT TO ANGUILLITA

BLOWING POINT is directly north of Marigot and is the closest and most convenient port of entry on Anguilla for yachts approaching from the east coast of St. Maarten/St. Martin, from Marigot, and from points in between. It is the terminal for ferries between Anguilla and St. Martin and anchorage for local trading boats. The Customs and Immigration office (open daily 7:00 A.M. to Midnight) is in the new, cream colored

Passenger Terminal behind the concrete pier about in the middle of the beach. Most cruising yachts pass by Blowing Point and clear in at Road Bay.

APPROACHES & ANCHORING The approaches to Blowing Point are free of offshore dangers except for ANGUILLITA ISLAND and BLOWING ROCKS off the southwest tip of Anguilla. There is a great deal of shore coral along much of the southern coast, but if you stand off a half mile, you will have no difficulty. Landmarks at Blowing Point include a group of three new one-story houses backed by a fourth that has a roof line of small arches to the west of the Passenger Terminal; up behind the Terminal and slightly to the east are the red roofs of houses in Blowing Point village; there are two modern houses on the shore west of Sandy Point.

Enter Blowing Point harbor midway between the beacons and lights on the isolated reef in the middle of the bay and on Sandy Point to the west; the beacon and light on the reef are green . . . not red . . . so be careful. Anchor off the pier in 10 to 14 feet of water and dive on your anchor to be sure your rode is not being chewed up by bottom coral. But leave plenty of room for the ferries using the pier. The anchorage is inclined to be rolly; for overnighting the anchorage behind Sandy Point is usually calmer and more peaceful.

ASHORE There are gas and diesel pumps at the end of the pier. Taxis are available behind the Passenger Terminal, and a few hundred yards up the road rental cars are available at Roy Rogers Car Rental. First Stop Grocery is near Roy Rogers, and Bennie & Sons is a little further along; both have provisions, and Bennie sells ice cubes.

A number of the beautiful Anguillan racing boats are normally beached to the east of the Passenger Terminal, and sometimes trading boats are under construction there. Take a few minutes and look around; you will be fascinated.

SANDY POINT ANCHORAGE just to the west of Blowing Point is a good anchorage for medium draft boats. Give Sandy Point a wide berth before heading in cautiously. On the shore is a conspicuous modern, rectangular white stucco house with a recessed strip of windows; 200 to 300 yards off this house is a coral patch that must be avoided.

BLOWING POINT HARBOR AND SANDY POINT   *Eiman photo*

MAUNDAY'S AND COVE BAYS *Derek Little photo*

Once past the point, feel your way in to the east of this house and anchor in 12 to 14 feet just inside the Point or in 8 to 10 feet closer up in the northeast corner. A fine anchorage with good protection from prevailing winds and seas.

RENDEZVOUS BAY Regulations prohibit yachts from anchoring in Rendezvous Bay. Mr. Jeremiah Gumbs, influential owner of the Rendezvous Bay Hotel, is reported to take an active, personal interest in enforcing the ban on anchoring; don't tempt him!

COVE BAY is a nice daytime anchorage immediately to the west of Rendezvous Bay. Buildings of the what was to be the Merrywing Resort mark its eastern point. Feel your way in around the reef that extends out to the west from this point and anchor off the beautiful beach. Snorkeling on the sea side of the reef is reported to be very good.

MAUNDAY'S BAY has a lovely beach and crystal clear water, but it is inclined to be rolly and uncomfortable as an overnight anchorage except when the wind is way around to the north. The shelling at the western end of the beach has been fantastic in past years, but we have no current reports on it. The gleaming white domes and buildings behind the eastern end of the beach are Cap Juluca . . . a very posh hotel; its Pimms Restaurant is quite elegant and has an excellent reputation.

SHOAL BAY to the west of Maunday's Bay has very little protection and is frequently rolly; you will probably want to use a stern anchor even during a daytime stop. Shoal Bay is identified by the very conspicuous and distinctive 2-story Cove Castles buildings along the beach. They are the most obvious and most visible landmarks on the southern coast of Anguilla. A good place for a swim.

ANGUILLITA ISLAND lies a few hundred yards off the southwestern tip of Anguilla. Go out and around Anguillita; there are submerged rocks, rocks awash, and strong currents in the passage inside. It is not a safe passage for strangers.

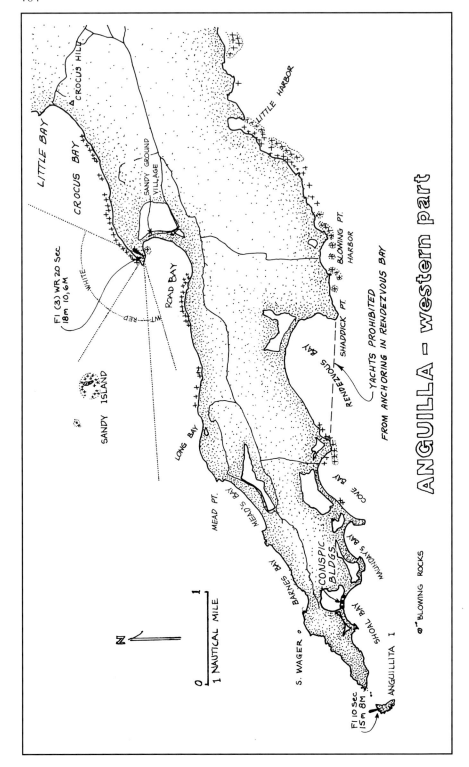

ANGUILLA — western part

LITTLE BAY

CROCUS HILL

CROCUS BAY

LITTLE HARBOR

SANDY GROUND VILLAGE

Fl (3) WR 20 Sec
18m 10,6M

WHITE

RED

ROAD BAY

BLOWING PT. HARBOR

SHADDICK PT.

RENDEZVOUS BAY

YACHTS PROHIBITED
FROM ANCHORING IN RENDEZVOUS BAY

SANDY ISLAND

LONG BAY

COVE BAY

MEAD PT.

MEAD'S BAY

BARNES BAY

CONSPIC. BLDGS.

MAKMAY'S BAY

N

0   1 NAUTICAL MILE

S. WAGER

SHOAL BAY

ANGUILLITA I

Fl 10 Sec
15m 8M

BLOWING ROCKS

MEADS AND BARNES BAYS *Derek Little photo*

NORTHWEST COAST--ANGUILLITA I. TO ROAD BAY

The coast from Anguillita I. to ROAD BAY consists of a breathtaking series of pristine beaches, rocky outcroppings, small coves, and spectacular cliffs. It is ideal for leisurely gunk holing or super sailing in smooth, protected water. The only danger beyond the normal rocks, coral, and shoals along the shore is SOUTH WAGER, a small rock some 200 yards off the land about a mile up the coast from the southwest tip. With that one exception, most cruising yachts can coast along fairly close to the coastline without difficulty.

BARNES BAY has a few tiny, isolated beaches and a several rocks close to the shore at its southern end where there are few, if any, others to disturb the tranquility. Another lovely Anguillan beach stretches to the north where the extensive Coccoloba Plantation hotel is situated. Snorkeling near the hotel is superb; reef fish are plentiful and occasionally enormous schools of small fry can be seen.

MEADS BAY is noted for its mile-long magnificent beach and the super-luxury Mallihouhana Hotel with over 50 double rooms and suites, 4 lighted tennis courts, and 3 fresh water pools. Although there are a few smaller, attractive hotels and villas along the shore, the beach rarely has more than a sprinkling of people along its entire length. If you have an urge for a refreshing swim in glorious surroundings, by all means give it a go.

ROAD BAY/SANDY GROUND

ROAD BAY is the principal harbor and the port of entry used by virtually all cruising yachts. The high ground surrounding the bay and the clear, gently sloping bottom make it a fine, protected harbor in normal trade wind weather, but it can be a little rolly if northern swells come along in winter. The sleepy village of SANDY GROUND lies behind the beautiful beach; the large commercial pier towards the southern end of the beach is used by trading sloops, freighters, tugs, etc., while the small pier to the north is for police boats and dinghies.

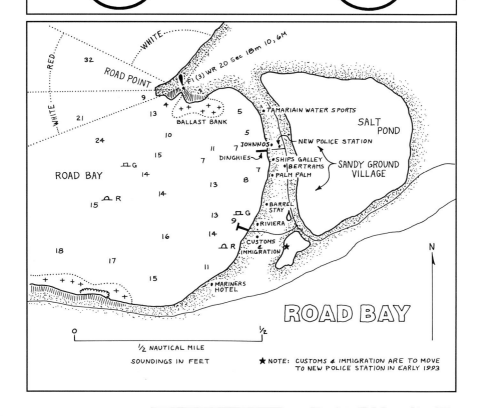

ROAD BAY

NOTE: CUSTOMS & IMMIGRATION ARE TO MOVE
TO NEW POLICE STATION IN EARLY 1993

½ NAUTICAL MILE
SOUNDINGS IN FEET

Very colorful and exciting races for the beautiful, fast Anguilla sloops during Carnival in early August are held at Sandy Ground. The races go on for days and attract large, happy, friendly crowds from Anguilla, St. Maarten/St. Martin, St. Barts as well as Anguillans from throughout the Caribbean and the States. The spirited partying and general celebration go on and on, and every body has a wonderful time.

ENTERING AND ANCHORING There are only a few dangers to avoid when approaching and entering Road Bay: About a mile and a half off shore is SANDY ISLAND that is surrounded by coral reefs, a small gravel island to the northwest, and SANDY SHOAL close by to its south. In addition, a series of reefs and shoals extends some 200 yards off the southern shore of Road Bay, and a shoal known as BALLAST BANK lies in the northeast part of the Bay just inside and south of ROAD POINT. The wrecks that littered the Bay have been moved well offshore and sunk for the benefit of divers. Anchoring in the northeast part of the Bay provides the best protection in case of infrequent northern swells, but near the dinghy dock the music and partying at Johnno's Beach Bar may bother you on Wednesday and Saturday nights and on Sunday afternoons. In settled weather you can anchor almost anywhere in good sand, but stay clear of the approach to the commercial pier. Tie your dinghy to the small dinghy dock; we have never heard of any dinghy thefts in Anguilla; a security wire may not be needed.

CLEARANCE Customs and Immigration are scheduled to move in late 1992 from the small building behind the commercial pier to the new Police Station behind the dinghy dock and Johnno's. Office hours are 8:30 A.M. to Noon Mondays through Saturdays and from 1:00 to 4:00 P.M. Mondays through Fridays. Cruising Permits are issued there,

108

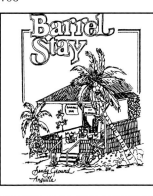

ROAD BAY   *Derek Little photo*

and the officers can give you all the latest information on the regulations, designated anchoring areas for yachts, etc.

SERVICES There are no yacht repair or supply services and no fuel in Sandy Ground, but ice, provisions, water, telephones, taxis, and a top-notch dive service are close at hand. The RIVIERA RESTAURANT near the commercial pier and BERTRAM'S YACHT SERVICE on the road near the Police Station sell ice; Bertram's monitors VHF Ch. 16,68, and 69 and can also provide water, taxis, fresh lobster, and island tours. Ice and limited provisions are available at 3-C's Grocery behind the big pier, and public telephones are just across the road. For the best provisioning take a very short taxi ride up the hill just past the roundabout to VISTA FOOD MARKET where you will find an excellent selection of choice and gourmet food items, meats, produce, liquor, and fine wines. HARRY'S TAXI SERVICE is very cruiser friendly and monitors VHF Ch. 16 . . . call signs Delta One/Delta Two; Harry's island tours are first rate, and he can get fresh fish and lobster for you. TAMARIAIN WATERSPORTS operates an excellent dive service on the beach to the north of the dinghy pier; owners Ian Grummitt and Thomas Peabody provide certified PADI instruction, dive and snorkel trips, tank fills, and dive and snorkel equipment. They have done much to develop diving in the area and have played major roles in sinking seven wrecked freighters offshore in over 40 feet of water for divers.

RESTAURANTS run the gamut from JOHNNO'S BAR & RESTAURANT behind the dinghy dock to The Mariners at the south end of the beach. Johnno's is like Foxy's on Jost Van Dyke . . . very informal and at times very active . . . with good local food; live and loud music gets rolling on Wednesdays and Saturdays about 8:00 P.M. and at 2:30 P.M. on Sundays. The excellent lunches, and dinners at The Mariners are served in a delightful and more restrained atmosphere; buffet/BBQ Thursday nights with steel band; Saturdays are West Indian nights with live music and dancing. Along the beach in between are SHIP'S GALLEY (Norita's specialties include Conch chowder, Lobster Thermador, and turtle steak; Caribbean music and dancing Thursday and Sunday evenings), Lucy's Palm Palm (seafood, Creole, and light dishes with live music

Tuesdays and Fridays), BARREL STAY (prime U.S. steaks, filet mignon, Creole specialties, seafood, and French wines), and RIVIERA (oyster bar in season; Sashimi, French, Creole, and seafood specialties; owner Didier makes terrific petit rum punch and other rum delights). Behind the commercial pier Millie's Place serves Caribbean and seafood dishes at reasonable prices and Ripples boasts an award winning chef, daily specials, fish, and lobster at 'the right price.' For tacos, nachos, buritos, and terrific margaritas, head for Que Pasa behind the new Police Station. Two fine restaurants a short taxi ride from Sandy Ground are Lucy's Harbor View overlooking Road Bay (top notch lobster, seafood & local specialties) and ROY'S in Crocus Bay (a great favorite with yachtsmen; super steaks, snapper, and — when available — superb local crayfish; roast beef special at Sunday lunch; reservations suggested; reasonable.)

ACTIVITIES More and more charterers are minimizing Cruising Permit expenses by anchoring (free of charge) in Road Bay, visiting the offshore islands by local catamaran or ferry, and/or touring the island by taxi or rental car. A drive around Anguilla with lunch in Island Harbor or Shoal Bay on the north coast makes a wonderful and interesting day. In The Valley (the largest town and capital of Anguilla) be sure to visit the Secretariat Building to see the extraordinary and very colorful murals by Robert Choisit depicting significant events from the discovery of the island by Columbus through the highjinks of St. Kitts Premier Bradshaw and the invasion by the British; at the Post Office you can buy the fascinating Anguillan stamps with beautiful renditions of Caribbean birds, reptiles, coral, and fish. The Valley has a number of groceries, bakeries, and other stores including the main branch of the ANGUILLA DRUG STORE that carries everything from cameras and cosmetics to sun screens and pharmaceutical.

The best snorkeling in Anguilla proper is in the coral gardens at Shoal Bay on the north coast; it is well worth the trip from Road Bay. There is good snorkeling in Sandy Hill Bay. Adventuresome types who want to get off the beaten track will enjoy a picnic lunch and/or a swim in the solitude of Savannah Bay with its beautiful crescent beach.

CROCUS BAY/LITTLE BAY/KARTOUCHE BAY

CROCUS BAY is in the center of a long indentation in the coast extending from Road Point to Flat Cap Point; LITTLE BAY is to the north, and KARTOUCHE BAY is to the south. The cliffs along the shore provide excellent protection from the wind, and anchorages in the area are lovely, serene, and quite calm except when infrequent northern swells roll in. Often when anchored there you can have the feeling of being on an inland lake; it can be that calm! Other attractive features include the views of the spectacular cliffs, the solitude along the mile-long beach, ROY'S PLACE (the only restaurant in Crocus Bay), and the impressive snorkeling off the cliffs on the northern shore of Little Bay. Watch out for the fish pot markers; all three bays are likely to be full of them; otherwise, there are no offshore hazards in Crocus Bay. Anchor directly off Roy's or to the south off the beautiful beach.

Roy's Place is a great island restaurant right on the beach in Crocus Bay; the only problem is that it's closed on Mondays and for lunch on Saturdays. Roy and Mandy serve burgers, sandwiches, and salads at lunch Tuesdays through Fridays; on Sundays their very popular lunches feature roast beef & yorkshire pudding, snapper, and lobster salad (reservations a must). Dinners feature snapper, lobster, steak, ham, pork, and chicken and tempting deserts all at attractive prices. Dinner reservations are advised; call on VHF CH. 16. Incidentally, Roy's has an endless stock of English draft beer (Double Diamond) and outstanding pina coladas.

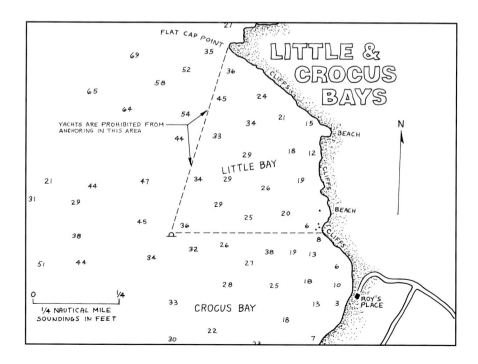

LITTLE BAY *Susan Pierres photo*

As noted earlier, yachts are not permitted to anchor in Little Bay (see sketch chart). To enjoy the excellent snorkeling along the cliffs on the northern shore, dinghy up from Roy's to the gem like beach in Little Bay, beach your dinghy, and snorkel out from the beach.

At the southern end of the beach in Crocus Bay there is an old wreck on the shore. The snorkeling on the shore reefs off this wreck is very good; some think it is as good as the snorkeling in Little Bay.

If you are short of supplies, you might walk up the hill behind Roy's to ASHLEY & SONS GROCERY that has recently expanded its facilities and selections; it is a good place to stock up on provisions of all sorts, cleaning supplies, etc.

OFFSHORE ISLANDS WEST OF ANGUILLA

SANDY ISLAND, PRICKLY PEAR CAYS, and DOG ISLAND are very special, uninhabited islands with lovely beaches, turquoise waters, and wonderful snorkeling. It is quite easy to visit any two of them in a day before returning to Road Bay before sunset. The government requires yachts anchoring near these islands to anchor only in designated anchor areas that are shown on our sketch charts.

SANDY ISLAND

It is impossible to sail up the coast of Anguilla towards ROAD BAY without being captivated by SANDY ISLAND, lying approximately 1-1/2 miles northwest of Road Bay. It is everyone's dream of the lovely, palm-studded, reef-fringed, deserted tropic island. With just eleven graceful palms along its 200 yards, it is a beautiful sentinel for Road Bay. Its pristine beauty is interrupted only by a refreshment stand that serves snacks, lunches, and drinks. Its beaches, the lagoon inside the reef, and the snorkeling along the reef to the west are out of this world; they are at their best in settled, sunny weather.

Be careful to avoid SANDY SHALLOW some 300 to 400 yards south of Sandy Island; it shoals to 5 feet and breaks in moderate to heavy seas. Also stay away from the

SANDY ISLAND   *Derek Little photo*

very small island less that a half mile to the northwest; it is surrounded by foul water.

In the designated anchor area outside the reef to the west of Sandy Cay there is 10 to 15 feet of clear, clear water over sand and grass. Entrances to the lagoon are very shallow and are suitable only for dinghies and shoal draft power boats. The entrance to the south is shallow and full of strong currents. It is better to use the entrance to the northwest; pick your way in carefully in deeper, calmer water. In the lagoon there is 4 to 6 feet of water; power boats are permitted to anchor there.

The reefs west of the lagoon are filled with Angelfish, Rock Beauties, Blue Tangs, Sergeant Majors, Parrotfish, Blue Headed Wrasses, and other colorful reef fish and many varieties of soft and hard corals that will delight everyone. On calm, sunny days you will find snorkeling at its very best.

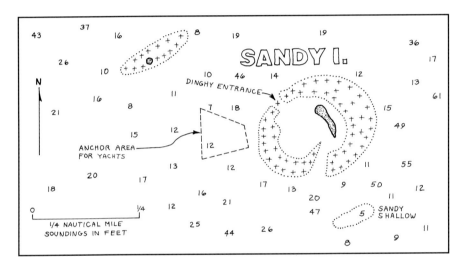

DOG ISLAND

DOG ISLAND, approximately 10 miles WNW of Road Point and some 2-1/2 miles WNW of PRICKLY PEAR WEST, is just far enough off the beaten track to escape the curse of beach bars and day trip catamarans. You will, in all probability, have it all to yourselves except, of course, for the wild goats that poke around in the scrub vegetation. The anchorage is inclined to be rolly, so it is best to visit only in settled conditions when the sea is calm.

Approach Dog Island from the east or southeast, and do not sail along the north coast between EAST CAY and MID CAY as there are some shoals and uncharted, scattered coral heads that can cause real trouble. Yachts are permitted to anchor only in Great Bay between BAY ROCK and the absolutely lovely beach (see sketch chart). Anchor in clear sand towards the southeastern end of the beach where the swell is least troublesome. Stay well off, as sizeable waves can build up just short of the beach.

In calm conditions dinghies can be landed with care along the beach and pulled well up on the sand; pick you time carefully and go for it! If the surf is too rough for your dinghy, don flippers and swim in from your boat provided, of course, the anchor is really well dug it. The beach in Great Bay is regarded by many as the most beautiful in the entire Caribbean; land behind it is private property, and we are advised that

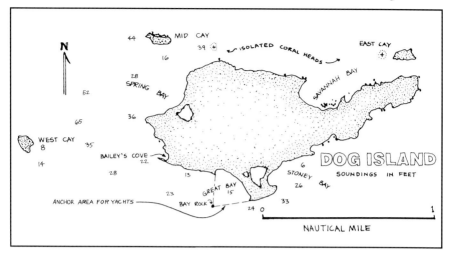

trespassing behind the beach is not permitted by the owner, Mr. Jeremiah Gumbs of Rendezvous Bay.

BAILEY'S COVE to the northwest of Great Bay is a good place to explore in a dinghy in calm conditions; the snorkeling is excellent, but watch out for the surge that can be troublesome. SPRING BAY is another good place to explore by dinghy; unfortunately, we have no information on the snorkeling there, but it might be good. You can explore the coast off Bailey's Cove and Spring Bay in your boat, but, as mentioned, avoid the north shore area.

Dog Island is best for a morning visit before an afternoon at the PRICKLY PEARS or SANDY ISLAND. But no matter when you go, you can celebrate the 1980 decision by the U.S. Navy to end its consideration of Dog Island as a weapons firing range; now we can all enjoy its beauty in peace and quiet.

PRICKLY PEAR CAYS

PRICKLY PEAR CAYS lie about 6 miles off Road Point and form the western end of a 6-mile string of jewel-like reefs and shallows that provide what some aficionados term the most wonderful diving this side of the Tobago Cays. The Prickly Pears themselves combine a varied assortment of pleasures that make them a highlight of almost any cruise in the area: Deserted islands surrounded by magnificent waters, lovely beaches, and spectacular snorkeling. To enjoy the Prickly Pears at their best, visit them in sunny, settled conditions when the breeze and the seas are moderate; it is best to avoid them when the wind or seas are high and whenever the infrequent northern swells are around.

APPROACHES AND ANCHORING The Prickly Pears should be approached only from the southeast, south, or southwest. The hazards, including NORTH WAGER, SEAL ISLAND REEFS, FLIRT ROCKS, etc., lie to the east and north. The usual approach from Road Bay to the southeast is trouble free once you are past Sandy Cay and the small gravel island to the northwest of it.

Yachts are permitted to anchor only on the southwest side of Prickly Pear East in the cove that is open to the west and south (see sketch chart). The water is 30 feet deep

116

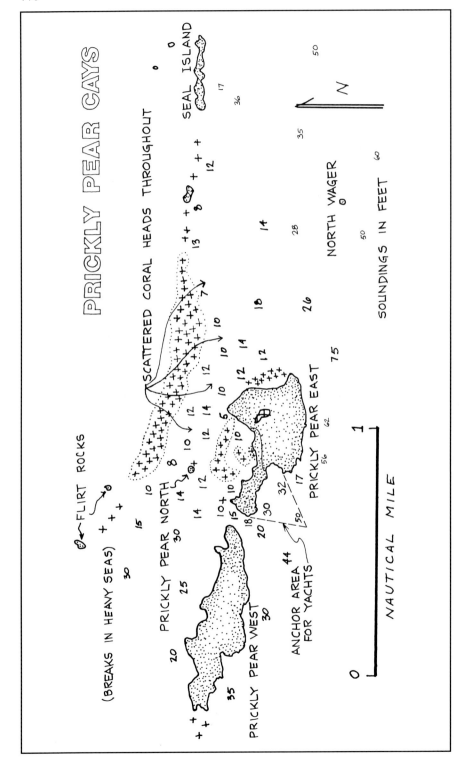

PRICKLY PEAR CAYS

SCATTERED CORAL HEADS THROUGHOUT

SEAL ISLAND

(BREAKS IN HEAVY SEAS)

FLIRT ROCKS

PRICKLY PEAR NORTH

PRICKLY PEAR WEST

ANCHOR AREA
FOR YACHTS

PRICKLY PEAR EAST

NORTH WAGER

SOUNDINGS IN FEET

N

NAUTICAL MILE

0   1

PRICKLY PEAR EAST & ANCHORAGE   *Derek Little photo*

or more 200 yards off the shore; feel your way along cautiously when you are closer in. It can be rolly and have a bit of a surge, especially when the wind is in the south. Anchors can be stuck in the rock and coral on the bottom; the best way to avoid leaving your anchor behind is to use trip line and buoy. You can, of course, motor through the channel between Prickly Pear East & West in your boat to check out the area up to Prickly Pear North, but you are not supposed to anchor there.

ASHORE There is a spot to land dinghies in the northeast corner of the anchor area, and a path there goes over to the main beach on the north side of the island. In settled conditions it is far better to motor around to the beach in your dinghy; along the north shore you will have to do a little eyeball navigation to weave around the coral. After rounding the western tip of Prickly Pear East, stay close to the shore until you see the opening in the reefs to port; motor through this passage and swing around in a big arc to starboard to the beach. The two moorings just off the beach are used by catamarans that bring vacationers from St. Maarten/St. Martin over for a day in paradise and lunch at the nearby beach bar. It is easy to get away from the crowd; just stroll along the beach to the north and east and you will be able to enjoy the fabulous surroundings in peace and quiet.

Another approach to peace and quiet is to dinghy over to PRICKLY PEAR WEST on a calm day. Wait for an opening in the breakers to land on the small beach on the northern side and pull the dinghy way up beyond the surf line for safety. Chances are you'll have the island all to yourselves; be sure to take along shoes for protection against burrs, prickers, and cactus. There are interesting layers of sedimentary rock on the northern shore and caves and blow holes on the southern shore. Hard to beat, if you like that sort of thing . . . and we do.

SNORKELING/EXPLORING Almost anywhere to the north of Prickly Pear East you will find endless and outstanding snorkeling. The curving reefs extending out to the northwest from the beach are filled with colorful fish and many varieties of coral all easily accessible from the beach. But perhaps the most spectacular variety of coral and fish can be found along the inner side of the line of reefs that separates Prickly Pear East from the open sea. Explore and snorkel the area from your dinghy; anchoring is not permitted, so take turns idling the dinghy along as the rest of your group enjoys the fish and the coral below. It's a great way to spend a morning or afternoon, but be sure to protect your backs from the burning sun.

Hardy explorers can have a great time on a good day poking cautiously along the south side of SEAL ISLAND and the adjacent reefs, but a flat sea and good sunlight are absolutely essential. Whether you go in a large sturdy dinghy with plenty of gas or in your cruising boat, keep a sharp eye out for coral heads and other surprises that don't show up on the charts. It is a shame that someone has to stay on board to look after the boat or dinghy because anchoring is verboten, but still the area can be exciting and rewarding and the snorkeling can be memorable.

NORTHWESTERN COAST — FLAT CAP POINT TO SNAKE POINT

The passage between Anguilla and Seal Island Reefs is known as SEAL ISLAND CHANNEL; it has a few spots where depths are 20 to 30 feet; in the past some charts have noted that these shoals, which make up MIDDLE GROUND, break in heavy seas. We have not been able to confirm this note in the last five years, but still it is good to keep the possibility in mind.

For most cruising yachts the prudent way to pass along coast between FLAT CAP POINT and SNAKE POINT is to stand off the shore a mile or more taking special care to avoid SHOAL (or SHAWL) ROCK that, according the British West Indies Pilot, lies almost 3/4 of a mile north of SHOAL POINT, has 8 feet of water over it, and breaks frequently. This part of the coast is full of offshore reefs, inshore reefs, and lots and lots of breakers. The inner passage between the reefs can be challenging and should be attempted only in good light by experienced reef pilots.

For approximately 1-3/4 miles to the northeast of Flat Cap Point the water a few hundred yards off the coast is deep (50 feet and more) and clear of hazards. Beyond that for the next three and a half miles there are reefs and breakers both along the shore and offshore with a deep water passage in between as shown in our sketch chart and aerial photo. Sometimes the sea breaks on the shore reefs and sometimes it doesn't, and the breakers offshore also can vary according to state of the sea. Water in channel is 45 to over 70 feet deep and is deep blue.

This passage should be used only in good conditions with good sunlight and only by hardy souls with good experience navigating among reefs. When heading to the east, drop your sails and proceed under power as tacking in the narrow channel can be quite difficult and trying. There is an 8 foot shoal about 600 yards off the western end of SHOAL BAY beyond the end of the beach; it is designated WEST SHOAL on our sketch chart WESTERN APPROACH TO ISLAND HARBOR and can be seen as a light spot in the water. Find West Shoal and get a good fix on it before entering the deep water passage; it will help stay in deep water away from the reefs. Then it is simply a matter of eyeballing your way through.

SHOAL BAY is easy to spot with its absolutely brilliant, mile-long stretch of beach with the prominent Shoal Bay Villas complex of luxury condominiums behind it. Additional accommodations and Trader Vic's and other restaurants are there as well. The beach is considered one of the finest on Anguilla, and snorkeling in the varied and colorful coral gardens along the shore is magnificent.

EAST SHOAL BAY is a mind-boggling daytime anchorage with vast areas of crystal clear water over pure white sand, and a superb beach. Enter a short distance to the northeast of Shoal Point through a wide open passage over clear sand between two small reefs (see photo). There is 9 feet of water at the entrance, but only 6 to 7 feet about 100 yards or so inside; a great anchorage . . . but only for shallow draft boats. Snorkeling enthusiasts can stroll along the beach to the spectacular coral gardens in Shoal Bay, or they can enjoy the sights along the protective reefs right at hand.

Back in the deep water channel proceed on past Shoal Bay East and head offshore between the reefs and breakers as shown on our sketch chart. Check your position by sighting the prominent new white houses on the high ground just to the west of ISLAND HARBOR and keep an eye out for fish trap markers. If you are going directly to SNAKE POINT, play it safe and go out around the NORTHERN OUTER REEF. If conditions are favorable and if you plan to enter Island Harbor, head for the EASTERN INNER REEF but stay well off the breakers to starboard.

ISLAND HARBOR is a mile and a half beyond Shoal Point; it is a beautiful, reef-protected harbor that is the center of Anguilla's lobster industry. The offshore reefs provide good protection, and local fishermen say there is always calm water in the harbor. Not many yachtsmen have visited Island Harbor primarily, we expect, because the entrance can be nerve-wracking for strangers. In any event, we recommend that you enter only when the sea is relatively calm and when the sunlight is good for eyeball navigation. Avoid entering around mid-day when the sun and its reflection off the water will make it extremely difficult to see the reefs and shallow spots ahead.

ENTERING Study our sketch chart and aerial photo of Island Harbor carefully and enter only when the sea is calm and the sun light is good. Drop your sails and proceed under motor from a position close to and just west of the EASTERN INNER REEF where the

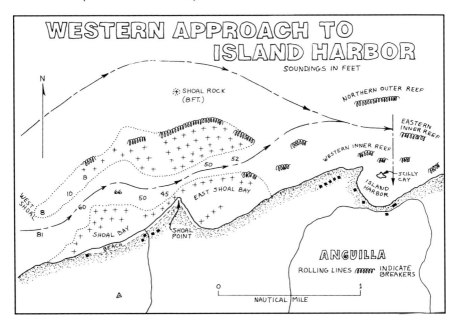

EAST SHOAL BAY, SHOAL POINT, AND SHOAL BAY   *Eiman photo*

depth is 30 to 36 feet. Head in on a base course of 185° magnetic to the long, 2-story building on the shore with a bright metal roof on the left side; to the right of this building you will see three prominent white, 3-story buildings with flat roofs.

The 185° course follows a path of clear sand into Island Harbor BUT it passes over one dark 6-foot spot, close to another dark patch with 9 feet over it, and over a third that has 12 feet of water over it; these are all shown on our sketch chart and photo. Using eyeball navigation, steer around these dark patches and proceed on staying in good water over clear sand. Once well past SCILLY CAY, turn to the west and anchor where you will in about 9 feet of water over clear sand.

Coming from the east, head in between the NORTHERN OUTER REEF and the EASTERN INNER REEF. When you are just past the Eastern Inner Reef, turn onto 185° magnetic heading to the long, 2-story building on the shore as described above.

ASHORE Island Harbor is a small fishing village where the fishermen head out to sea very, very early in the morning and return in the early afternoon, so do not be surprised to see all their colorful boats pulled up on the beach near a grove of palm trees; they are a friendly, good natured group and are always willing to be helpful.

Smitty's is a combination bar, snack bar, and restaurant nestled among the swaying palms where you can enjoy the freshest fish and lobster; live music Thursday nights and Sunday afternoons and lots of high spirits and dancing on the beach. Just across the road from Smitty's is The Fish Trap Restaurant where Chef Leduc features lobster, crayfish, bouillabaisse, veal, and wonderful breads and desserts all served al fresco. HIBERNIA is in a lovely West Indian house just to the east overlooking the harbor where Mary Pat and Chef Raoul earn raves for their French Creole cuisine

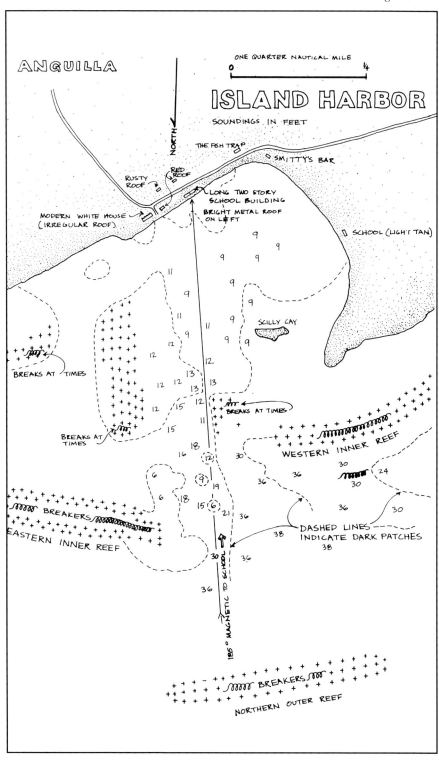

ANGUILLA

ONE QUARTER NAUTICAL MILE

0   1/4

ISLAND HARBOR

SOUNDINGS IN FEET

NORTH

THE FISH TRAP

SMITTY'S BAR

RUSTY ROOF

RED ROOF

LONG TWO STORY SCHOOL BUILDING

BRIGHT METAL ROOF ON LEFT

MODERN WHITE HOUSE (IRREGULAR ROOF)

SCHOOL (LIGHT TAN)

9

9   9

9

11

9

9

11

9   9

SCILLY CAY

11

9

11   12

12

12

BREAKS AT TIMES

12   13

13

12   12   13   13

12

BREAKS AT TIMES

12

BREAKS AT TIMES

15

15

11

WESTERN INNER REEF

16   18

12

30

30

30

24

6

9

19

30

36

36

36

30

EASTERN INNER REEF

BREAKERS

6

18

15   6

21

36

DASHED LINES ------

INDICATE DARK PATCHES

38

30

36

36

38

185° MAGNETIC TO SCHOOL

36

BREAKERS

NORTHERN OUTER REEF

ISLAND HARBOR   *Skeoch photo*

flavored with their home grown herbs; delicious dining at moderate prices. Gorgeous Scilly Cay in the middle of the harbor is open for lunches only; chicken, lobster, and crayfish are the favorites; live music Wednesdays and Sundays.

Bull, a well known ex-fisherman, operates Anguilla Divers with his partner Jess; they run daily dive trips to Scrub Island and rent dive equipment.

ISLAND HARBOR TO SNAKE POINT Once past the reefs near Island Harbor you will find good water on to Snake Point. Halfway between Island Harbor and SNAKE POINT is a perfectly lovely small beach in a little cove called CAPTAIN'S BAY. The surge there is usually very bad and landing a dinghy can be hazardous, so it is best not to try it.

SCRUB ISLAND

SCRUB ISLAND is about two miles long and almost a mile wide and at present is deserted. Like Dog and Tintamarre Islands, Scrub is less than 100 feet high, has an old airstrip and ruins of buildings, is rumored to have been a transfer point for contraband, and has its best and most popular beach and anchorage on its west side. There was a small hotel on the eastern end of Scrub but it closed a few years ago, and we haven't even heard any rumors about its future.

There is good water between Anguilla and Scrub Island and between Scrub and Little Scrub; porpoises like this area and sometimes will swim along with you for a while. In approaching the beach on the west coast of Scrub, follow the clear sand passage in the middle of the beach and anchor in 15 feet of water avoiding the grass and shallow water on either side. Anchor well off, as there is often a big surge running in all but the calmest condition; you may want to set a stern anchor. Be very careful when landing your dinghy; the waves can be quite rough and swamp you in a flash.

SOUTHEASTERN COAST — WINDWARD POINT TO BLOWING POINT

There are shore reefs all along this stretch of coast, and it is usually a lee shore. Stand off a half mile and you will clear all dangers. This is not a popular cruising area as there are only three possible places to anchor. SAVANNAH BAY has a beautiful, long, deserted beach; it has no protection and is usually a dead lee shore. Local boats sometimes use SANDY HILL BAY and FOREST BAY, but local knowledge is important as both are full of reefs and isolated coral heads. adventuresome gunk holers might want to explore these anchorages, but our recommendation is to sail on by.

WEST COAST SCRUB ISLAND *Skeoch photo*

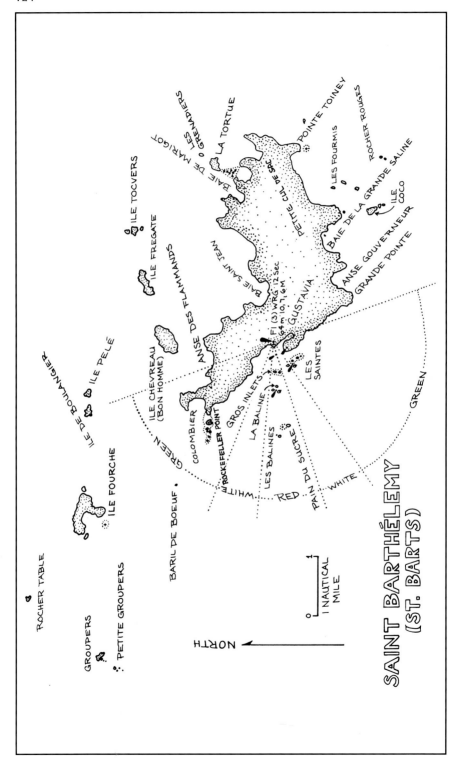

ROCHER TABLE

GROUPERS

PETITE GROUPERS

ILE DE BOULANGER

ILE PELÉ

ILE FOURCHE

BARIL DE BOEUF

ILE CHEVREAU
(BON HOMME)

GREEN

COLOMBIER

ROCKEFELLER POINT

GROS INLETS

LA BALINE

LES BALINES

PAIN DU SUCRE

WHITE

RED

WHITE

GREEN

LES SAINTES

GUSTAVIA

Fl (3) WRG 12 Sec
64 m 10, 7, 6 M

ANSE DES FLAMMANDS

BAIE SAINT JEAN

ILE FREGATE

ILE TOCVERS

BAIE DE MARIGOT

ILE 0 GRENADERS

LA TORTUE

PETITE CUL DE SAC

POINTE TOINEY

LES FOURMIS

BAIE DE LA GRANDE SALINE

ROCHER ROUGES

ILE COCO

ANSE GOUVERNEUR

GRANDE POINTE

1 NAUTICAL MILE
0   1

NORTH

SAINT BARTHÉLEMY
(ST. BARTS)

SAINT BARTHELEMY — ST. BARTS

CHARTS: U.S. DMA 25600, 25608, 25613

British 955, 2079

Dutch 2110

French 6090

YACHTSMAN'S PLANNING CHART 63-18

Imray-Iolaire A24

ST. BARTS is clearly among the most alluring and captivating islands in the Caribbean where hedonism and sensuality draw increasing numbers of sophisticated vacationers. It does not cater to the mass tourism industry; it has no casinos and very little glitz and artificial night life. By some standards it is an expensive island, but hardly anybody seems to mind. In our view, St. Barts is a most enticing island that will make you feel good all over for a long, long time.

Christopher Columbus supposedly discovered or sighted ST. BARTHELEMY (along with Dominica, Les Saintes, Guadeloupe, Antigua, Nevis, St. Kitts, St. Maarten, Anguilla, Saba and the Virgin Islands) during his second voyage to the New World in 1493 and named it after his brother Barthelemeo. The first European settlers arrived in 1648 in the form of some 60 Frenchmen from St. Kitts, and the French influence and indeed dominance have been paramount ever since. The only interruption began in 1785 when King Louis XVI ceded the island to Sweden in return for huge trading warehouses in Gothenburg and ended in 1878 when the Swedes decided to cut their losses and returned the island to France. The Swedes had bestowed free port status on St. Barts in 1875; that fortunate designation still applies and is a great boon to the island ecomony.

St. Barts has somehow survived Carib Indians intent on massacre; Spanish, English, and French men-of-war; swashbuckling buccaneers and freebooters (including the fearsome Montbars the Exterminator and the renowned Jean Lafitte); Huguenot colonists from Normandy and Brittany; Swedish settlers; fishermen, seafarers, and

GUSTAVIA - 1953   *Eiman photo*

traders of many persuasions; and, more recently, stimulating vacationers from Europe, England, and the Americas. The island has been enriched by the enormous variety of these visitors who have enjoyed her hospitality, her famed free port status, and her many considerable charms.

Lacking adequate rainfall and level ground for commercial agriculture, St. Barts has relied on the sea for its livelihood. Its convenient location, sheltered harbor, and free port status made it a favorite port of call for commercial shipping and helped establish it as the most famous . . . or infamous . . . transshipping point in the Caribbean. During the American Revolution and the War of 1812, St. Barts was a source of supply for the Colonies and an operating base for American privateers preying on British shipping. In more recent times, it traded in huge quantities of cattle, tobacco, rum, and other commodities that supposedly were smuggled into other islands to avoid bothersome import duties.

Today St. Barts is a commune of France with her affairs administered by Guadeloupe. Its 4,000 inhabitants are predominantly white and are largely descendants of Norman, Breton, and Swedish settlers; influences of these roots can occasionally be noticed in the speech, customs, and dress of the residents today. The industrious nature of the islanders together with the enormous increase in vacation business help give St. Barts the highest per capita income in the Caribbean. The principal language is a unique patois that scholars say is classic 17th century French flavored will accents of Brittany and the provence of Poitou, but English is spoken throughout Gustavia and virtually anywhere a visitor might travel.

APPROACHES TO ST. BARTS

St. Barts is surrounded by more than two dozen smaller islands and rocks; alert yachtsmen should have no difficulty in avoiding them in good daylight visibility even though some are awash, and a few are only 3 or 4 feet above the water. The east coast from GRANDE POINTE north and around to POINTE L'ORIENT has quite a few hard-to-see rocks awash and small, low islands; be especially careful if you sail there. If approaching St. Barts from the northwest, keep a sharp eye out for ROCHER TABLE, GROUPERS, PETITE GROUPERS, BARIL DE BOEUF, and the small island and the rock awash near ILE FOURCHE.

When sailing to St. Barts from St. Maarten/St. Martin, it is best to leave from the Tintamarre/Orient Bay area so you can make it on one tack. If you sail from Philipsburg, you will normally have an 11 mile slog to windward to what is known locally as ROCKEFELLER POINT at the northwest end of St. Barts. As mentioned earlier, it is good to stay on the port tack until near THE GROUPERS; then tack over towards ROCHER TABLE for better wind and water but do not sail between The Groupers and Petite Groupers. Go back on the port tack when you can lay ILE FOURCHE. Close in to St. Barts take care to avoid the rocks and reefs extending off ROCKEFELLER POINT before heading in to GUSTAVIA.

From the east, the south, and the southwest one mile off the shore clears all dangers except ROCHES ROUGES off the southeast coast and LES BALINES and PAIN DE SUCRE off the southwest coast.

Strangers should approach St. Barts at night only from the east, south, or west and only with the greatest caution. The lights along ANSE DE GRAND FOND and in and around GUSTAVIA should help you stand well off until you can pick up the white sectors of the WRG light at Gustavia that lead safely into the harbor.

ILE FOURCHE

About two miles to the northwest of St. Barts, ILE FOURCHE is sometimes referred to as FIVE ISLANDS because its hills can have the appearance of being quite separate; the highest peak is to the west and rises almost 350 feet above the sea. The island is inhabited only by wild goats and is quite barren except for a few scruffy bushes and low ground cover. Its rocky peaks and rugged shoreline give it a wonderful, wild, craters-of-the-moon feeling; the views from the peaks are fabulous. It is a great place for a lunch stop or for overnight.

The approach to the anchorage in the northeast corner is midway between the two points of the island. This will keep you clear of the rock/reef awash off to the southwest of the southern point. Anchor in close off the gravel beach in 20 to 40 feet of water that is usually crystal clear. Sometimes a slight swell wraps around the southern point, so if you spend the night, you may be more comfortable with a stern anchor. When the water is not stirred up, the snorkeling at Fourche is excellent, especially along the northern shore; we have seen beautiful varieties of fish there that we have not encountered anywhere else in the islands.

GUSTAVIA

Gustavia is the picturesque and colorful port of entry and capital of St. Barts; it has an enchanting, stage set quality about it. There is a pleasing blend of beautiful old buildings and contemporary structures in the French West Indian style. The steep and narrow streets are frequently filled with a wild assortment of small cars, scooters, and motorcycles, but everything flows along smoothly and happily. The benign government has adjusted skillfully to recent growth with thoughtful improvements to the town and the port facilities as well.

ILE FOURCHE   *Derek Little photo*

GUSTAVIA   *Eiman photo*

APPROACHES The small islands, cays, and rocks awash in the approaches to Gustavia are all quite easy to see in normal daylight conditions. Charts show them all clearly together with the white sectors of the Gustavia light where the water is good. Yellow and black buoys with quick flashing lights mark LA BALINE about a third of a mile west of GROS ILETS and a small rock north of LES SAINTES.

From the northwest avoid BARIL DE BOEUF and the rocks off ROCKEFELLER POINT and proceed in along the coast; the hills cause fickle winds, so you will be better off under power. From the west leave LES BALINES and PAIN DE SUCRE and GROS ILETS to port and LES SAINTES and the buoy north of it to starboard.

From the south you can pass between Les Saintes and St. Barts, but avoid the shallow water and the rock north of Les Saintes. But it is better to stay outside both Les Saintes and the buoy north of them . . . i.e. leave them to starboard.

The fairway into the harbor is marked to port by green buoys between CORROSOL and ANSE PUBLIC and to starboard by four red buoys between the commercial pier and FORT OSCAR; the outer red buoy has a flashing red light on it. Anchoring in the fairway is prohibited.

ANCHORAGE AND DOCKING The most popular anchorage is off Fort Oscar where there is protection from the normal swells; the holding is good in sand and mud in 8 to 20 feet of water. To the northwest of the Fort you may want to use a stern anchor to prevent swinging around when the backwinds swirl over the hills. If you anchor anywhere inside the line from Fort Oscar to the light at Fort Gustavia (see sketch chart), regulations require that you set a stern anchor.

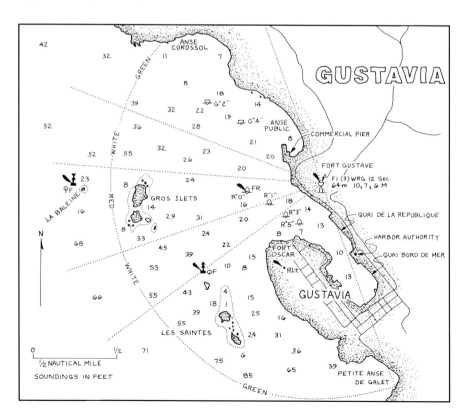

Some prefer to anchor further out along the northeast coast near Corrosol.It is peaceful and quiet there, but watch out for the 7 and 8 foot shallow spots off the village. And again, do not anchor in the fairway.

Other options include anchoring in the inner harbor and tieing stern-to along QUAI DE LA REPUBLIQUE. The inner harbor is convenient, but it is usually very crowded in the winter season and can be noisy. STARDUST CHARTERS keeps its large charter yachts along the Quai, but there is plenty of room for visiting yachts. Setting your bow anchor securely well off the Quai and backing in between other boats can be difficult in the usual cross winds. Have plenty of fenders ready and keep off the Quai to guard against the swells that roll in occasionally. Some bareboat fleets do not permit their boats to tie to the Quai; others require the use of two bow anchors. The Quai, incidentally, is the place to land and tie your dinghy no matter where you anchor.

Modest harbor fees (about $2.50 per day) are charged for anchoring outside the line from Fort Oscar to the Gustavia light; higher fees apply inside this line, and even higher fees are charged to yachts at the Quai. An official launch from the Port Authority will come along side in the morning to remind you about these fees in case you forget.

CLEARANCE Clearing in and out of St. Barts is easy and pleasant; the staff of the Port Authority is most helpful and will provide you with copies of the local newspaper and brochures that will help acquaint you with the island and what is going on; the office monitors VHF channels 16 and 10. In season office hours are 7:30 A.M. to 12:30 P.M. and 3:00 P.M to 5:00 P.M Mondays through Fridays; on Saturdays hours are the same except that the office opens at 8:30 A.M.; Sunday hours are 10:30 A.M. to 12:30 P.M. Off season hours are the same for all days except Sundays when the office is closed. The Port Authority may expand its office hours even more in the future. Crewed charter yachts should note that French cabotage laws prohibit foreign vessels from chartering between French ports or islands without special permits; offenders are subject to serious penalties.

SERVICES Gas, diesel, and water are available from 8:00 A.M. to Noon Mondays through Fridays and on Saturday mornings at the commercial pier (VHF Ch 77). Water is available on Quai De Gaulle through the Port Authority office, and trash containers,

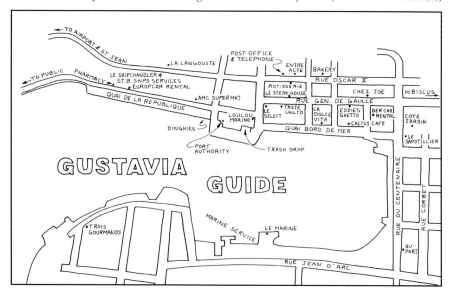

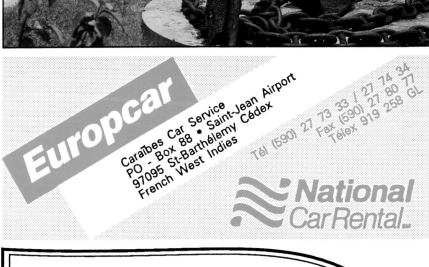

showers, and toilets are there as well. Ice cubes and blocks can be bought at AMC Libre Service just behind the Quai De La Republique.

   LOULOU'S MARINE, the oldest chandlery in town, is operated by LouLou Magras who has done much to further the development of sailing in St. Barts and who has been very helpful to visiting yachtsmen for many years; he carries a good selection of paint, varnish, marine hardware, cordage, charts and guides as well as those great striped French sailor's shirts, T shirts, and canvas bags, etc. Ther new LE SHIP CHANDLER DU PORT FRANC (VHF Ch 16) behind Quai De La Republique stocks marine hardware, fittings, anchors, paints and varnishes, cordage, tools, fastenings, gas tanks, and all sorts of accessories. ST. BARTHS SHIPS SERVICES are agents for North Sails and Zodiac and provide communications and other support services for yachts. For anything in the way of hardware and housewares and related supplies, head for the fabulous Alma Quincaillerie behind the Commercial Pier in Public.

   People who can repair engines, electronics, outboards, etc. come and go in St. Barts. The two chandleries and the people at the Port Authority can usually tell you who can help with any problems you have.

   Provisioning is simple and easy. Just behind the Quai De La Republique is AMC LIBRE SERVICE, the best and most convenient supermarket in Gustavia; it has fresh produce, meats, dry/boxed/canned/bottled groceries, wonderful cheeses and pates, wines, ice cubes and blocks, and lots of other French goodies. When supplies are adequate, fresh fish and langouste (local lobster) can be bought from fishermen along Rue du Bord de Mer between 8:00 A.M. and 10:00 A.M., and a few stalls offer fresh fruit and vegetables almost daily; when a trading vessel arrives from Guadeloupe (usually

GUSTAVIA HARBOR VIEW *Eiman photo*

Tuesdays and Thursdays in season) the selection of fresh produce is wide and wonderful.

Freshly baked croissants and French bread can be purchased at the bakery (boulangerie) on Rue Roi Oscar, the Rotisserie/Tratteur across from the Post Office, and at Taste Unlimited on Rue General de Gaulle. If you want your croissants and bread warm and right out of the oven, get to the bakery between 6:00 and 8:00 A.M.

Very efficient telephone service is available at the Post Office on Rue Roi Oscar. You can reach any phone in the world quickly and easily; no problem.

RESTAURANTS St. Barts has an outstanding array of restaurants to please every palate and pocketbook. Whether you prefer haute cuisine with candlelight and crystal, a delicious cold lobster on the beach, or tempting red snapper in an old West Indian house, the chefs of St. Barts are ready, willing, and able to serve you with imagination and flair. You may want to check the prices before you commit; to paraphrase the New York Times, St. Barts is known not only for its breathtaking beaches, but also for its breathtaking restaurant prices.

But do not despair; there are quite a few good restaurants around the harbor in Gustavia where prices are more reasonable including La Marine (fresh mussels and Dover sole flown in from Paris on Thursdays), La Langouste (wonderful lobster, seafood, and Creole food), Cote Jardin (Italian), and Eddies Ghetto (delicious, classic French menu), and La Dolce Vita (swordfish, grouper, pizza). Or you can dine on your yacht and still enjoy delicious French food via the take out service at Taste Unlimited, L'EntreActe, and Rotisserie/Tratteur at very reasonable prices; it is best to leave your order in the morning to allow time for preparation. For 'hamburgers in paradise' etc. don't miss Le Select, a Gustavia landmark that is a great hang out for yachtsmen, Jet Setters, and all sorts of waterfront types; things get very active and very colorful there when the late night crowd gets rolling.

Out of town we like the Marigot Bay Club in Marigot (really fresh seafood caught by the owner; lovely candle light setting) and LE PELICAN at Bay St. Jean where lobster is featured both at lunch and dinner overlooking the fabulous beach; lunches are informal in the grill, while fine dinners are served in the dining room. Bon appetit.

SHOPPING Gustavia, the airport shopping complex, and St. Jean boast many stylish dress shops, jewelry stores, and chic boutiques that will please the ladies and make budget-minded spouses groan. Most stores on St. Barts open at 9:00 A.M. and close at noon and reopen from 2:00 to 5:30 P.M. daily, but all are closed tight on Sundays. Free port prices prevail, but on style and luxury items bargain basement pricing is nowhere in sight. The best buys include liquor and wine, French perfume, French fashions and beach wear, crystal, jewelry, porcelain, and other luxury items. Famous designers, brand names, and boutiques are very much in evidence. The wonderful original hand-blocked fabrics and clothes of Jean Yves Froment are available in his shop in Colombier.

FUN AND GAMES For water skiing, SCUBA diving, snorkel trips, and underwater photography head for MARINE SERVICE across the harbor from the center of town where you will find just about anything you want including a very friendly, helpful staff. For thrilling, spectacular birds-eye views of the island and a chance to make your own breathtaking photographs its beaches, anchorages, and countryside, contact Heli St. Barts at the airport. You only go around once, and you may never have another chance to see St. Barts by helicopter, so go for it!

It is good sport to join the group in the late afternoon at the road intersection overlooking the airport to watch the Air Guadelope planes and others come in for landings on the 1,250-foot runway that starts half way down a hill and ends at the beach in Bay St. Jean. Planes landing and taking off remind one of carrier operations in "Victory At Sea." It is a unique and wonderful diversion, and the photo opportunities are terrific.

Shell Beach in Petite Anse de Galet is just a five minute walk from the head of the inner harbor in Gustavia . . . most convenient for a quick swim before, during, or after shopping . . . and the shelling there is still very good. In addition, we understand there is good snorkeling around Gros Ilets where there are lots of colorful fish to be seen.

BAIE ST. JEAN is the primary playground of St. Barts and has an unmistakable St. Tropez

AIRPORT - 1953   *Eiman photo*

TOURING ST. BARTS *Eiman photo*

flavor. The beach that stretches for almost 1,000 yards behind protective reefs attracts visitors and locals alike the way honey attracts bees. Swimming, sunning, snorkeling, windsurfing, Hobie cats, Sunfish, beach paddle, and other games, al fresco lunching, strolling, and bird watching keep the active and attractive beach goers happy and smiling. There is plenty of activity . . . topless and otherwise . . . for everyone in the sparkling water and along the creamy beach. The most popular area is between the airport runway and the Eden Roc Hotel sitting on a knoll just off the beach; that's where most of the restaurants, bars, hotels, and beach rentals are concentrated. On the other side of the runway the beach is less crowded and more sedate . . . if one can use that word for anything in Baie St. Jean. Habitable boats are not permitted to anchor in Baie St. Jean, so you'll have to take the overland approach.

TOURING ST. BARTS If you have seen only Gustavia and Baie St. Jean, you have just

ANSE DES FLAMANDES *Eiman photo*

scratched the surface of St. Barts; there are many, many more delights awaiting you around the island. For first timers and others not ready to tackle roller coaster driving on steep, narrow, twisting roads, we recommend a taxi tour. Except when cruise ships are in port, taxis are usually available in Gustavia at the stand alongside LouLou's Marine; taximan Hugo Cagan is one of the very best for island tours. If you are up to the driving challenge and want to set your own pace and route, rent a car, Mopped, motorcycle, or scooter. EUROP/NATIONAL CAR RENTAL (Phone: 27.73.33) has an office at LE SHIPCHANDLER on Quai De La Republique. In town Budget has an office in a swish shop on Rue De La France as few steps from Le Select; cars and scooters can be rented from Beringer on Rue De Gaulle near the head of the harbor and from Rent Some Fun near the Anglican church. Additional rental agencies are clustered around the airport and in St. Jean. Drive carefully and defensively!

The scenery and views are breathtaking; the houses range from charming and colorful to fabulous; the topography varies from lovely, windswept grassy slopes to dense and beautiful tropical valleys; and each of the beautiful beaches has its own distinct character. You'll want your camera and plenty of film.

One approach is to start off at the northwest end of the island stopping at Corossol, the small fishing village where the ladies make and sell wonderful straw hats, bags, etc. and then drive to see Yves Froment's impressive designs (fabrics, beachwear, & resortwear) in Colombier. From there wend your way around to visit the beautiful beach at Anse Des Flamands.

Next head east circling past Baie St. Jean, Anse L'Orient, Point Milou, Vitet, Marigot, Cul De Sac, and Grand Fond. As you drive towards Grande Saline, you might stop for lunch at Le Tamarin Restaurant or the Saline Creperie before heading to the beach. Although nudism (i.e. total nudity) is against the law in St. Barts, many of the bathers at Saline seem blissfully unaware of the legalities; in any event, is a wonderful place to spend an hour or two.

NORTHWESTERN & NORTHERN COASTS

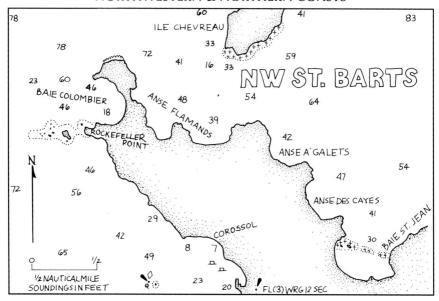

138

BAIE COLOMBIER   *Derek Little photo*

BAIE COLOMBIER on the northwest tip of St. Barts is lovely, relaxing place to overnight or spend a day or two and is doubly attractive as an alternative anchorage when Gustavia is crowded or rolly. On the south the bay is bounded by ROCKEFELLER POINT, ILE DE LA POINTE, and rocks and reefs extending out to the west; give them all a good berth and do not attempt to pass between Rockefeller Point and Ile De La Pointe. Much of the land around Colombier was owned by David Rockefeller who built the house and modernistic structure on the point that bears his name; presently the property is owned by the Rothschilds. To the north is POINTE COLOMBIER that has a turkey/goose/peacock farm near the beach where the birds frequently entertain with cackles, calls, and screeches.

Colombier is usually peaceful and uncrowded; only a foot path at the northern end of the beautiful beach connects it with Anse Des Flamandes and the rest of St. Barts. Proceed straight in and anchor off the beach in the northeast corner . . . or anywhere you like . . . in sand and grass; there is 8 to 10 feet of water a hundred yards or so off the beach and off the shore along Pointe Colombier. Backwinds can swing you around, so you might want to put out a stern anchor. Snorkelers will find great varieties of corals and colorful reef fish along the inside of Pointe Colombier; the snorkeling is also very good on the reefs around Ile De La Pointe, but currents are sometimes strong and the water can be rough.

ANSE DES FLAMANDES is around past Colombier on the north coast; it has a lovely, wild beach that is backed by a sprinkling of hotels and restaurants. The bay is wide open to the north and thus may not be comfortable for overnight anchoring. But it is a wonderful place for a lunch stop and a swim. Off Anse Des Flamandes is ILE DU CHEVREAU (or ILE BONHOMME) where there are shore reefs along the southeastern and southwestern shores; snorkeling there is reported to be very good, but the surge has made it impossible for us to check it out.

BAIE ST. JEAN lies in the middle of the northern coast. As mentioned, habitable boats are not permitted to anchor in the Baie, and the opening in the protective reef is narrow and shallow. If you are determined to visit it from your boat, you'll have to anchor outside the reef and dinghy ashore. We wouldn't try it; it's a little too crazy for us.

EAST OF BAIE ST. JEAN the north coast of St. Barts is quite inhospitable to cruising sailors; most bareboat charter fleets designate it a prohibited area. The only possible anchorage is in MARIGOT BAY where the entrance snakes in through hairy reefs that almost block the narrow channel completely; don't try it unless you know the channel very well. Beyond Marigot stand well off the coast taking care to avoid LA TORTUE and the reefs between it and the shore and LES GRENADIERS where, we understand, sharks can be a problem.

SOUTHEASTERN COAST

From the northern point of land near Petit Cul De Sac to BAIE DE LA GRANDE SALINE and ILE COCO the waters off the southeastern coast are strewn with a number of rocks awash and small, low islands that can be especially dangerous when visibility is limited. Keep a sharp eye out if you sail among them; better still, stand well off and avoid the trauma.

The beaches in BAIE DE LA GRANDE SALINE and ANSE GOUVERNEUR are

GRANDE SALINE *Berry photo*

AH!   *J.W. Eiman photo*

magnificent, but they are exposed to the southeast and thus are usually dead lee shores. Do not anchor off them unless the breeze is light and the sea is quite calm; anchoring at night is not permitted.

The beach and bay of GRANDE SALINE are indeed grand. The beautiful, clear blue water is uniquely lovely, and the fabulous beach is backed by wind-blown dunes between rugged hills with virtually no signs of civilization. Bathers frequently ignore the law prohibiting total nudity; c'est la vie. Our favorite anchorage is in the northeast corner near the two rocks awash 100 to 200 yards off the shore. There is another anchorage that sometimes has a little more protection; it is off the small beach beyond the large rock outcropping to the northeast. Whichever you select, set your anchor securely in the sand and use plenty of scope; this is no place to drag. Snorkeling along both sides of the bay is reported to be excellent when the surge is not bad. We are told there is also good snorkeling in ANSE DE GHAUVETTE between Saline and Gouveneur.

ANSE GOUVERNEUR is an attractive, clear bay with a lovely beach. The land behind the bay rises steeply and is dotted with attractive homes. The bay has no obstructions, crowds, or congestion. Anchor where you will in clear sand, and enjoy it all. It is a wonderful daytime anchorage in very calm conditions.

BAIE ST. JEAN & AIRPORT   *Eiman photo*

SABA

CHARTS: U.S. DMA 2550, 25600, 25607

British 130, 487, 955

Dutch 2110, 2716

Imray-Iolaire A25

SABA is a dramatic, enchanting island that lies off by itself some 25 miles the southwest of St. Maarten/St. Martin. Like many Caribbean islands, it is the top of an ancient volcano, but in other ways it is quite unique and indeed seems to be part of another world. Covering just over five square miles, it is a jumble of precipitous ravines and rugged mountains thrusting up almost perpendicularly from the sea to the peak of Mount Scenery at an elevation of 2854 feet. The island is steep-to and has no sandy beaches; also, it has nothing even faintly resembling the typical Caribbean harbor.

The early history of Saba seems almost as clouded as the top of Mount Scenery. After the traditional sighting by Columbus in 1493, nothing much is clear for more than 100 years, and even then the clouds part only slightly; nobody seems to be able to explain with certainty or precision when, how, or why Saba was settled. Some presume that colonists from near by St. Eustatia (Statia) landed on Saba during fishing expeditions to the SABA BANK in the 1630s. Supposedly, they took possession of the island in the 1640s, and the Dutch extended formal control over it in the 1650s. Then, true to the pattern of the Caribbean, Saba changed hands among the French, Dutch, and English a dozen times or so until finally it came under Dutch control once and for all in 1816. During this time of tumult and transition, the inhabitants used the ingenious Rolling Stones Defense: When the attackers began to scramble up the hillsides, the local forces simply removed the restraining timbers that had kept huge quantities of boulders in readiness for such emergencies, and that was the end of the that!

SABA   *Joan Curtis Borque photo*

On their magical island the Sabans, with the help of the Dutch government, have won some impressive victories over the environment. In 1972 a 277-foot pier was completed in FORT BAY, giving the island its first-ever real docking facility. Until the completion of that seemingly impossible engineering and construction feat, everybody and everything arriving by sea had to be landed through the surf on a rocky beach in small surf boats handled by skilled local surfmen.

Even more impressive in many ways are the nine miles of twisting roads built entirely by hand on extremely difficult terrain to the designs of Josephus Lambert Hassell, a Saban who took a correspondence course on road building. Some twenty years in the making, these incredible roads have had an enormous impact on all of Saba, enabling Jeeps and other motor vehicles to replace the porters who had for centuries carried on their own backs or on the backs of their donkeys everything landed on the shore and destined for the villages 800 to 1800 feet up from the sea. The first Jeep came in through the surf in 1947 and was named 'The Donkey With Wheels' by the porters. Carleton Mitchell has called that landing of the Jeep the greatest event in the history of Saba, and he is undoubtedly right.

In the past the limited resources of the island were not able to support the population, with the result that Saban men traditionally left to find work abroad. For

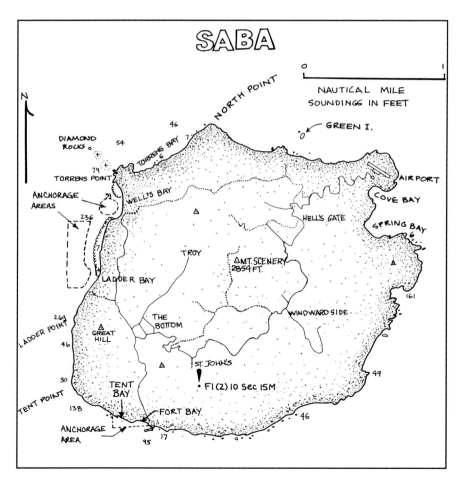

generations many joined the merchant marine, working on vessels throughout the world; others gravitated to the oil refineries on Curacao and other islands of the Caribbean. With many men of working age pursuing their fortunes away from home, the proportion of women was unusually high, and thus at times Saba was referred to as an island of women. The men abroad did not forget their homes, their island, or their loved ones; husbands sent money back regularly to their wives, and bachelors frequently returned to marry their childhood sweethearts and raise families.

SABA MARINE PARK, established in 1987 to preserve the island's marine resources in perpetuity, has done an impressive job not only developing ecologically sound diving and recreational regulations but also assisting divers and visiting yachtsmen as well. Strict regulations have been established to protect fish, coral, conch, and turtles. A multiple use zone, five dive zones, one all purpose recreational zone, and three anchorage areas have been designated. Anchoring is permitted only in the three anchorage areas that are shown on our sketch chart. The Marine Park has put down 36 moorings at the best dive sites to facilitate diving and to protect the coral; white buoys are for boats up to 50' LOA; orange buoys are for boats 50' to 100' LOA; there is a two hour limit on use of these dive moorings. There are five yellow overnight mooring buoys in LADDER BAY and WELLS BAY; they are available on a first-come-first-served basis; use is limited to seven days. Crewed charter yachts are limited to four visits a year. For more information contact Manager Susan White or the staff at Saba Marine Park office in Fort Bay or out on patrol Mondays through Fridays and on Saturday and Sunday mornings; they are very friendly and helpful and can tell you the best ways to deal with the local conditions and get the most from your stay.

APPROACH Saba is quite steep to; the only offshore hazards are DIAMOND ROCKS off TORRENS POINT to the northwest and GREEN ISLAND off the north coast. Yachtsmen should avoid SABA BANK, a large shoal area about 2-3/4 miles southwest of Saba extending 25 miles to the south of the island and some 30 miles to the west of it with depths varying from 24 to 60 feet. Winds and currents often cover the Bank with short, steep, dangerous seas; yachts should not attempt crossing the Bank going to windward.

CLEARANCE/SERVICES Clear in (Immigration only) at the Harbor Office in Fort Bay where Harbormaster Hugo Levenstone is in charge; hours are 8:00 A.M. to Noon and 1:00 to 5:00 P.M. Mondays through Fridays. When Mr. Levenstone is not available, you can clear in at the Marine Park office nearby. In any event, be sure to pick up current information on the Marine Park at its office.

If you want to use the large red buoy off Fort Bay or come alongside one of the piers while checking in, you must obtain permission from the Harbormaster (VHF Ch 11) or contact Saba Radio (VHF Ch 16). Otherwise, anchor out and dinghy into the pier. Fuel is available at the gas station in Fort Bay; SABA DEEP DIVE CENTER has an office near the pier, and taxis are usually available there.

DOCKING/ANCHORING The Leo Chance pier at Fort Bay has made a tremendous contribution to Saba by providing a vital facility for handling marine freight; it is a load-and-unload, in-and-out facility and is not to be used for lenghtly tie-ups. Primarily used by commercial traffic, it can be helpful to yachts; permission to use it must be obtained from the Harbormaster (Ch 11). The surge behind the pier can damage boats by bashing them against the pier or against one another. Stout fenders and lines are needed, and some fenders should be placed low to guard against the lower timbers along the pier. Water inside the pier varies from about 20 feet at the outer or western end to 12 feet at its eastern end, and the bottom shoals to about 6 feet in close to the rocky shore. Normal

WELL'S BAY *Joan Curtis Borque photo*

FORT BAY *Eiman photo*

easterly or southeasterly winds blow boats away from the inside of the pier toward the fishing boats moored over towards the shore. There is not much room for visitors to maneuver. Give the end of the pier a wide berth as a shoal has been reported there. The large, red buoy a few hundred yards off the pier is reserved for the Windjammer head boats but can, as noted, be used by yachts with permission from the Harbormaster.

The Leo Chance pier has been enlarged recently, and another pier for fishing and dive boats has been built to the east. This new pier is also a load-and-unload facility; use must be cleared with the Harbormaster.

In the **FORT BAY/TENT BAY** designated anchor area the sand bottom drops off to 50 feet and more quite near the shore. If you anchor in close, set a stern anchor to make sure you don't swing ashore. If you anchor farther out, take care to keep clear of the three moorings in the adjacent dive zone and keep a sharp eye out for swimmers & divers. This area is best when the wind is north of east, but even then it can be uneasy. SMP does not recommend overnight anchoring here. Usually, you will be better off anchoring along the west coast.

When the wind is from the east or southeast, the anchorage areas in **LADDER BAY** or **WELL'S BAY** can be fairly calm and pleasant. Shore parties can be dropped off at Fort Bay, or they can—conditions permitting—dinghy back there, or they can make the tough climb up to THE BOTTOM. From Ladder Bay you have to huff and puff up some 800 steps cut into the hillside; from Well's Bay you must climb a mile or so up a steep road usually closed to taxis by fallen rock. In Ladder Bay the bottom is sand, and the depth is 20 feet close to the shore, but stay off a bit to avoid the big rocks in the shallows and down drafts that can waltz your boat around all over the place. The holding is good. A stern anchor is advised and, again, keep clear of the dive moorings nearby. The bottom drops off to 50 feet + north of Ladder Bay and up to Well's Bay. You may be lucky enough to use one of the yellow overnight mooring buoys for boats up to 50 feet in length put down there by the Saba Marine Park.

SABA COTTAGES *Eiman photo*

The best anchorage in most conditions is in Well's Bay. In the anchor area depths are 15 to 30+ feet, and the bottom is clear, hard sand; be sure to dive on your anchor to make sure it is well set. As in Ladder Bay the yellow overnight SMP mooring buoys are a great addition. The scenery is fantastic, and the snorkeling around Torrens Point is spectacular with tunnels and caves and wonderful fish and coral; SMP has marked an underwater snorkel trail there and provides a trail map at its office in Fort Bay.

If you don't want to spend one day sailing to Saba and another sailing back, or if you are put off by the anchoring situation, you can still enjoy the enchantment of Saba with ease. Windward Island Airways has five flights a day from St. Maarten starting at 7:00 AM; the last return flight leaves Saba at 5:00 PM. Thus it is a simple matter to spend a memorable day . . . or two . . . on Saba. In a day it is possible to see the spectacular sights on land and to make a dive or two in the unforgettable waters of the Marine Park.

ASHORE The capital and main settlement on Saba is THE BOTTOM, an attractive Dutch village with neat, picturesque houses, gabled red roofs, and lovely gardens. The name is derived from the Dutch word 'botte,' which means bowl and refers to the valley in which the town is located; it does NOT, as the popular story has it, refer to the lower floor of a volcano crater. The village is about 800 feet above the sea and is the site of the Commissioner's official residence, the facilities of SABA RADIO, Landsradio (telephone) office, and Cranston's Antique Inn, an attractive, small hotel with a restaurant and the Birds of Paradise Disco. Also there is a popular gathering place, the Lime Tree Bar & Restaurant (formerly Bougaloo), known for its local fish, lobster, vegetables, soursopp ice cream, and for Saba Spice, a unique, spicy liqueur that is smooth and delicious. The Serving Spoon restaurant features local dishes and

THE BOTTOM *Eiman photo*

occasionally a steel band. At the Saba Artisans Foundation boutique locally designed hand screened resort fashions are available in an assortment of interesting patterns.

Another thousand feet or so further above sea level is WINDWARDSIDE, Saba's second largest village and the location of two fine hotels, a few restaurants, SEA SABA DIVE CENTER, and the island's only museum. Captain's Quarters Hotel is built around a restored 19th century sea captain's home; it has ten large guest rooms (half of which have antique four poster beds), a tennis court, skeet range, restaurant and bar, swimming pool, and terrace in a beautiful setting jutting out towards the sea. Scout's Place is a bit more informal and has fifteen guest rooms, restaurant and bar; it is popular with day visitors and local people alike and describes itself as "Bed 'n Board; Cheap and Cheerful." The Saba Museum is in a lovely old sea captain's home and is filled with antiques circa 1890 and family memorabilia. Windwardside also boasts the Saba

Tourist Bureau, Island Craft Shop, Saba Chinese Restaurant, and Guido's Pizzeria, Big Rock Market, Saba Drug Store, and a number of other handicraft, souvenir, and clothing shops.

The Tourist Bureau provides helpful information about anything and everything on the island including the popular hiking opportunities on well-groomed and marked trails. The most ambitious and rewarding is the hike up the 1,064 handhewn steps to the top of MOUNT SCENERY that starts near Windwardside; watch the weather as the upper elevations are in the clouds about half the time; on clear days the views are absolutely spectacular. Other hikes are less taxing but filled with fabulous views and rain forests with lovely tropical trees and flowers.

Between Windwardside and HELL'S GATE the incredible road makes its way through gorges dotted with wild philodendron, elephant ears, orchids clinging to trees, and masses of luxurious subtropical growth that include yellow sage, mountain cotton, Surinam cherry, and Eucharist lilies. Both Windwardside and Hell's Gate cling precariously to the mountainside and have scores of charming white houses with red roofs, contrasting shutters, gingerbread, and picket fences, as well as other homes with weathered shingles that are reminiscent of Nantucket and Cape Cod. Neat and tidy with carefully tended gardens, they make a delightful contrast to the powerful backdrop of massive mountains, plunging ravines, and sweeping vistas that make the island a living fairyland.

The women of Saba have made beautiful drawn thread work (or lace work) ever since it was introduced by Gertrude Johnson in the 1870s. Also called Spanish work because Miss Johnson learned it from Spanish nuns in a convent school in Caracas, it

AIRPORT AND HELL'S GATE *Eiman photo*

SABA MUSEUM, WINDWARD SIDE *R.M. Glover photo*

involves drawing and tying selected threads on a piece of linen to produce ornamental designs. It is extremely delicate and requires careful laundering. The Island Craft Shop in Windwardside and the Community Center in Hell's Gate have extensive selections for sale, and it is available in most of the other shops in Windwardside.

Diving is a major activity in Saba; experts regard it as an outstanding dive site because of its clear waters, underwater peaks, caves, tunnels, coral gardens, spectacular walls, and the variety of its colorful fish. Some say it is one of the five best dive locations in the world! Saba Marine Park not only protects and preserves the underwater world but also provides extensive facilities and services for divers and yachtsmen. At Fort Bay it has recently set up a four person recompression chamber that is staffed by trained divemasters and other volunteers headed by Dr. Jack Buchanan.

Saba has two top flight dive services--SEA SABA in Windwardside and SABA DEEP in Fort Bay-- that have everything novice or experienced divers and snorkelers could want or need....certified instructors, dive masters, well equipped dive boats, resort and certification courses, night dives, equipment rentals, retail shops, complete dive packages, etc., etc. Owner Mike Myers is in charge at Saba Deep. Owners Joan and Louis Borque operate Sea Saba; Joan is an accomplished photographer and provides expert instruction in underwater photography. Both services monitor VHF channel l6.

Saba is a unique, spectacular, and fascinating island. A visit will surely be a memorable high point of any cruise.

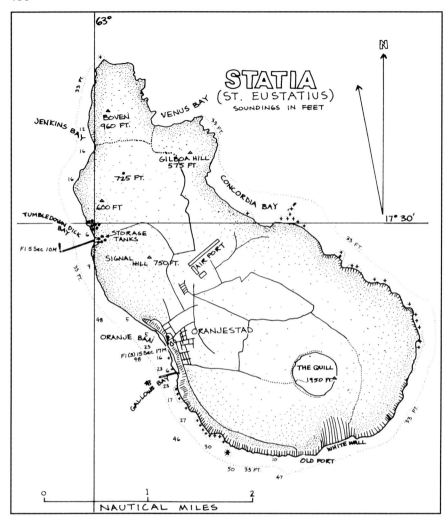

STATIA
(ST. EUSTATIUS)
SOUNDINGS IN FEET

N

63°

17° 30'

33 FT.

JENKINS BAY
12
16
16

BOVEN
960 FT.

VENUS BAY
33 FT.

GILBOA HILL
575 FT.

725 FT.

CONCORDIA BAY
23 FT.

600 FT

TUMBLEDOWN DICK
BAY 6

STORAGE
TANKS

Fl 5 Sec 10M

SIGNAL
HILL 750 FT.

33 FT.
9

AIRPORT

48 5

ORANJE BAY
5
23
16
48

Fl (3) 15 Sec 17M

23 6

GALLOWS BAY
18
23
17
27
46
30
50 33 FT.
10
47

ORANJESTAD

THE QUILL
1950 FT.

WHITE WALL

OLD PORT

33 FT.

0   1   2

NAUTICAL MILES

STATIA   *Eiman photo*

STATIA (ST. EUSTATIUS)

CHARTS: U.S. DMA 2550, 25600, 25607
   British 487, 955
   Dutch 2110, 2716
   Imray-Iolaire A25

In the 17th and 18th centuries Statia earned its place in history as a famous transit point for merchandise, partly because its central location among English, Spanish, Dutch, and French colonies was ideal in an era when cargo ships were dominated by winds and currents. Today it is well situated for sailors of a different sort, and cruising yachtsmen will find it an intriguing and rewarding port of call. Located approximately 29 miles south of St. Maarten/St. Martin, 23 miles south and west of St. Barts, 14 miles east of Saba, and 7 miles off the northwest coast of St. Kitts, it is ideal for island hopping in short steps.

PAST GLORIES, NEW ERA

In the 1700s Statia was the leading trans-shipping and trading center in the Caribbean with such enormous and lucrative trade that it was known as "The Golden Rock." England and European powers required their colonies to do business only with their Mother Countries and would not allow them to trade directly among themselves. But the crafty Dutch, who controlled Statia, breached these restrictions by making the island a free port where goods of all nations and colonies could be traded without question or restriction as long as the paperwork was in order. As a result corn, tobacco, and lumber from North America, sugar, rum, and tobacco from Caribbean islands, slaves from Africa, and furniture, textiles, weapons, gunpowder, clothing, and manufactured wares from Europe and Asia were traded actively. Slave trading peaked in the 1730s, but commerce in other merchandise was greatest in the last half of the

FORT ORANJE AND SABA   *Eiman photo*

152

ORANJESTAD AND THE QUILL   *Eiman photo*

century. In the busiest of times more than 3,500 ships called at Statia in a single year, and frequently 200 or more were anchored off the town; trading was fast and furious along the waterfront where pandemonium was the norm.

In this Golden Era Oranjestad was a town divided: Fort Oranje, the Dutch Reform Church, the synagogue Honen Dalim, and most residences were in the Upper Town atop the 130-foot cliff, while bulging warehouses, the slave house, shops, and other commercial operations clustered amid the hustle and bustle in the Lower Town along the shore. A Lady of Quality, Janet Schaw, visited from Scotland in 1775 and made the following observation:

> " . . . From one end of the town to the other is a continuous mart, wherein goods of most different uses and qualities are displayed before the shop doors. Here hang rich embroideries, painted silks, flowered muslins, with all the manufactures of the Indies. Just by hang sailor's jackets, trousers, shoes, hats, etc. The next stall contains the most exquisite silver, the most beautiful indeed I ever saw, and close by these, iron pots, kettles, shovels . . . I bought a quantity of excellent French gloves for fourteen pence a pair . . . We purchased excellent claret for less than two shillings a bottle . . . "

Free port shoppers today might make similar observations about St. Thomas or St. Maarten.

Statia earned a very special place in the history of the United States by supplying the colonies with everything they wanted and needed including vast and continuing shipments of European weapons and gunpowder to resist and overcome the British. This essential trade flourished in spite of 'stern orders' from the Netherlands that it cease and in spite of efforts of the British fleet. And as if that were not enough, Fort Oranje is credited with firing the first foreign salute to a U.S. ship carrying the Great Union Flag of the newly formed United States. Commander Johannes de Graffe was in command on November 16, 1776 when the U.S. Brig-of-War ANDREW DORIA arrived off Lower Town and saluted with flag and cannon; Fort Oranje returned the salutes in kind, and history was made. According to the bronze placque at Fort Oranje presented by President Franklin Delano Roosevelt, "Here the sovereignty of the United States of America was first formally acknowledged to a national vessel by a foreign official."

The illegal trade in Statia had long infuriated the English in London, and the famous salute was the crowning blow. The British declared war on the Netherlands in December, 1780, and Admiral Rodney of the Royal Navy plundered the island in February, 1781. After keeping the Dutch flag flying on Fort Oranje for a month to lure additional merchant ships, Rodney confiscated all the goods and merchandise on the land as well as the ships at anchor off Oranjestad and auctioned off the lot in one of the greatest public auctions of the century. By tradition Rodney shared in the proceeds, but he spent years fighting lawsuits brought by his outraged countrymen from nearby St. Kitts who suffered huge losses as a result of his actions.

The island recovered quickly from the British raid. Between 1784 and 1795 trade flourished once again, and the population increased to just over 8000, its highest point ever. But as the end of the century approached, Statia's trade with other islands and with the independent United States began to dwindle. By 1816, according to historian Dr. J. Hartog, the economy of Statia was ruined and has never recovered. As the golden days receded into history, Statia lost her allure for foreign governments and merchants alike and the island slid into a deep decline.

After struggling through the doldrums for more than a century, the island has been moving towards better times of late. Since the 1950s roads have been built throughout the island; a modern concrete pier and fishery complex have been built in Gallows Bay; electricity has been introduced; a new airport has been built and enlarged, and a number of small inns, shops, and restaurants have appeared. The St. Eustatius Historical Foundation, started in 1947, has been in the forefront of intensive and impressive efforts to preserve and restore beautiful reminders of the days when Statia was one of the wealthiest islands of its size in the world and was indeed The Golden Rock.

Interestingly, Statia in the early 1980s began an entirely new era as a transshipping center. In sharp contrast to the 1700s when an enormous variety of goods was traded, her new transit business involved one commodity only—oil. American interests have established Statia Terminals, Inc. to build and operate an oil terminal. Storage tanks and a 3,000+ foot pier have been built in Tumble Down Dick Bay to accommodate very

VISITORS RECEPTION CENTER   *Eiman photo*

large supertankers. More recently a small oil refinery has been put in operation in the hills where it does not spoil the view. The oil industry is now the largest private employer on the island.

STATIA FOR YACHTSMEN

Statia is like a huge western saddle pointing towards the southeast. The QUILL, a beautiful extinct volcano that is said to be one of the most perfectly symmetrical in the world, towers some 1960 feet at the southeast end of the island, while BOVEN HILL rises almost 1000 feet above the northwest coast. LOWER TOWN and UPPER TOWN combine to make up the principal settlement, ORANJESTAD, that nestles on the west coast in the central seat of the saddle. Statia is off the beaten tourist track and totally unspoiled; it is a peaceful and quiet haven where the friendly people delight in welcoming visitors to their charming island.

APPROACH Statia is generally quite steep to, and there are only a few off-lying hazards to note: Along the northern shore to the southeast of CONCORDIA BAY, reefs and shoals extend out a few hundred yards from the shore. A rock awash is reported to lie about 350 yards off the southern coast to the southwest of the Quill. Yachts standing off the coast 500 yards or more will clear all rocks and shoals. Everyone should, of course, give a wide berth to the 3,000+-foot oil terminal pier in TUMBLE DOWN DICK BAY. There is a flashing light (5 sec.) at its head; north going currents of 2-1\2 knots and south going currents of 1-1/2 knots have been observed at the pier.

ORANJE BAAI is backed by the Lower Town and a narrow strip of land near sea level and the Upper Town atop the 130-foot cliff. A group flashing light (15 sec.) is reported at FORT ORANJE in the Upper Town . An 1,100-foot commercial pier is at the southern end at GALLOWS BAY with a small concrete pier just to the north of it.

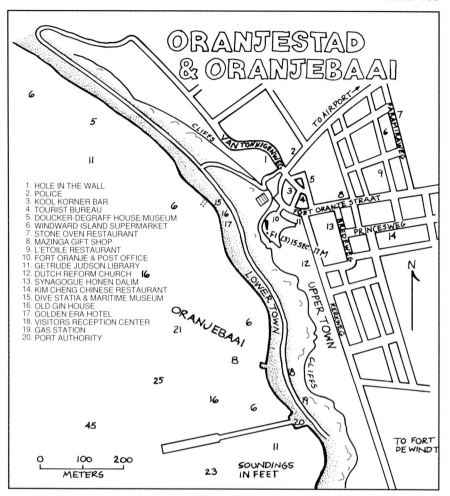

ORANJESTAD & ORANJEBAAI

1. HOLE IN THE WALL
2. POLICE
3. KOOL KORNER BAR
4. TOURIST BUREAU
5. DOUCKER-DEGRAFF HOUSE/MUSEUM
6. WINDWARD ISLAND SUPERMARKET
7. STONE OVEN RESTAURANT
8. MAZINGA GIFT SHOP
9. L'ETOILE RESTAURANT
10. FORT ORANJE & POST OFFICE
11. GETRUDE JUDSON LIBRARY
12. DUTCH REFORM CHURCH
13. SYNAGOGUE HONEN DALIM
14. KIM CHENG CHINESE RESTAURANT
15. DIVE STATIA & MARITIME MUSEUM
16. OLD GIN HOUSE
17. GOLDEN ERA HOTEL
18. VISITORS RECEPTION CENTER
19. GAS STATION
20. PORT AUTHORITY

SOUNDINGS IN FEET

METERS

Foundations of old warehouses extend out 50 yards or more into the water all along the shore, and a 7-foot shoal is reported 400 to 500 feet north of the commercial pier and 400 feet off the land. Otherwise, the Baai is free from obstructions.

ANCHORING The best anchorage for yachts is to the north of the commercial pier in 15 to 30 feet of water. The anchorage is protected from normal trade winds, but it is an open roadstead where the surge frequently makes life very rolly and at times downright uncomfortable. Be sure your anchor is well dug in and use a stern anchor to minimize the roll.

As scrambling up the ladder on the north side of the big pier from a dinghy can be difficult, it is often better to land at the small concrete pier to the north; it has steps on its northern side. If a surge is running, use a light stern anchor to keep your dinghy from bashing against the pier. And if you plan to be ashore after dark, it is good to remember that the swells can be troublesome when it comes time to board your dinghy; flashlights can be very helpful!

If Oranje Baai is too rolly for overnighting, you can move to JENKINS BAY up above Tumble Down Dick Bay on the northwest coast. The anchorage there can be calmer and less rolly, and we are told there is good snorkeling along the shore reefs.

Construction of a new pier and a proper breakwater in Oranje Baai have been discussed for quite some time, and happily work is to begin late in 1992. That is the best possible news; a breakwater that will provide a calm anchorage and end the rock and roll will answer the prayers and curses of seamen since Statia was discovered.

CLEARANCE Mr. Carlyle Millard handles clearance at the Harbor Office at the head of the commercial pier. He advises that the office "will be open at all times for your convenience." If, by chance, it is closed, go to the Police Station in the Upper Town to clear in.

SERVICES Fuel and water are available at the Shell station near the commercial pier. Provisioning can be done at the MAZINGA GIFT SHOP and the Windward Island Supermarket; Mazinga now stocks cheeses, cold cuts, pastries, liquor, and beer, etc.

ASHORE The Visitors Reception Center is in the neat West Indian style house just across the road from the small concrete pier. The friendly, helpful staff can provide maps, booklets, and information on taxis, and hiking. Be sure to pick up the Historical Foundation folder, "Walking Tour of Lower and Upper Town;" it contains interesting comments and an excellent map highlighting many points of interest in both elevations of Oranjestad.

The Historical Foundation is responsible for the attractive park along the shore; its beautiful flowering oleander bushes are both attractive and practical as they are quite toxic and thus are not eaten by the hungry goats. The park contains ruins of many 17th and 18th century warehouse foundations and cisterns; some are submerged, some are

FORT ORANJE   *Houser photo*

awash, and some are on the dry land. Snorkeling among the ruins is interesting and, although the area has been pretty well picked over, there is a chance of finding blue slave beads or other small relics of the olde days.

Beyond the park is another pleasing sight with a practical twist: The CLAES GUT PROJECT, an attractive cascade of stone terraces and oleanders descending the cliff that separates Upper Town from Lower Town. It not only prevents dangerous erosion of the cliff but also acts as part of a catchment system that channels valuable rainwater runoff from the streets above to a cistern in Lower Town where it is available for construction and agricultural uses. Opposite the Claes Gut Project is the new 20-room GOLDEN ERA HOTEL complete with restaurant, bar, cable TV and swimming pool. It serves West Indian food, seafood, steaks, and chops at reasonable prices. Neat as a pin and comfortable, it is a welcome, year round addition to Statia's accommodations for visitors.

A few steps further along are the tasteful buildings of The Old Gin House Hotel that is the result of years of devoted labors by John May and the late Martin Scofield, delightful and vibrant refugees from Connecticut and New York City, respectively. The restaurant has the most sophisticated menu on the island; it is best to make dinner reservations in the afternoon to allow time for careful preparation. If you are fortunate, John might show and tell something of his fantastic collection of blue slave beads that came from Africa during the days of the slave trade. John has a wonderful wealth of information about the island past and present.

Just beyond The Old Gin House DIVE STATIA provides equipment sales and rentals, SSI, PADI, and NAUI instruction, and snorkel and dive trips to Statia's many and varied sites. Owners Mike and Judy Brown will show you the impressive underwater sights all around the island including wrecks, reefs, rays, turtles, eels, and huge angelfish. Call them on VHF Channel l6.

To reach Upper Town, hike up the short, steep, cobblestone SLAVE TRAIL that starts just past Dive Statia or take a cab up FORT ROAD. The Upper Town has an air

DUTCH REFORM CHURCH *Eiman photo*

of Dutch tidiness about it and is filled with quaint, narrow streets and picturesque West Indies/New England cottages with gingerbread trim and brightly painted shutters and a host of 18th century buildings that are well worth visiting. The centerpiece for many is Fort Oranje, which has been preserved and restored with great care. Nearby are the Gertrude Judson Library, Three Widows Corners with its lovely courtyard, the restored ruins of the Dutch Reform Church, and the remains of the synagogue Honen Dalim. The beautiful Doncker-De Graaff House includes the Historical Foundation Museum; the old maps, prints, photographs, porcelain, and other memorabilia are intriguing.

A few steps along Fort Oranje Straat will bring you to the MAZINGA GIFT SHOP that stocks not only a wonderful selection of duty free island handicrafts, gifts, souvenirs, chocolates, perfumes, and beach wear but also, as mentioned earlier, cheeses, sausages, cold cuts, pastries, liquor, and beer. The Deli Cooler prepares picnics and beaches lunches. Mazinga is adding a new wing, and plans for a French Cafe are being considered. Leontine Durby, who is in charge, is a great, friendly source of information about the island.

Restaurants in the Upper Town are modest and inexpensive. Kool Korner is a very congenial gathering spot with fine local fare when the chef is on hand. Kim Cheng's Chinese Restaurant, The Stone Oven (West Indian), and L'Etoile (local and seafood) have been joined by new al fresco restaurants such as the popular Sonny's Place and King's Well. Sailing enthusiast Wyn and Laura at King's Well overlooking the bay serve good seafood and German wonders (pot roast, snitzels, dumplings, etc.) at dinner and super sandwiches (sausage is a specialty) at lunches . . . all with Becks beer; yachtsmen can expect a warm reception.

Hiking is very popular especially the trip up the QUILL and down into its crater. Trail maps can be found at the Tourist Board in Upper Town. The highest point on the Quill is about 2,000 feet above the sea, but the trail down into the crater starts a few hundred feet lower. From the rim the views of Statia, Saba, St. Kitts, Nevis, St. Barts, and St. Maarten are spectacular on clear days. Deep inside the crater is a lush tropical rain forest filled with orchids, mahogany trees, wood doves, yellow butterflies, banana trees, and land crabs. The crabs come out of their holes only at night; catching them by torchlight or moonlight is great sport and eating them is a great delight.

Miscellaneous Notes: The round stones in the walls of the Dutch Reform Church are called face stones because of their size and shape . . . The larger old graves contain the remains of 10 to 15 people; bodies were interred in layers as the need arose. The people on Statia are guided by traditional values and respect for other people's property; there is virtually no theft or other crime on the island. We are told that there is so much iron in the beach at Oranje Baai at times that the sand can be picked up with a magnet....The rusting pilings on the same beach are the remains of an unsuccessful attempt in 1906 to build a permanent pier.

THE QUILL   *Eiman photo*

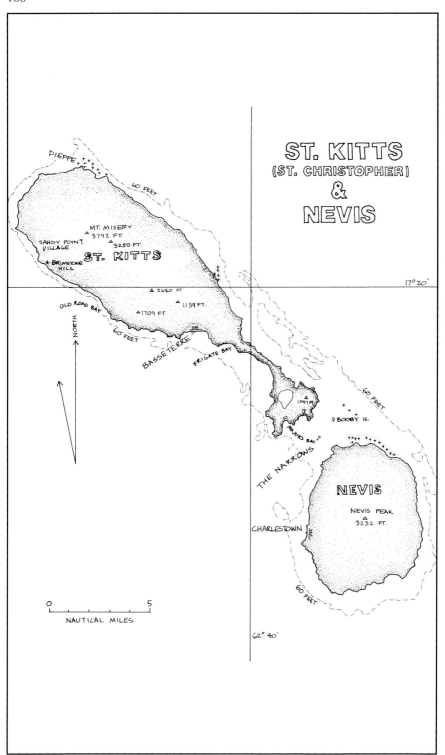

ST. KITTS
(ST. CHRISTOPHER)
&
NEVIS

DIEPPE

60 FEET

MT. MISERY
3792 FT.
3250 FT.

SANDY POINT
VILLAGE
ST. KITTS
BRIMSTONE
HILL

17°20'

2620 FT.

OLD ROAD BAY

1159 FT.

NORTH

1709 FT.

60 FEET

BASSETERRE

FRIGATE BAY

1047 FT.

0 BOOBY IS.

MAIDES BAY

THE NARROWS

NEVIS

NEVIS PEAK
3232 FT.

CHARLESTOWN

60 FEET

60 FEET

0   5
NAUTICAL MILES

62° 40'

INTRODUCTION TO ST. KITTS — NEVIS

The shores of ST. KITTS and NEVIS lie 37 (nautical) miles to the south and east of ST. MAARTEN, 27 miles south of ST. BARTS, 7 miles southeast of STATIA, 25 miles northeast of MONTSERRAT, and 36 miles west of ANTIGUA. They sit on a bank that extends from 10 miles southeast of Nevis to about 2 miles northwest of Statia; this bank rises abruptly from surrounding depths of 600 to 2,000 feet and more. Depths approximately 1-1/2 to 2 miles off St. Kitts and Nevis are in the range of 35 to 90 feet; some 8 miles to the southeast of Nevis there is a shoal area with 45 to 55 feet of water over it. At the northeast end of THE NARROWS between the two islands there are breaking reefs and dangerous shoals about 2 miles off the shores.

The formal name of the larger island is ST. CHRISTOPHER. This name does appear on some postage stamps, charts, maps, and other documents, but ST. KITTS is the popular name and is used almost universally.

WEATHER

Weather in St. Kitts/Nevis is about the same as in St. Maarten (see Introduction to the St. Maarten/St. Martin Cruising Area). Annually, trade winds in St. Kitts blow from the north-northeast to east-southeast over 90% of the time, but typically they swing more to the north in fall and winter and to the south in spring and summer. Average wind velocities are relatively constant but increase to highs in June and July before falling to annual lows in September, October and November.

SUMMARY OF CLIMATOLOGICAL DATA FOR
ST. KITTS-NEVIS

From Observations at Golden Rock Airport,

St. Kitts 1971-1978

Caribbean Meteorological Institute

| | Mean Wind Speed | | Mean Dry Bulb Temperature | | Mean Relative Humidity | | Mean Cloud Cover | | Mean Sea Level Pressure | |
| | Knots | | Degrees F | | % | | OKTAS | | mb | |
	0800 LST	1400 LST	0800 LST	1400 LST	0800 LST	1400 LST	0800 LST	1400 LST	0800 LST	1400 LST
January	12.1	13.3	75.7	80.0	76	67	4.6	4.3	1018.0	1017.0
February	10.8	12.7	75.8	80.1	74	66	4.6	4.2	1017.8	1016.8
March	12.1	13.0	76.6	80.6	74	65	4.7	4.1	1017.5	1016.5
April	11.6	12.8	78.1	81.7	73	66	5.0	4.4	1017.0	1015.9
May	12.2	13.3	79.8	83.0	73	70	5.1	4.9	1017.3	1016.4
June	13.8	14.7	81.1	84.4	76	67	5.3	4.8	1017.6	1017.0
July	14.0	14.6	81.2	84.9	75	68	4.9	4.3	1017.9	1017.1
August	13.4	14.1	81.5	84.5	77	71	4.9	4.7	1016.6	1016.0
September	10.5	11.2	81.3	84.2	79	72	4.8	4.9	1015.6	1014.7
October	9.4	10.8	81.2	83.6	77	73	5.1	5.2	1014.9	1013.4
November	10.3	11.4	79.4	82.3	79	72	4.7	4.7	1015.1	1013.6
December	11.3	13.1	76.8	80.4	77	70	4.7	4.5	1016.5	1015.2
Mean	11.8	12.9	79.0	82.5	76	69	4.9	4.6	1016.8	1015.8

We are indebted to Climatologist B. A. Rocheford of the Caribbean Meteorological Institute for the data from Golden Rock Airport on St. Kitts. Please remember that averages give an overview of conditions and do not indicate daily or unusual conditions with precision; they are very helpful, but they do not tell the whole story.

Marine weather forecasts are broadcast daily by VON Radio (Voice of Nevis) on 895 KHz-AM at 7:45 AM, 10:45 AM, and 12:45 PM. ZDK in Antigua (1100 KHz-AM & 99.0 MHz-FM) broadcasts marine weather daily at 6:55 PM and provides general weather information Monday through Friday approximately 15 minutes after 8:00 AM, 9:00 AM, 10:00 AM, and 2:00 PM. SABA RADIO broadcasts hurricane advisories and warnings on VHF channels 16 and 26.

COMMUNICATIONS/RADIO

International direct dialing is available and greatly facilitates calls to the islands; to call St. Kitts from abroad simply dial 1-809-465 + four local numbers; to reach Nevis dial 1-809-469 + four local numbers. To make outgoing overseas calls, dial "0" and place your call. In St. Kitts the USA Dial Direct operator can be reached directly by dialing 1-800-872-2281, or by using USA Direct phones that are located at the Deep Water Port, Ocean Terrace Inn (O.T.I.), Jack Tar Village Hotel, and at the SKANTEL office in Basseterre. In Nevis USA Direct phones are outside the SKANTEL office in Charlestown.

SABA RADIO can be reached on VHF Channel 16 (call and emergency) and Channel 26 (routine traffic) between 6:00 AM and midnight from south of a line between BRIMSTONE HILL and NAG'S HEAD on St. Kitts and from south of CADES BAY on Nevis. To the north of this line and Cades Bay, the land mass of St. Kitts and/ or Statia makes communication with Saba Radio difficult or impossible.

EMERGENCIES

In serious emergencies requiring outside assistance call on VHF Channel 16; Police Control, the Captain of the fast inter-island ferry CARIB QUEEN, the OCEAN TERRACE INN, OUALI BEACH CLUB, and others monitor Channel 16 routinely. Someone close by will be listening 24 hours a day. The Skipper of the CARIB QUEEN is an extremely knowledgeable, competent, and reliable man named BROTHER; he and his vessel perform rescue operations in the waters of St. Kitts and Nevis when necessary.

CHARTS & MAPS

There are several English language charts with adequate detail of St. Kitts and Nevis; all are quite satisfactory:

U.S.D.M.A.	**25601**	**Approaches to Saint Christopher, Nevis, Montserrat, and Redonda — 1:75,000**
	25607	**Saba, Sint Eustatius and Saint Christopher — 12:75,000 (with details of Saba and St. Eustatius)**
	25608	**Plans of the Leeward Islands — Plan of Basseterre, St. Kitts — 1:15,000 and others**

British Admiralty	487	Saba, St. Eustatius, St. Christopher, Nevis, — 1:56,000 (with details of Oranje Baai, St. Eustatius and Basseterre Bay, St. Christopher
	489	Approaches to Nevis — 1:50,000
Imray-Iolaire	A25	St. Christopher, St. Eustatius, Nevis, Montserrat & Saba (with details of Fort Baai, Saba; Oranje Baai, St. Eustatius; Basseterre Bay, St. Christopher; and Plymouth, Montserrat

The following English language charts are suitable for interisland cruising:

U.S.D.M.A.	2550	St. Barthelemy to Guadeloupe --1:250,000
British Admiralty	995	Sombrero to Dominica --1:475,000
Imray Iolaire	A3	Anguilla to Guadeloupe

The British Directorate of Overseas Surveys has published some handsome maps of St. Kitts and Nevis that contain a great deal of practical and fascinating information that will delight interested visitors. Ask the Tourist Bureau in either Basseterre or Charlestown where they can be purchased.

RUBBISH

The only trash containers in the area are located at the Deep Water Port in Basseterre Bay and outside the town pier in Charlestown. If you cannot dispose of rubbish there, it is best to dump biodegradable items, tin cans and bottles, etc. in deep water far from the shore in locations where wind and water will not deposit them on an island. Cans should be holed at both ends, glass containers should be broken, and bags should be holed and weighted so they will sink promptly. Please take styrofoam and other items of indestructible plastic to a port where they can be disposed of properly.

HOLIDAYS

Virtually all businesses close down during holidays in the islands:

Carnival Week December 26 to
   January 1
Carnival Day December 31
New Year's Day January 1
Good Friday
Easter Monday*
Labour Day 1st Monday in May
Whit Monday

Queen's Birthday & Parade 2nd
   Saturday in June
August Bank Holiday 1st Monday in
   August*
Independence Day September 19
Christmas Day December 25
 Boxing Day December 26*

*Horse Racing in Nevis

CURRENCY

The Eastern Caribbean Dollar (E.C.$) is the official currency on St. Kitts and Nevis, but U.S. dollars and recognized travellers checks are accepted by many shops, restaurants, hotels, and services dealing with vacationers and other visitors. The rate of exchange is usually about $2.65 E.C. for $1.00 U.S. or $1.00 E.C. for about 38¢ U.S.

Eiman photo

ST. KITTS

ST. KITTS (ST. CHRISTOPHER)

CHARTS: U.S. DMA 2550, 25601, 25507, 25508

British 487,955

Imray-Iolaire A25

ST. KITTS absolutely dominates the northern section of the Leeward Islands (British definition) by dint of its dramatic size and breathtaking beauty. From the deck of a yacht it appears as a gigantic luxurious green tent rising out of the sea with a ridge line towering from 3,800-foot MT. MISERY on the northwest to 2,600-foot OLIVEE MOUNTAIN and 1,200-foot MONKEY HILL on the southeast. The tropic sun gives its gentle green slopes of waving sugar cane a soft but vivid green that surely ranks among the most lovely sights in the world. St. Kitts has been blessed with a combination of rich soil and ample rain (55" a year on average) which accounts for its Carib Indian name LIAMUIGA . . . FERTILE ISLAND.

St. Kitts is filled with enormous visual luxury, impressive reminders of the past and an assortment of facilities and natural assets which add greatly to the pleasure of visitors. Although tourism is on the increase, most of the island outside of the southeastern peninsula and bustling Basseterre provides an intriguing and unspoiled view of rural Caribbean life as it has existed for decades. The island has many reminders of the incredible labors and achievements of past generations and is sprinkled with delightful small hotels, a few resorts, and fine restaurants that will please a wide range of tastes.

Columbus added St. Kitts to his collection of discoveries on his second voyage in 1493, and according to which story one hears, gave it either his Christian name or the name of the patron saint of travellers, St. Christopher. The first permanent settlers arrived in 1623 when Thomas Warner, his son and wife, and 14 others landed at what is now Old Road Town and established the first British settlement in the Caribbean. Two years later the French settled Basseterre and were welcomed by Warner who saw them as valuable allies against the indigenous Carib Indians and the intolerant Spanish. A long history of slaughter on the island started promptly when the English and French ganged up on the Caribs and massacred most of them in 1626; shortly thereafter they signed a treaty that gave the central part of the island and its excellent water supply to the English and the extremities to the French, with joint rights to the salt ponds at the extreme southeastern end of the island.

Once the Caribs were largely eliminated, the slaughter continued with intermittent warfare involving Spanish, French, and British that lasted until the Treaty of Versailles in 1783 finally restored St. Kitts to the British for good. Since then the English have had the island all to themselves and were free to raise cane and consolidate their fortunes until St. Kitts became independent in 1983. The most impressive remaining memorial to the 150-odd years of fighting is the fortress at Brimstone Hill that has been aptly dubbed the GIBRALTAR OF THE CARIBBEAN.

Perhaps the main reason so much blood was shed over St. Kitts was that it was reported to have the highest yield of superior quality sugar in the world. Sugar displaced tobacco as the island's main crop in the late 17th century and has been the commercial king of St. Kitts ever since. The sugar economy flourished in the 17th and 18th centuries when plantations covered the gentle slopes and enormous revenues flowed to their owners. But competition, absentee ownership, the independence of the American colonies, and the abolition of slavery caused profits to decline sharply in the 19th century. But sugar is still king in St. Kitts, accounting for some 40% of all employment and 75% of its export business. The entire industry, including plantation fields, narrow gauge railroad, sugar factory, docking facilities, etc., has been nationalized and thus is owned and operated by the government. Still cane choppers can make only about $3,000 U.S. for their brutally hard work during harvest from January to July.

St. Kitts and Nevis gained independence and became a Sovereign and Democratic Federal State on September 19, 1983 with full status within the Commonwealth. The government is basically a cabinet system with a Prime Minister, appointed by the Governor-General, and an elected House of Assembly and Legislature. St. Kitts has approximately 35,000 residents; half live in the capital, Basseterre, while the others are scattered in towns and villages along the coast.

Tourism is an increasingly important business in St. Kitts, and many developments in recent years have made the island more attractive to vacationers. New shopping malls and plazas have been built in Basseterre; port facilities for cruise ships have been improved. And a new hard-surface road . . . the Dr. Kennedy Simmonds Highway . . . has been built on the southeast peninsula to provide rolling access to Cockleshell, Banana, Major's, and White House Bays; new hotels and other tourist facilities are sure to follow.

APPROACHING ST. KITTS

It is essential to clear in with Customs and Immigration in Basseterre before you anchor or go ashore anywhere on St. Kitts, so in effect the approach to St. Kitts is the approach to Basseterre. From the north and west approach Basseterre along the southwest coast in the lee of the island. The water is calmer in close to shore; there are no off-lying obstructions, but winds can be irregular and gusty. Some prefer to stand off a bit to take advantage of the steady winds and spectacular views of St. Kitts. From the south it is best to leave Nevis to starboard and sail directly to Basseterre; in rough weather this same course should be taken when coming from Antigua. Under all conditions it is advisable to stand well off the east/northeast coasts of both islands; they are normally lee shores and have no good, protected harbors or anchorages for yachts.

When conditions are favorable and the seas aren't kicking up, yachts from the east will have no great difficulty going through THE NARROWS south of St. Kitts. The main problem is to avoid the nasty reefs and shoals one to two miles east and slightly south of MOSQUITO BLUFF. As you approach the southern end of St. Kitts, head for ST. ANTHONY PEAKS (1,047 Ft.) on a southwesterly course; when about a half mile off the coast, turn south and follow the coast around staying about a half mile off. This will lead inside BOOBY I. and north of COW ROCKS and will keep you in good water. Swing wide around NAG'S HEAD before proceeding directly to Basseterre.

Do not attempt to enter The Narrows between Booby Island and Nevis unless you are very familiar with the waters; the area contains numerous dangerous shoals and reefs and is frequently filled with breaking seas.

BASSETERRE

Basseterre was established by the French in 1625 and became the capital of the entire island when the British moved their government there from Old Town in 1727. Even though it was largely destroyed by fire in 1867 and has been battered by floods, pestilence, earthquakes, and hurricanes, it retains a great deal of old world charm that is heightened by a number of gracious and intriguing reminders of the distant past such as the Government House (1850s), the new St. George's Anglican Church (1859), Berkeley Memorial Drinking Fountain and Clock in the Circus (1883), and the Treasury Building (1859).

In addition to reflecting centuries of British influence, Basseterre today is a busy commercial port with an increasing interest in the vacation/visitor business. Shops carry duty-free merchandise, china and silverware, books and maps, sketches and paintings, fashions and fabrics, and straw goods and other handicrafts that are attractive and appealing. Shopping is concentrated along Bay Road near the Treasury Building and along Fort, Princess, and Central Streets and on Liverpool Row. Normal shopping hours are 8:00 AM to Noon and 1:00 to 4:00 PM Monday through Saturday except on Thursday when some shops are not open after Noon. Pharmacies remain open through the lunch hour.

ENTRANCE BASSETERRE BAY is wide open to the south and is notorious for swells that frequently make it an extremely uncomfortable anchorage. The rocking and rolling increase the more the wind shifts farther south of east; they are especially bad off the middle of the town.

Depths average 20 to 30 feet across the entrance to the Bay, and the sand and grass bottom shoals gradually to the shores with no surprises. Holding is generally good, but the water is murky. The center of the town is marked by the two-story Treasury Building built of brown stone with white trim and a white cupola, by the bright turquoise Customs Building, and by three piers. The Customs Pier (in the middle) is the only one in use; the others have deteriorated badly and are abandoned. Over the years we have rarely seen any of the navigation lights shown in British, U.S., and Imray Iolaire charts and in our sketch chart. It is best not to count on them.

ANCHORING Anchor in the eastern end of Basseterre Bay near the Deep Water Port and the Coast Guard pier where there is maximum protection and minimum swells and rolling. Leave plenty of room for cruise ships and other vessels using the facilities there. Dinghies can be secured at the ladder as the head of the Deep Water Port pier.

BASSETERRE   *Eiman photo*

168

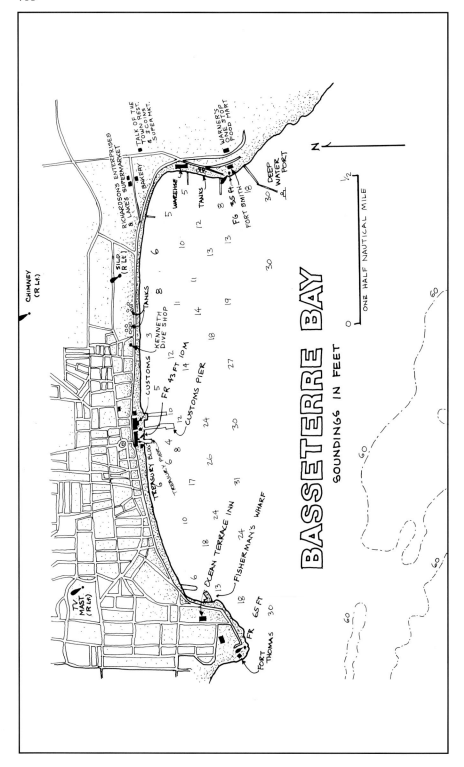

BASSETERRE BAY

SOUNDINGS IN FEET

ONE HALF NAUTICAL MILE

Dinghies, incidentally, should always be secured, day and night, with security cables or chains and locks to minimize the risk of theft.

To get to town walk around the shore or call a taxi on VHF channel l6; cab drivers Big Mac and Perci are very knowledgeable and very helpful. We do NOT recommend leaving your dinghy at the Customs Pier; we have had reports of characters there demanding outrageous payments for watching dinghies and threatening damage or theft if their demands are not met!

ALTERNATE ANCHORING If, after clearing in and taking care of essentials in town, you want to escape from Basseterre Bay, head for calmer waters down the southeastern peninsula and anchor near the new road in White House Bay or Major's Bay. To get back into Basseterre or to tour the island, etc. just call a cab on Channel l6, and you will have the best of both worlds.

CLEARANCE Clear in through Customs and obtain a Cruising Permit for St. Kitts anchorages at the turquoise Customs Building in the middle of the town. If you plan to cruise to Nevis, pick up a Boat Pass as well. Customs Office is open from 8:00 AM to Noon and from 1:00 to 4:00 PM Monday through Friday. U.S. and Canadian citizens can present proof of citizenship, such as a birth certificate or a voter registration card, or they can use a valid passport. All others must have valid passports. Vaccination Certificates are not required except for visitors coming from an infected area. Pets are not permitted ashore, and firearms are prohibited. Entrance fees that cover both St. Kitts & Nevis are $20EC for vessels up to 20 tons, $35EC 20 to 30 tons, $38EC 30 to 50 tons, and $56EC 50 to 100 tons. If you arrive when Customs is not open, have a taxi driver take you to a Customs Officer; overtime charges are $5.00EC per hour. After clearing

DEEPWATER PORT   *Eiman photo*

Ocean Terrace Inn

ST. KITTS, WEST INDIES

Ken McLeod
Manager

- 1 mile from the center of Basseterre in a quiet residential neighborhood
- 53 spacious and luxurious double rooms and apartment suites all with air conditioning, color cable TV, and direct dial phones
- Excellent cuisine with Continental and Caribbean specialities
- Swimming pool and Quarter Deck Bar
- Entertainment 2 nights weekly in season
- Golf, tennis, sailing, snorkeling, SCUBA diving, water skiing, hiking, beach picnics, and Island tours available thru hospitality desk
- Pelican Cove Marina and Fisherman's Wharf Restaurant
- Personal attention and friendly atmosphere

RESERVATIONS — American/Wolfe International, toll-free (800) 223-5695. N.Y. (212) 730-8100. In Canada: International Reservations Worldwide, Don Mills, Ontario — Toll Free (800) 387-8031 or (413) 447-23355.

OCEAN TERRACE INN
P.O. Box 65, Fortlands, St. Kitts, West Indies
Phones: (809) 465-2754; (809) 465-2380   Cable: OTI ST. KITTS   Telex: 681 OTI KC

YACHTSMEN WELCOME — WE MONITOR V.H.F. CH. 16

in through Customs, you must also clear through Immigration at the Police Station; formalities there cover both St. Kitts and Nevis.

If all this sounds like a drag, enlist the help of a cab driver like Big Mac or Perci (VHF Ch. 16) right at the start; they can smooth out a lot of bumps and help you through the entire process quickly and easily.

SERVICES Although Basseterre sis not a yachting center, cruising sailors can find virtually everything required to satisfy basic needs. Water is available at the Deep Water Port via the Harbormaster there; gas and diesel can be bought at gas stations near the Deep Water Port, on Adlam Street, and on Canyon Street.

For provisions we recommend Warner's One Stop Food Mart and Lake's Supermarket near the Deep Water Port and the Public Market, Scotch House and Rams Supermarket on Bay Street in town. Block ice is available at Richardsons Enterprises near Lake's and at the Government ice plant on Canyon Street; cubes can be bought at Warner's Food Mart and at most liquor stores.

Gumbs Hardware on Bay Road and TDC Hardware on Central Street have impressive and very extensive stocks. For propane gas refills stop at St. Kitts Gasses on Bay Road or at any Shell gas station. Mr. Douglas Brookes at Brookes Boats near the D.W.P. can help with fiberglass and mechanical problems and other boat repairs. For Diesel engine work see Mr. Richard Caines at Caines Garage, Mr. Sammy Lake at St. Kitts Masonry Products, or Mr. Stanley Franks at the Technical School; Mr. Franks also works on gas engines.

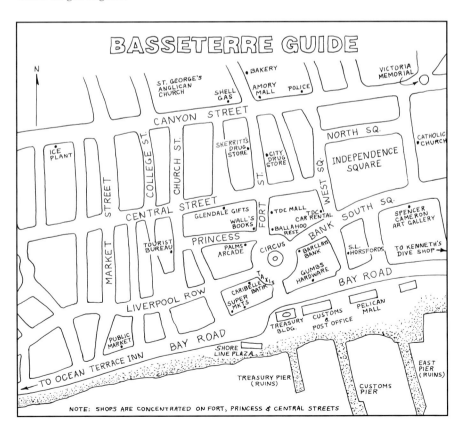

172

GEORGIA HOUSE   *Eiman photo*

KENNETH'S DIVE CENTER is on Bay Road between the town and the Deep Water Port and has a satellite operation in Frigate Bay. Owner Kenneth Samuel has been diving in St. Kitts for over 20 years and provides instruction, equipment, and reef and wreck dive trips as well as ferry service to Nevis. Call him on VHF Ch. 16; he will pick you up from your boat. Pro Divers, with bases at Fisherman's Wharf and Turtle Bay, is another full dive service; they monitor Ch 16 also.

Basseterre has some wonderful taxi drivers like Big Mac and Perci who can drive you around the town, give interesting guided tours around the island, show you where to get what you want quickly and easily, and, as noted, be very helpful in getting you through the Customs and Immigration process quickly and easily. The Taxi Association publishes standard rates to all popular points and for island tours. The taxi stand in town is at The Circus; many cabs monitor VHF Channel 16.

ASHORE Basseterre is a pleasing blend of old and new, of energetic hustle and quiet charm, of tradition and tourism and is well worth exploring at a leisurely pace. Interesting, comprehensive, and current information about Basseterre and all of St. Kitts is available at WALL'S RECORD AND BOOK SHOP on Fort Street and at The Tourist Board on Church Street; both have a wealth of information covering everything from rain forest hikes to shopping, side trips, SCUBA, and taxi rates.

Our favorites in Basseterre include Palm Crafts in the Palms Arcade on Princess Street (wonderful tropical fashions and unusual, attractive Caribbean handcrafts), A Slice of The Lemon also in Palms Arcade (duty free perfumes, watches, jewelry, china, crystal), Palms Patisserie in the TDC Mall, Caribelle Batik on the Circus (fabulous locally designed and made and designed batik and tie dye fabric and beach and casual wear),

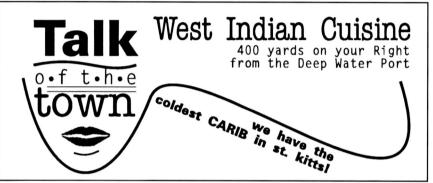
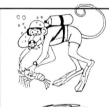

Pandora's Box on Fort Street (gifts, hand painted T shirts, souvenirs), WALL'S RECORD & BOOK SHOP on Fort Street (fiction and non-fiction, cruising guides, maps, and great Caribbean music), and Spencer Cameron Art Gallery on South Independence Square (original works by Caribbean artists, prints, and silk screens). The new Pelican Shopping Mall on Bay Road near Customs houses the Philatelic Bureau and a host of attractive shops; it seems destined to be a major shopping center.

THE BALLAHOO RESTAURANT on the Circus is a delightful 'landmark' in the center of everything . . . a great favorite luncheon and dinner spot for visitors and local residents alike. Relax on the veranda overlooking the Circus, enjoy wonderful seafood, local dishes, and snacks, and watch the colorful passing parade.

THE OCEAN TERRACE INN at the western end of Basseterre Bay, known universally as the O.T.I., continues to earn its reputation for gracious hospitality, excellent luncheons and dinners, and the best rum punches in the world; live entertainment Wednesday and Friday evenings in season; spectacular views of Basseterre and Nevis all the time. On the shore just below O.T.I. FISHERMAN'S WHARF is a popular evening gathering spot that specializes in seafood; there is a secure dinghy landing right at the front door. O.T.I., incidentally, monitors VHF Channel 16 24 hours a day.

At the other end of town near the Deep Water Port TALK OF THE TOWN features West Indian fare at reasonable prices. Just south of the D.W.P. the Lighthouse Gourmet Restaurant is adjacent to the Bird Rock Beach Hotel; anchor right off the restaurant while you enjoy the varied menu prepared by a European chef and spectacular views of the harbor. Further down the peninsula in the Frigate Bay area, The Patio restaurant is popular for well prepared duck, roast beef, and seafood. On the beach in Frigate Bay COCONUT CAFE serves wonderful local produce and seafood with a Caribbean flavor in a beautiful setting where you might see the Green Flash!

Ottley's Plantation Inn, a 20 minute taxi drive from Basseterre up the Windward Road, is a beautiful old plantation Great House inn set among waving cane fields and manicured gardens. Excellent, Caribbean inspired dinners are the work of Culinary Institute graduate Pamela Yahn. For reservations phone 465-7234. The White House is a charming plantation inn nestled in the foothills behind Bassetere below Monkey Hill just 10 minutes from town. Visitors and the largely British resident clientele alike enjoy the fine, sophisticated cuisine and cheerful service. For reservations phone 465-8162.

TOURING ST. KITTS

The countryside beyond Basseterre is filled with spectacular natural beauty, fabulous fortifications, picturesque villages, lovely old stone churches, sugar plantation Great Houses, and a host of historic points of interest. Perhaps the best way for most to enjoy the sights is to tour the island by taxi with a good driver and an excellent luncheon at Rawlins Plantation or the Golden Lemon (phone ahead for reservations). Hikers and nature buffs may be more interested in exploring the spectacular rain forest; guides and transportation can be provided by veteran Greg's Safaris (phone 465-4121) or Kriss Tours (phone 465-4042).

A clockwise tour from Basseterre will include the following in order of their appearance: Fairview Inn, Trinity Anglican Church, Bloody Point, Old Road Town, Wingfield Carib Indian petroglyphs, Wingfield Estate, Caribelle Batiks at Romney Manor, St. Thomas Anglican Church and tomb of Sir Thomas Warner in Middle

BRIMSTONE HILL   *Eiman photo*

Village, Brimstone Hill (the Gibraltar of the West Indies), Sandy Point Town, Fig Tree, Rawlins Plantation, Dieppe, the Golden Lemon, Black Rocks, Behavioral Science Foundation at Estridge Estate, Bayford Estate, St. Peter's Church, and the Sugar Factory. Along the way you will cross and recross the narrow gauge railroad tracks used to carry cane to the central Sugar Factory for processing; you may also see school children playing soccer, cane choppers, and fishermen with their nets; and you may also catch sight of the St. Kitts version of scarecrows that are used to frighten the vervet monkeys that roam the higher elevations.

Brimstone Hill Fortress is the most spectacular historical site on the island. The massive fortifications command sweeping views of the countryside, the coastline, Saba, Statia, and Nevis from atop the 750-foot Brimstone Hill. Started in 1690 when Sir Timothy Thornhill first dragged a few cannon up from the coast below, construction of this Gibraltar of the West Indies stretched over 100 years and included a series of bastions, barracks, Officers Quarters, messing facilities, ammunition stores, a hospital, a cemetery, and a water catchment system with a 100,000 gallon cistern. In 1782 before the fortifications were completed, Brimstone Hill was attacked by some 6,000 French troops supported by 29 ships-of-the-line under Count de Grasse. During the month-long siege the British garrison of less than 1,000 men fought gallantly and inflicted great damage on the French, but in the end they were forced to sue for peace. Ironically, the French used English cannon and ammunition in their assault on the Hill. Shortly before the siege the English government landed badly needed cannon and munitions at the foot of the fortress, but local planters, outraged over losses they suffered when Rodney sacked Statia, refused to provide labor to move them up to the bastions. Thus they fell into the hands of the French and were promptly turned against the defenders.

Although the siege of Brimstone Hill ended in defeat for its heroic garrison, the battle made a crucial contribution to a larger victory for the British. The month-long defense of the Hill pinned down the French fleet in St. Kitts, preventing it from joining forces with the Spanish to dominate the Caribbean. As a result Rodney was able to engage the French fleet alone off Les Saintes a few months later, winning a historic victory that gave the British undisputed control of the West Indies.

The fortifications on Brimstone Hill were abandoned in the middle of the 19th century but in recent times have been beautifully preserved and restored through the efforts of the Brimstone Hill Fortress National Park Society. Information on the fortifications is available in the Visitors Center in the Prince of Wales Bastion where a gift shop and restaurant are also located.

Less dramatic than Brimstone Hill but equally impressive is the grave of Sir Thomas Warner at St. Thomas Anglican Church in Middle Town. Resting quietly under stately palms in the lovely church grounds, the tomb of the founding father of the first English settlement in the Caribbean bears this tribute:

> *First read then weep when thou art hereby taught*
> *That Warner lyes interr'd here, one that bought*
> *With losses of Noble bloud Illustrious Name*
> *Of a Commander Greate in Acts of Fame,*
> *Trayned from his youth in Armes, his courage bold*
> *Attempted brave exploites, and uncontrolled*
> *By Fortunes fiercest Frownes, hee still gave forth*
> *Large narratives of Military worth*
> *Written with his swoards poynt, but what is man*
> *In the midst of his glory, and who can*
> *Forsee this life a moment since hee*
> *From Perils by Sea and Land, so long kept free*
> *Through dreadful Mortal strokes at length did yield*
> *With Knightly grace to conquering Death the field*

VIEW FROM BAYFORD ESTATE   *Eiman photo*

COASTWISE CRUISING

Don't forget you must have a Cruising Permit that lists all the places outside Basseterre Bay where you will anchor. If you don't have one when the local Coast Guard comes along, you could be in big trouble.

St. Kitts northwest of Basseterre is a marginal cruising area at best. Some yachts anchor occasionally off OLD ROAD TOWN and SANDY POINT TOWN, but the anchorages are open and are often quite uncomfortable. DIEPPE (or DEEP) BAY and THE PUNCH BOWL at the northwest tip of the island do have protection for small boats behind offshore reefs, but the area is full of coral and requires local knowledge. It is not recommended for strangers.

All of the best beaches and anchorages on St. Kitts are concentrated on the peninsula that extends some 6 miles to the southeast of Basseterre to SCOTCH BONNET. The first are in **FRIGATE BAY** just 2 miles from Basseterre. Be sure to avoid the 120 foot steel freighter River Taw that sank in 1982 off the hill at the northwestern end of Frigate Bay. Her masts no longer protrude above the surface of the sea, so she is especially hard to spot; keep a sharp eye out for her. The approach to Frigate Bay is straightforward; the only dangers are a few rocks awash some 50 yards off the northern end of the beach. The bottom is sand with patches of grass, and the holding is good. Unfortunately, when Basseterre is uncomfortable, Frigate Bay is usually the same.

Behind the beach in Frigate Bay there is an assortment of hotels, condos, and restaurants plus a casino and golf course that are open to the public. As mentioned, KENNETH'S DIVE CENTER has a base there, and popular restaurants include El Patio and . . . right on the beach . . . COCONUT CAFE.

SOUTH FRIARS BAY with its lovely, mile-long beach is just south of SIR TIMOTHY'S HILL. Sail right in and anchor where you will; in close the bottom is clear sand. The little sharp rise in the sand along the beach is a tell-tale sign of surge; you may roll a bit without a stern anchor. But if the sea is calm, it is a delightful and spectacular anchorage; against a backdrop of swaying palms you can revel in breathtaking views of the towering heights and cane fields of St. Kitts to the north and west and of Mt. Nevis to the south. The beach is popular with local residents on holidays and weekends, but it is never crowded; there is plenty of lovely space for all.

FRIGATE BAY *Eiman photo*

WHITE HOUSE BAY   *Eiman photo*

The new hard-surface road down the southern peninsula has not only added greatly to the convenience of cruising sailors but also opened the entire area to development. The Turtle Beach Bar & Grill has opened in MOSQUITO BAY complete with lunch and dinner service, a dive operation, and popular DJ dancing, etc., on Saturday nights in season. The 300-room Casablanca Hotel is under construction ('92) east of COCKLESHELL BAY, and other resort hotels are expected in WHITE HOUSE BAY and in COCKLESHELL and BANANA BAYS. Tune in next year to see what happens; in the interim, enjoy the peninsula as it is now . . . lovely, peaceful, and serenely quiet.

WHITE HOUSE BAY, about 4-1/2 miles from Basseterre, is a small indentation in the coast just north of the 150-foot hill on GUANA POINT; it is one of the best and most comfortable anchorages when Basseterre has too much rock and roll. The curving white beach boasts a new dock, and the new road passes close by. The only hazards are an old wreck along the southern shore and the rock and coral around it where the snorkeling is good. Anchor anywhere in sand and grass keeping in mind that the tide rises and falls about 2 feet.

White House Bay is a good starting point for inland exploring and jogging along the new road. By all means walk across the north end of Great Salt Pond and follow the old path over to SAND BANK BAY on the east coast to enjoy the splendid solitude and beauty of its gem-like beach behind offshore reefs. To get into Basseterre or tour the rest of St. Kitts by cab, call a taxi on VHF Ch. 16 or arrange for a rental car delivery.

Just south of White House Bay and GUANA POINT is **BALLAST BAY**, another anchorage that is well protected from normal winds and seas; it is usually quite comfortable even when the trades swing quite far to the south and Basseterre is unsettled. Stand well off Guana Point to avoid the nasty reef that extends a quarter of a mile or more off to the southwest (see the aerial photo). Also to be avoided are fish nets, poles, and markers in place from time to time in the southern part of the Bay. Within 150 yards of the shore the depth is 12 to 15 feet, and the bottom is sand and grass; closer in the grass gives way to vast areas of clear sand. The preferred anchorage

BALLAST BAY *Eiman photo*

is at the north end in close behind the reef that provides some protection from the seas and good snorkeling as well. You will find peace and quiet in Ballast Bay; unfortunately, the beach is all gravel. At the very southern end of the Bay near GREEN POINT snorkelers will find rewarding sights along the shore.

Between Green Point and NAG'S HEAD is a long indentation in the coast; the northern part is **SHITTEN BAY**, while southern section is sometimes called **BUGS HOLE**. In any event, the area offers excellent protection from winds from the southeast, east, and north, and will appeal to everyone who likes the wild feeling of anchoring under steep, rugged hills covered with all sorts of flowers, trees, vines, and scrub growth. There are a few large rocks 2 to 4 feet below the surface about 100 feet off the point at the northern end of the Bay. In addition, TURTLE REEF, a shoal with 10 to 12 feet of water over it, lies off the small point in the middle of Shitten Bay in line with the points of land that are its northern and southern boundaries. Otherwise, the water is good throughout; we found 14 to 16 feet of water some 100 to 150 yards off the shore. In close the bottom is generally clear sand with occasional patches of rock; further off it is sand and grass. If you anchor in close, avoid the rock patches and guard against backwinds swirling over the hills. In calm conditions the water is incredibly clear and snorkeling along the shore is wonderful. There are no beaches or landing places in Shitten Bay or Bugs Hole.

British and U.S. charts and our own sketch chart show a sunken wreck about a mile to the west and a bit south of HORSE SHOE POINT. This is the estimated location of the M.V. CHRISTENA that sank on Saturday afternoon, August 1, 1970 while carrying a Bank Holiday Weekend crowd from Nevis to St. Kitts; 227 persons perished in the tragic sinking. Her hull reportedly lies in 70 to 80 feet of water.

THE NARROWS

St. Kitts and Nevis are separated by approximately two miles of water aptly named THE NARROWS. The western end and the middle section have plenty of water for

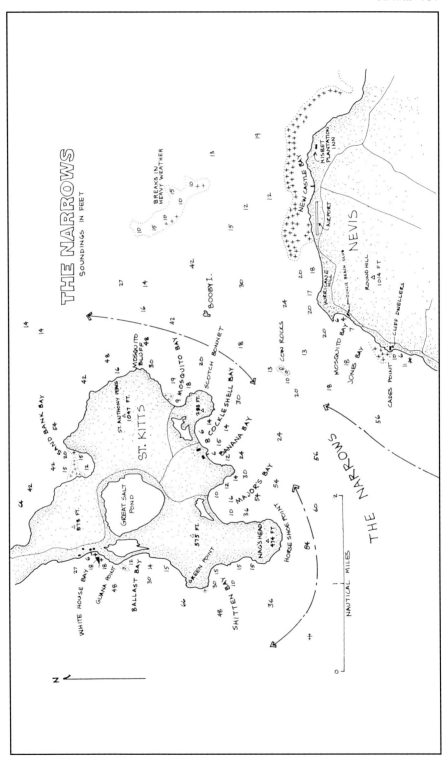

THE NARROWS
SOUNDINGS IN FEET

cruising yachts that stand well off the shores of both islands and avoid COW ROCKS in the middle of the passage and slightly to the south of midchannel. But the eastern end is quite a different matter; an extensive and dangerous reef straddles the eastern entrance about a mile to the east of BOOBY ISLAND, and between this reef and the coast of Nevis there are a number of shoals with depths of 12 to 15 feet. When the wind is from the east and blowing 12 knots or more, the seas break frequently on the reef and the shoals to the south of it. Yachts should not pass south of Booby Island and between the reef and Nevis unless conditions are ideal and there is an experienced local guide on board.

The safe passage through the eastern end of The Narrows lies between the coast of St. Kitts on the north and COW ROCKS and BOOBY ISLAND on the south as indicated on our sketch chart. Stand a half mile off HORSE SHOE POINT, SCOTCH BONNET, and MOSQUITO BLUFF until you are north of ST. ANTHONY PEAKS, and all will be well.

MAJOR'S BAY is a very popular anchorage for visiting yachts. It is convenient to Basseterre and Charlestown and all anchorages and beaches in between, and it is perhaps the calmest and most protected bay in the area in virtually all conditions. St. Kitts shields it on the east, north, and west while Nevis protects it on the south. On rare occasions when swells might come in, a stern anchor will usually insure a peaceful night for all. There is a nice, long, totally deserted beach with low scrub growth behind it at the head of the bay; the eastern third of the beach is gravel, but the rest is all sand. One branch of the road to Basseterre ends just behind the eastern end of the beach; taxis and rental cars can drive right up.

The water is 10 feet deep some 200 yards off the eastern end of the beach, 300 yards off the middle section, and about 400 yards off the western end. Most yachts anchor well up in the Bay as close to the beach as their drafts will permit. Although the

MAJORS BAY   *Eiman Photo*

bottom is covered solidly with grass, anchors can be set without great difficulty and the holding is quite good once you are dug in well; it is best to dive on your anchor to be sure you have a good night.

Good snorkeling is reported along the western shore of Major's Bay, especially in the small cove near Horse Shoe Point. You might want to sweep back and forth over the grass bottom of the western shore near the head of the Bay; with luck you may be able to find a few conch and perhaps some white sea urchins (the ones with good roe). Snorkeling is also said to be quite good around the point that separates Major's Bay from BANANA BAY to the east.

The visual pleasures to be enjoyed in Major's Bay are considerable. The texture and colors of the surrounding hills vary constantly under the influences of rainfall, cloud cover, and the movements of the sun providing a great array of delights from dawn to dusk. For other dramatic vistas you need only turn south and gaze across The Narrows to the towering peak of Nevis and her lush and lovely plunging slopes and coastal plains.

BANANA and COCKLESHELL BAYS are not quite as deep or quite as well protected as Major's Bay, but they can provide quiet, attractive, and hospitable anchorages and equally fine views of Nevis. Both are headed by sweeping white sand beaches that are favorites of local citizens and visitors alike. As mentioned earlier, The Casablanca Hotel is being built ('92) east of Cockleshell Bay; rumor has it that Sandals of Jamaica will do another biggie behind Banana and Cockleshell Bays sometime . . . Keep your fingers crossed.

The bottom in both Banana Bay and Cockleshell Bay is almost entirely covered with grass, but as in Major's Bay, setting anchors is not too difficult. The waters are free of dangers, and in normal conditions the best anchorage is in the northeast corner of Cockleshell Bay in about 10 feet of water where some protection is offered by SCOTCH BONNET. Snorkelers will enjoy the reefs at Scotch Bonnet.

It is a short and easy walk over to Mosquito Bay from Cockleshell to enjoy surf bathing and/or lunch or dinner at the Turtle Beach Bar & Grill. Joggers can, of course, work out on the road that connects these two lovely bays with Basseterre.

ST. KITTS—NEVIS LIGHTER　　　　　　　　*J.W. Eiman photo*

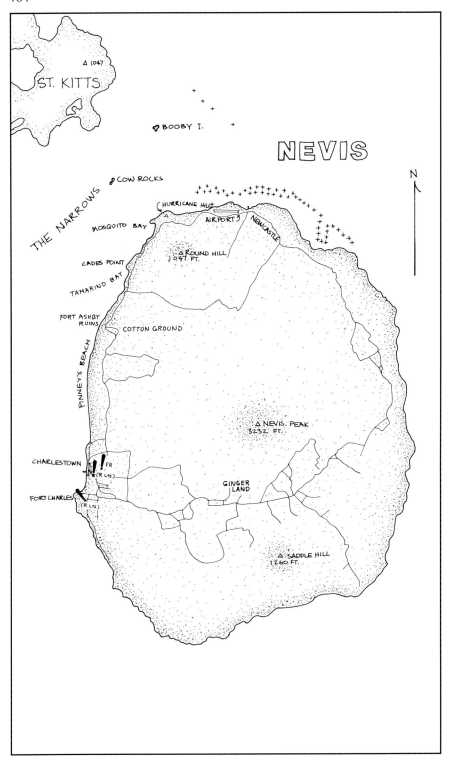

NEVIS

CHARTS: U.S. DMA 2550, 25601, 25607

           BRITISH 487, 489, 955

           Imary-Iolaire A25

The words of Henry Coleridge, son of the poet, written shortly after he discovered Nevis in the early nineteenth century, are quite apt in the 1990s:

> *The appearance of Nevis is perhaps the most captivating of any island in the West Indies. From the south and west it seems to be nothing but a single cone rising with the most graceful curve out of the sea and piercing a fleecy mass of clouds which sleeps forever around its summit. It is green as a heart can conceive . . . and enlivened with many old planters' houses of a superior style and churches peeping out in the most picturesque situations imaginable.*

Nevis has won a place in the hearts of a select group of discriminating West Indian travellers who consider it the quintessence of the beautiful and charming Caribbean island. But it is not for everyone: It is long on tranquility, natural and man-made beauty, friendliness and grace; it is short on high life and night life, on condos, on casinos, on television, and on ostentation of all varieties. If you enjoy quiet delights and the idyllic atmosphere of the Caribbean the way it used to be, you will find Nevis richly rewarding even though the winds of change are beginning to reach its gentle slopes and beautiful beaches.

No one challenges Columbus as the discoverer of Nevis, but there is some question about the original name. Some believe it was San Martin . . . a name that ultimately drifted some sixty miles to the northwest. But the more popular version has it that the cloud cap on the peak reminded Columbus of snows in the Pyrenees, and thus he named it Nuestra Senora de las Nieves, Our Lady of Snows.

The island was first settled in 1628 by Captain Anthony Hilton and 80 planters from St. Kitts. The ruins of Fort Ashby and Fort Charles on the west coast are weathered reminders of the battles with the Spanish and French that started in 1629 and continued off and on until 1805. When early settlers were not fighting off enemy attacks, they turned to the lucrative cultivation first of tobacco and later of sugar.

Nevis reached the height of its prosperity in the 18th and early 19th centuries; in the best of times some 80 large plantations covered her graceful slopes, and enormous fortunes were made from the waving fields of sugar cane.

Her natural mineral baths helped make her the social center of the West Indies and earned her the title, "Queen of the Caribees." Captain John Smith of Jamestown, Virginia fame is credited with discovering the hot mineral waters and their almost magical powers in 1607 during his voyage to America. To accommodate the great numbers of West Indian planters and Europeans attracted by the 108 degree medicinal baths local merchant John Huggins built the Bath House Hotel in 1778; its handsome facilities were the focal point of social activity for one glorious decade after another until it was closed in 1870. The baths themselves were reopened in 1983 for the public's pleasure.

Nevis was the birthplace of Alexander Hamilton, drafter of the Constitution of the United States and first Secretary of the Treasury. The illegitimate son of Scottish merchant James Hamilton and Creole Rachell Fawcett, Hamilton and his family moved to St. Croix when he was five years old; at age fifteen he sailed alone to North

America where he completed his education and became one of the Founding Fathers of the United States. Hamilton's birthplace has been reconstructed in Charlestown at the northern end of Main Street; it houses a museum devoted to the history of Hamilton and of Nevis.

Another famous name linked historically with Nevis is that of Horatio Nelson, hero of the Battle of Trafalger. While serving at English Harbor in Antigua, Nelson frequently brought his ship H.M.S. Boreas to Nevis for fresh water. During these visits the dashing captain met and courted the widowed Frances Herbert Nisbet, niece of the President of the Nevis Council. They were married at Montpelier Estate on the 11th day of March, 1787.

After decades of peaceful slumber the pace of change in Nevis has increased in recent years. In l988 Mt. Nevis Hotel provided the first accommodations with air conditioning, cable TV, and direct dial phones. 1991 marked the opening of the Four Seasons Resort on Pinney's Beach with almost 200 rooms and suites, an 18 hole golf course, ten tennis courts, restaurants, and lounges. This doubling of accommodations for visitors and other developments that will follow will increase employment on the island and will provide pleasure for thousands of visitors, and they will have great impact on the island and its lovely people. Those who treasure the unspoiled, natural charm of the Caribbean should be sure to enjoy Nevis without delay.

APPROACHING NEVIS

The approaches to Nevis are straightforward and free of obstructions a half mile off its shores except along the north/northeast coast where shoals and a dangerous reef extend out two miles from the land. See the section on THE NARROWS for information on this latter area.

If you approach from the south, take care to avoid the reef that extends out a half mile or so from FORT CHARLES just south of Charlestown. Otherwise there are no offshore dangers as you approach CHARLESTOWN. Ferries and sailing lighters that connect Charlestown and Basseterre use the concrete pier in the center of the town so it is best to anchor to the south of it to avoid the traffic. The most popular anchorage is off the petroleum tanks; another is a bit further south off the beach where fishing boats are often pulled up under the palm trees. The bottom is sand and grass and rises evenly to the shore. The island provides protection from normal trade winds, and Fort Charles Point helps block swells from the south. Charlestown fortunately is usually calm and comfortable; when it does rock and roll, TAMARIND (or CADES) BAY and MOS-QUITO BAY to the north are quiet alternatives. Rumor has it that a marina and hotel complex will be developed at Fort Charles Point, but nobody seems to know when or if it will be completed.

There is a minimum of 11 feet of water off the end of the town pier and for 50 feet along both sides, and there are landing steps on both sides. Dinghies can be tied to the south side of the pier out of the way of commercial traffic, or they can be hauled up on the beach to the south. Relatively few trading schooners and sloops from other islands call at Charlestown, and the environment is quite different from Basseterre; we have had no reports of dinghy thefts, but still security wires and locks can increase peace of mind.

CLEARANCE The Customs Office in the beautiful old building across Main Street at the head of Prince Charles Street is open from 8:00 A.M. to Noon and 1:00 to 4:00 P.M. Monday through Friday. Entry Fees, which cover both Nevis and St. Kitts, are $20EC for

CHARLESTOWN *Eiman photo*

boats up to 20 tons, $34EC up to 30 tons, $38EC up to 50 tons, etc. All visitors are required to have valid passports except U.S. and Canadian citizens who may present proof of citizenship such as a birth certificate or a voter registration card. When clearing in be sure to get a Cruising Permit for Nevis anchorages you will visit and a Boat Pass for St. Kitts. (To anchor in St. Kitts, you have to get another Cruising Permit in Basseterre!) If you went through Immigration in St. Kitts, it is not necessary to do it again in Nevis; otherwise you must go to the Police Station to the south on Main Street for Immigration clearance.

CHARLESTOWN

Half of the 9,000 residents of Nevis live in or around the capital Charlestown, a lovely, drowsy town of picturesque West Indian buildings, narrow streets, and quiet charm that until 1989 had changed very little in the last thirty years. The atmosphere is peaceful, hospitable, courteous, and friendly; the only signs of impatience and urgency are in the colorful excitement of the public market on Tuesday, Thursday, and Saturday mornings and during the arrivals and departures of the high speed ferry — the Carib Queen--to and from Bassseterre twice a day except on Thursdays and Sundays.

The pier is not only the center of town but also the focal point of commerce for all of Nevis. Virtually everybody and everything arriving in Nevis or leaving its shores are loaded or unloaded there. The Carib Queen, under the extremely capable command of Captain Arthur Anslyn (who much prefers to be known simply as Brother), carries freight and passengers between Nevis and St. Kitts; her arrivals and departures are times for joyful greetings, sad farewells, and a great deal of general hubbub. The pier is also the terminal for the traditional sailing lighters and other local cargo boats that ply the waters between Charlestown and Basseterre hauling cargo that includes everything from fruit, vegetables, and cotton to automobiles, building materials, soft drinks, and goats. When the lighters and the Carib Queen are being worked together on the pier, it seems like a wild and wonderful three ring circus. Friends greet arriving passengers

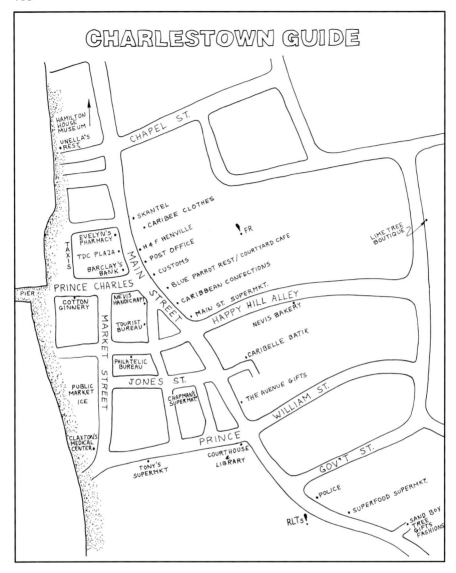

CHARLESTOWN GUIDE

HAMILTON HOUSE MUSEUM

UNELLA'S REST.

CHAPEL ST.

SKANTEL

CARIBEE CLOTHES

FR

LIME TREE BOUTIQUE 2

EVELYN'S PHARMACY

H & F HENVILLE

TAXIS

TDC PLAZA

POST OFFICE

BARCLAY'S BANK

CUSTOMS

PRINCE CHARLES

BLUE PARROT REST/ COURTYARD CAFE

PIER

CARIBBEAN CONFECTIONS

COTTON GINNERY

NEVIS HANDICRAFT

MAIN ST. SUPERMKT.

MAIN STREET

HAPPY HILL ALLEY

TOURIST BUREAU

NEVIS BAKERY

MARKET STREET

PHILATELIC BUREAU

CARIBELLE BATIK

JONES ST.

PUBLIC MARKET

THE AVENUE GIFTS

ICE

CHAPMAN'S SUPERMKT.

WILLIAM ST.

CLAXTON'S MEDICAL CENTER

PRINCE

COURTHOUSE LIBRARY

GOV'T ST.

TONY'S SUPERMKT

POLICE

SUPERFOOD SUPERMKT.

RLTs

SAND BOX TREE GIFTS FASHIONS

and bid farewell to those departing, while dockworkers hustle to unload tons of cargo, and trucks and cars push through the crowds in search of incoming shipments. There is a great deal of hubbub, and the scene is pure and fascinating pandemonium. CAUTION: Some of the workers become VERY excited and agitated if their pictures are taken.

The public market is also colorful and fascinating. All kinds of local produce-- beans, yams, bananas, limes, christophene, mangos, breadfruit, papayas, etc.--are carried in from the countryside and sold at the market. Solid buckets of ice are available at the Fish Department. Saturdays are the biggest market days with a superabundance of people, fresh produce, fish, socializing, and activity. The market presents an unequalled opportunity to stock up on fresh fruit and vegetables and to participate in one of the time honored happenings essential to island life.

Our Plan of Charlestown locates the landmarks, offices, shops, restaurants, etc. we believe most interesting and useful to cruising people. The shops are generally small and interesting; the Sandbox Tree and Caribelle Batik have especially lovely merchandise. The restaurants in town are modest and tend to feature West Indian food; Unella's, the Courtyard Cafe behind Caribbean Confections, and Muriel's are local favorites. Superfoods is the largest supermarket, and Claxton's Medical Center is an excellent pharmacy. Normal business hours in Charlestown are 8:00 A.M. to noon and 1:00 to 4:00 P.M. Monday through Saturday, except on Thursday when everything closes for the day at noon. For additional information visit the Tourist Bureau office on Main Street.

The Cotton Ginnery on Prince Charles Street operates during the harvest season in July and August; sea island cotton has been the largest cash crop on the island for years and provides employment for many residents. Another special operation is the Philatelic Bureau on lower Happy Hill Alley that sells the colorful and fascinating stamps of Nevis (quite different from the stamps of St. Kitts) that depict local historical sites, plantations, flowers, fish, scenic views, points of interest, etc. And be sure to visit the Hamilton Museum just north of town.

SERVICES Charlestown has no specialized facilities for yachts and yachtsmen, but basic tools, household supplies, pharmaceuticals, provisions, and beverages can be purchased conveniently. As mentioned, fantastic buckets of solid ice can be bought at the Fish Department of the public market. Water is available at the pier; gas and diesel are sold at the Shell station (bring your own jerry jugs). If you have serious boat problems, contact Brother; he can tell you where to get help.

Three special assets of Charlestown for sailors: Contact with Saba Radio is loud and clear; direct dial telephone contact with the U.S. is available at the Skantel office on Main Street; and marine weather forecasts are broadcast daily on Radio VON (Voice Of Nevis) at 895 on your AM dial at 7:45 AM, 10:45 AM, and 12:45 PM.

HAPPY HILL ALLEY *Eiman photo*

NEVIS BEYOND CHARLESTOWN

Anyone who is charmed by Charlestown will be greatly delighted by rural Nevis, its luxurious vegetation, stirring scenery, historic sites, beautiful country churches, and plantation houses, both ruined and restored. It is good to browse through the "Motoring Guide to Nevis" booklet (available at the Tourist Bureau) before a leisurely taxi tour of the island with luncheon at Montpelier Estate, Golden Rock Estate, or Nisbet Plantation Inn. There is no better way to get the real feeling for the way the island was when plantations flourished and Nevis was indeed Queen of the Caribees. The taxi drivers of Nevis are knowledgeable and helpful; two who have been commended to us are Billy Laughlin and Ralph Hutton. But no matter who you engage, it is important to agree on the currency and price before you start off.

Highlights of a trip around the island are listed here in the order in which they will be encountered heading south from Charlestown and proceeding counterclockwise; all are on the main road or very close to it:

FORT CHARLES	Modest, weed-covered ruins; impressive cannon; spectacular views. Site of rumored marina and hotel development.
BATH HOUSE HOTEL & BATHS	Handsome ruins; step cautiously inside. Modest charge for bathing in the wonderful mineral waters.
GOVERNMENT HOUSE	Home of the Secretary to the Nevis Council and site of state functions; visitors welcome.
NELSON MUSEUM	Reported to be the largest collection of Nelson memorabilia in the western hemisphere. Gift of Mr. Robert Abrams of Philadelphia in a new location adjacent to Government House.
FIG TREE CHURCH (ST. JOHN'S CHURCH)	Perfectly beautiful church with record of Nelson's marriage to Frances Nisbet.
MONTPELIER ESTATE	Site of Nelson-Nisbett nuptials. Most attractive 16-room hotel built on ruins of sugar works with lovely gardens and beautiful stone work. Excellent cuisine. Visitors welcome for lunch and dinner; reservations advised for dinner.
CRONEY'S OLD MANOR ESTATE	Outstanding restoration of plantation Great House and sugar buildings complete with fascinating machinery; now a lovely inn with formal gardens and old world atmosphere.
GOLDEN ROCK ESTATE	1815 sugar plantation; charming inn with spectacular views, wonderful West Indian atmosphere, and magnificent gardens. Guides to Nevis Peak available. Visitors welcome for breakfast, lunch, and dinner; wonderful cuisine. Reservations advised for dinner. Honeybees string band plays at dinner Saturday nights Dec. through May.
NEW RIVER ESTATE	One of the last plantations to cease sugar operations; a good deal of machinery still in place; fascinating tours on ecology, the sugar industry, etc.

COCONUT WALK ESTATE Ruins of the largest sugar mill on Nevis; stonework this relatively intact estate dates back to the mid-18th century.

EDEN BROWN ESTATE Impressive ruins of a plantation house that, tragically, was never occupied; reported to be haunted.

ST. JAMES CHURCH Active country church that contains one of the few black Christs in the Caribbean.

NISBET PLANTATION INN Stately palm groves surround this former home of Frances Nisbet and, more recently, of the late, legendary Mary Pomeroy who opened the Great House as a splendid inn decades ago. A beautifully appointed inn with breathtaking grounds, lovely beach, and fine cuisine. Visitors welcome for luncheon at the beach bar, restaurant, and pool and for dinner; reservations for dinner advised. String band music at dinner Tuesday and Friday evenings in season.

NEWCASTLE POTTERY Mrs. Jones and other ladies make unglazed pottery baked over open fires . . . pots, jugs, dishes, animals, birds, etc.,etc. Wonderful!

COUNTRY DINING Luncheon is also served in various other locations along the north coast and Pinney's Beach. Near Newcastle Cla Cha Deli is a modest, friendly family operation with great West Indian fare at bargain prices. Waves/Gourmet Pizza does its thing at Newcastle Marina. Further west, Oualie Beach Club at Mosquito Bay, PRINDERELLA'S at Tamarind Bay, Fort Ashby Restaurant near Nelson's Spring, Montpelier Beach Club at Cotton Ground, the Four Seasons Hotel, and Golden Rock's Carousel Beach Bar on Pinney's are all good luncheon spots. The curries, paw-paw with cheese, and breadfruit at the Fort Ashby Restaurant are really wonderful!

PINNEY'S BEACH *Eiman photo*

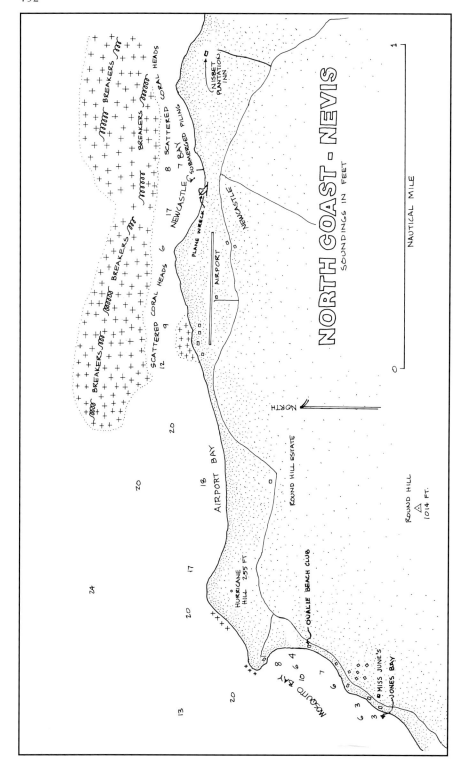

NORTH COAST - NEVIS

SOUNDINGS IN FEET

NAUTICAL MILE

NORTH

BREAKERS

SCATTERED CORAL HEADS

BREAKERS

BREAKERS

SCATTERED PILING

NEWCASTLE BAY

PLANE WRECK

SUBMERGED PILING

NISBET PLANTATION INN

NEWCASTLE

AIRPORT

SCATTERED CORAL HEADS

BREAKERS

BREAKERS

AIRPORT BAY

ROUND HILL ESTATE

ROUND HILL
1014 FT.

HURRICANE HILL 255 FT.

OUALIE BEACH CLUB

MOSQUITO BAY

MISS JUNE'S

JONES BAY

Dinners at the plantation inns noted above and at Four Seasons can be thoroughly delightful and indeed memorable; dress codes are observed; reservations are advised/necessary; about $40-$50US per person. Along the north coast there are some very good, less expensive restaurants. Ian and Charlotte Intrim's PRINDERELLA'S BAR & RESTAURANT is known for its warm and cheerful atmosphere, varied/Mediterranean menu, reasonable prices and, in season, its live Saturday night music that draws an enthusiastic crowd. Oualie Beach Club specializes in Caribbean seafood in an informal setting at Mosquito Bay. Local inn keepers advise that Miss June's at Jones Bay is a wonderful addition to the restaurant scene that definitely should be considered for fine dining ashore; reservations required.

COASTAL CRUISING

The west coast north of Charlestown and the north coast over to NEWCASTLE BAY are the only areas suitable for cruising yachts; miles of beautiful beaches, good snorkeling, anchorages, and absolutely fantastic views abound. The rest of the coast offers little to attract yachts, and most of it is a dead lee shore.

Stretching north from Charlestown for about three miles is **PINNEY'S BEACH** that is surely one of the most lovely in the Caribbean with spectacular views of St. Kitts. Pinney's Beach is a very popular anchorage; conditions are usually the same as off Charlestown. Keep an eye out for fish trap buoys and anchor well off to avoid interfering with the fishermen who put their nets out along the beach. At the southern end is Pinney's Beach Hotel with its unmistakable turquoise roof...a modest and comfortable hotel with good food and drinks and a friendly welcome for one and all; taxis can often

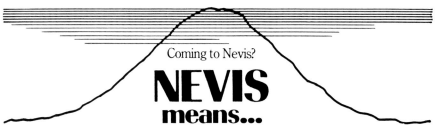

be picked up there. See our comments above regarding the beach bars and other restaurants along Pinney's.

The new luxurious Four Seasons Hotel is the only major development . . . so far...along Pinney's Beach. Its 18 hole golf course, 10 tennis courts, and two restaurants are open to the public on a space-available basis; a dress code is observed. A guard advised recently that visitors' dinghies should not be tied to the dock.

Some three miles north of Charlestown is the site of Jamestown, the first settlement on Nevis, and a few cut stones that are the remains of Fort Ashby near Nelson's Spring. The village of Jamestown was destroyed by an earthquake and/or tidal wave in 1680 just 52 years after it was established by Anthony Hilton and 80 planters from St. Kitts. There have been reports that the remains of the town could be seen by snorkelers and SCUBA divers, but careful searches by the Smithsonian Institute and others found nothing, so we assume Jamestown lives on in memory only. As noted, Fort Ashby Restaurant serves excellent lunches.

CADES POINT lies approximately three and a half miles north of Charlestown; it is identified by the ruins of what was the Cliff Dwellers Hotel before it was largely destroyed by hurricane Hugo. Plans for the future of Cliff Dwellers are vague.

Just to the south of Cades Point is **CADES or TAMARIND BAY** that is protected in normal trade winds conditions and has a nice beach. The only dangers in the bay are a rocky patch and a few rocks awash about 100 yards off the beach to the south of a low stone wall at the southern end of the bay. Anchor in sand and grass in the northern half of the bay; the depth is 10' to 11' about 200 yards off the shore and 5' to 6' some 100 yards off. PRENDERELLA'S RESTAURANT (described above under Country Dining) is on the beach at Tamarind Bay and monitors VHF Ch. 16; you can tie your dinghy to the pier and use the showers when they are completed; in season Saturday nights with live music are very popular.

There is good snorkeling off Cades Point and along the shore reefs to the north of it. The reefs include both rock and coral and extend out perhaps 200 to 300 yards off the shore and continue north to a small gravel point and a small sandy beach. When

MOSQUITO BAY *Eiman photo*

the sea is calm, this is a great spot for snorkelers, but yachts should stand well off to avoid troubles.

To the north of Cades Point is a slight indentation in the coast known as **JONES BAY**; there are a few houses overlooking it. The bay is shallow (3 to 6 feet about 300 yards off) and should be avoided. Stand well off and proceed on by.

MOSQUITO BAY lies to the northeast of Jones Bay and southwest of HURRICANE HILL, an isolated, 225 ft. hill that is the most prominent landmark on the north coast of Nevis. It is a good, protected, but shallow, anchorage with a bottom of sand and grass and depths of 6' to 8' some 200 yards off the beach. The best protection is in the northern part; proceed in slowly and anchor when you start to run out of water. Good snorkeling is reported off the point at the north end of Mosquito Bay and off the point at the foot of Hurricane Hill.

OUALIE BEACH CLUB in Mosquito Bay is owned and operated by John and Karen Yearwood who have welcomed visiting sailors for years. The Club has six attractive double rooms and serves breakfast, lunch, and dinner to guests and visitors alike at very reasonable prices. The atmosphere is informal and friendly, and dinners feature seafood with both West Indian and Continental flair. Ellis Chaderton operates Scuba Safaris at Oualie . . . a full service PADI dive center with dive charters, instruction, and equipment rentals. The Club monitors VHF channel l6.

When conditions are favorable, the north coast of Nevis from Hurricane Hill to Newcastle Bay is a wonderful area to explore; its white sand beaches, swaying palms, and breaking offshore reefs give it a definite South Seas feeling. Just to the east of Hurricane Hill is a lovely bay we have been told is called **AIRPORT BAY**. Proceed in cautiously keeping a sharp eye out for possible isolated coral patches. Anchor off the beautiful beach in good water and enjoy the protection of the offshore reefs that provide spectacular snorkeling; they are filled with coral rising abruptly from the depths, underwater canyons, and beautiful coral formations.

Behind the offshore reefs a passage extends east to **NEWCASTLE BAY.** There is good water in this passage, but there are also a lot of coral heads and isolated patches of coral that cold ruin your whole day. Wonderful for a slow dinghy, but definitely NOT for cruising yachts. Don't feel badly if you see a large boat or two in Newcastle Bay; there is an entrance through the offshore reefs, but only experienced, local experts know it. It is no place for strangers.

Take your dinghy into Newcastle Bay and enjoy beachcombing, more snorkeling, lunch at Waves/Gourmet Pizza, and a walk to Newcastle Village and the Pottery. If a deep, well-marked channel into Newcastle Bay is ever dredged, it will be a great place for visiting yachts . . . but not until then.

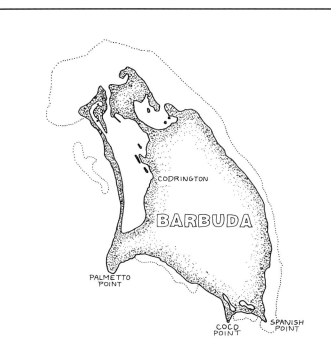

ANTIGUA & BARBUDA

INTRODUCTION TO ANTIGUA — BARBUDA

Antigua and Barbuda lie 23 (nautical) miles apart on the Barbuda Bank that straddles 61 deg. 50' W. Longitude just north of 17 eg. N. Latitude. They are approximately 85 miles southeast of St. Maarten/St. Martin, 50 miles to the east of St. Kitts and some 40 miles north of Gudeloupe. The Barbuda Bank rises quickly from surrounding depths of 900 to 2,400 feet and in general has offshore depths of 30 to 90 feet. Dangerous shoals, reefs, and small islands are found within 3 to 4 miles off the coasts of both Antigua and Barbuda; thus both islands should be approached with great caution especially at night and when visibility is limited.

WEATHER

Antigua and Barbuda share, along with neighboring islands in the Leewards, superb sailing weather unmatched by few, if any, other areas in the world. The remarkably steady trade winds blow from between Northeast and Southeast from 90% to 96% of the time in St. John's, Antigua according to government data. Mean wind speed at the V.C.Bird Airport in Antigua is between ll and ll.25 knots from December through May year after year; in June, July, and August it reaches 12 to 13.5 knots before falling off to 9 to 10 knots in September, October, and November. Days are generally sun-drenched with cloud cover approximately 5%.

Antigua has an average of 44 inches of rainfall annually; the seasons are not always distinct, but January through June are usually the driest months, while July through November are typically the wettest. Visibility is normally 10 to 20 miles or more, but is under 5 miles about 5% of the time primarily in intense squalls and hurricanes. Dust blown over from Africa can occasionally reduce visibility to 5 to 10 miles.

Large northern swells, usually generated by winter storms in the North Atlantic, reach Antigua and Barbuda from time to time between early December and the end of March. They increase in height in shallow water and wrap around the land making anchorages expose to the north, east, and west uncomfortable or untenable. Their arrival is unpredictable, but they should be kept in mind when planning where to anchor.

In the Caribbean 85% of the hurricanes occur in August, September, and October, while to remaining 15% usually . . . but not always . . . come in June, July, and November. Their counterclockwise winds of 64 knots and more, torrential rains, high seas, and extremely restricted visibility should be avoided at all costs. From June through November it is essential to listen to daily weather foreasts for storm and hurricane warnings and to take shelter before conditions deteriorate. Weather information broadcasts by the following sources are received in Antigua and Barbuda:

AM 895 kHz - VON - Nevis - Marine Weather 7:45 A.M., 10:45 A.M., and 12:45 P.M.

1100 kHz - ZDK, Antigua - Marine Weather 6:55 P.M.; Weather 8:15 A.M., 9:15 A.M., 10:15 A.M., 2:15 P.M.

VHF Channel 6 - English Harbor Radio - Marine Weather 9:00 A.M.

SSB 08294.0 - Nicholson Yacht Charters - Weather 9:00 A.M.

COMMUNICATIONS

VHF RADIO is the link of choice among yachts and shore stations in Antigua and Barbuda. VHF Channel 16 is used for calling and distress on the high seas but its use is not permitted while at anchor or dockside in Antigua and Barbuda. In these latter situations VHF Channel 68 is the calling frequency; practically everybody in the yachting community monitors VHF Ch 68 routinely.

SSB RADIO is used by Nicholson Yacht Charters and by many crewed charter yachts and others. Nicholson monitors 08294.0 daily from 8:30 A.M. to 4:30 P.M.

TELEPHONE - To phone Antigua from the U.S. dial 1-809 + seven local numbers. International and local calls can be placed at the Cable and Wireless offices in St. John's and just outside Nelson's Dockyard in English Harbor. Also just outside the Dockyard are USA Direct phones and public phones for credit card and collect calls. Boatphone service is available in Antigua and Barbuda. To phone Antigua from the U.S. dial 1-809 + seven local numbers.

CHARTS

The following charts can be helpful to yachtsmen cruising the waters of Antigua and Barbuda. They should be used with caution as much of the data is based on British surveys made many, many decades ago; data on the waters around Barbuda are described in some publications as unreliable.

U.S.D.M.A.	25550	Saint Barthelemy To Guadeloupe - 1:250,000
	25570	Approach To Antigua - 1:75,000
	25575	St. John's Harbor To Parham Harbor - 1:25,000
	25608	Plans of The Leeward Islands - Approach To Barbuda - 1:75,000; Baie Marigot, Port de Gustavia, Plymouth, and Basseterre - 1:15,000
British Admiralty	254	Montserrat And Barbuda - 1:150,000; Barbuda - 1:60,000; Montserrat - 1:50,000; Plymouth Anchorage - 1:15,000
	955	Sombrero To Dominica - 1:475,000
	2064	Antigua - 1:60,000; Plan of Falmouth & English Harbors 1:20,000; Plan of Mamora Bay - 1:10,000
	2065	St. John's Harbor To Parham Harbor - 1:25,000

Imray-Iolaire publishes three charts of the area: A3 - Anguilla to Guadeloupe -1:394,000, A26 - Barbuda - Southwest Coast - 1:28,000 with Plan of Gravenor Bay, and A27 - Antigua - 1:57,000 with Plans of Nonsuch Bay, Mamora Bay, Falmouth & English Harbors. They are good charts but tend to disintegrate when wet; they are available from selected chart stores for about $18.00 US.

In Antigua The Map Shop on St. Mary's Street in St. Johns carries a good inventory of charts. In the U.S. one of the best and most reliable sources of Caribbean charts and cruising guides is BLUEWATER BOOKS & CHARTS, 1481 S.E. 17th Street, Ft. Lauderdale, FL 33316; phone (305) 763-6533.

DIRECT DISTANCES

The following approximate distances in nautical miles are provided to assist in planning itineraries. When estimating sailing time between points, allowences should be made for wind direction and strength, tacking, and sea conditions.

ENGLISH HARBOR WESTAROUND TO:		ENGLISH HARBOR EAST AND NORTH TO:	
Carlisle Bay	4.5	Nonsuch Bay	9
Mosquito Cove/Jolly Harbor	11.5	Barbuda - Spanish Point	39
Five Islands Harbor	13	**INTERISLAND FROM**	
Deep Bay	15	**ENGLISH HARBOR:**	
St. John's	18	Guadeloupe - Deshaies	40
Dickinson Bay	18	Montserrat - Plymouth	35
Diamond Bank Tower	19	St. Kitts - Basseterre	63
Barbuda - Cocoa Point	43	St. Barts - Gustavia	85
North Sound/Crabbs	25.5	St. Maarten - Philipsburg	98

NAVIGATION AIDS

Whenever a buoyage system is used in the Caribbean, it is usually the IALA "B" system . . . 'red-right-returning' when entering harbors and black and yellow markers on shoals. Orange or white racing buoys and other private markers (white plastic Clorox bottles, spars, stakes or whatever) are often encountered in the waters of Antigua; they should not be mistaken for official aids to navigation.

Information on lights is based on government charts and other sources considered reliable, but the lights themselves are often not working. Throughout the Caribbean, navigation aids are frequently UNRELIABLE and should be treated with great caution.

SECURITY

As at home, it is adviseable to take simple precautions routinely to minimize the risk of theft. Close and lock your boat whenever you leave it unattended; lock your outboard to your dinghy and lock your dinghy to the dock when you go ashore and to your yacht at night. Do not leave valuables unattended in public places including beaches.

RUBBISH

There are rubbish/trash/garbage recepticles at English Harbor, Mamora Bay, St. John's, and all marinas in Antigua. ALL rubbish should be bagged and left in the recepticles provided. Biodegradable garbage (not including wrappers & packages) can be tossed overboard well offshore where it will not wash ashore on an island, but plastic items should never be thrown overbord under any circumstances. And don't even think about throwing anything overboard in anchorages and harbors. Please.

CURRENCY

U.S. dollars are widely accepted in Antigua and Barbuda, and recognized credit cards can be used in many restaurants and tourist-oriented shops in Antigua. The official currency, however, is the Eastern Caribbean Dollar (E.C.$). The exchange rate is generally about $1.00 U.S. = $2.65 E.C or $1.00 E.C. = $0.38 U.S. Be sure to check which curency is being used before buying or agreeing to anything.

CUSTOMS & IMMIGRATION

For clearance purposes Antigua and Barbuda are one jurisdiction. All yachts must clear in and out of Antigua/Barbuda and must obtain a Cruising Permit to cruise the waters of the islands. In Antigua this can be done at C & I offices at English Harbor, Jolly Harbor (after 11/92), Crabbs Marina, and St. John's. Yachts must clear in in Antigua before cruising to Barbuda but can clear out at the C & I office in Barbuda. Clearance from the last port of call is required from arriving yachts, and ship's papers may be requested. Passports are required for all on board except for U.S. citizens who may use a driver's license or birth certificate. A "Q" flag should be flown and crew members should stay aboard until the Captain has completed clearance procedures.

The following fees are charged: Entry Fees are $2.00US for boats up to 20',

$4.00US for 21'-40', $6.00US for 41'-80', $8.00US for 80'-100', etc. Monthly Cruising Permits are $8.00US for boats up to 40', $10.00US for 41'-80', $12.00US for 81'-100' etc. See the sections on English Harbor and Falmouth for additional charges for yachts staying there.

YACHT RACING

Thanks largely to the Antigua Yacht Club, there is more racing in Antigua than anywhere else in the Caribbean. Special races and regattas are held almost every month throughout the year, and 'regular' races are scheduled weekly and on various Sundays each month. Visiting yachts are welcome to participate in the races held every Thursday evening; contact AYC for information.

The granddaddy of all Caribbean yacht racing...and the most action-packed, stylish, colorful, and fun-filled . . . takes place during Antigua Sailing Week held annually in late April or early May. Dreamed up by Desmond Nicholson and Howard Halford some 25 years ago, Sailing Week marks the end of the winter charter/tourist season with a week of very hot, spirited racing that draws perhaps 150 competitive yachts from Europe, North America, and the Caribbean together with thousands of hedonistic sailors, spectators, and assorted camp followers. Races concentrate along the coast and always end with enthusiastic partying at luxury hotels or restaurants. The highjinks are topped off on the last day by what are described as "Fun and Games" in Nelson's Dockyard, the presentation of Prizes by His Excellency The Governor General, and Lord Nelson's Ball at The Admiral's Inn. If you never make Antigua Sailing Week, you'll just have to eat your heart out.

Sadly, the Caribbean is not immune to the ravages of the drug problem. Possession and/or use of drugs is a serious problem in Antigua and is delt with harshly. The authorities in Antigua have been reported to use agents posing as friendly drug dealers during Race Week to lure the unsuspecting into buying drugs and then WHAMMO! prosecuting them for possession and throwing the key away.

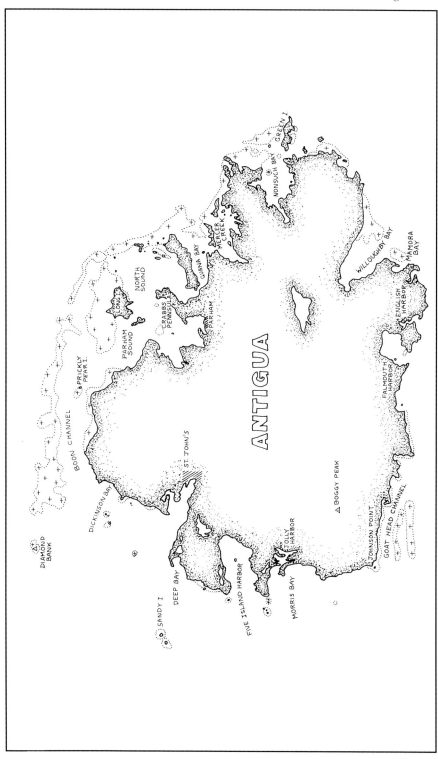

ANTIGUA

CHARTS: U.S. DMA 25550, 25570, 25575

British 955, 2064, 2065

Imray Iolaire A3, A27

Antigua . . . pronounced An-TEE-ga . . . is at the heart of the Leeward Islands just half way between Anguilla to the northwest and Dominica to the south; it boasts more attractive beaches and anchorages than any other island in the Caribbean. While most of the island is a low, gently rolling plain, there is a series of high peaks and hills generally along the southern coast topped by Boggy Peak that reaches 1,319 feet near the southwest end of the island. Its deeply indented, 60-odd mile coastline, minimal rainfall, and steady cooling trade winds help make it a near-perfect haven for cruising yachtsmen; many knowledgeable skippers have long considered Antigua THE yachting center of the Caribbean.

Although Amerindians, including the peaceful Arawaks and the warlike Caribs, inhabited or visited Antigua since at least the second century before Christ, Europeans knew nothing of it until Columbus sighted the island in November, 1493 and named it after the famous statue of The Virgin in the Seville Cathedral. The first permanent settlement was established in 1632 in the area of Old Road on the southern coast by English colonists from St. Kitts under the direction of Thomas Warner. Except for a brief occupation by the French in 1666-67, Antigua remained a British possession until it gained independence in 1981.

By 1672 sugar became the leading crop on Antigua and, beginning with the importation of untold thousands of slaves from Africa, dominated every aspect of life on the island for almost the next three hundred years. The enormous value of sugar on Antigua and other Caribbean islands led to continuing warfare between the British and French from the 1600s until the Battle of Waterloo in 1815. To protect their sugar interests, the British fortified some forty sites on Antigua and built the Royal Dockyard at English Harbor to service their warships patrolling the Eastern Caribbean.

Sugar production peaked in Antigua in the late 1700s when Europe found cheaper sources, and the economy started a long decline that continued well into the 20th century. In 1834 Antigua became the first British colony in the Caribbean to free its slaves unconditionally. In the 1950s universal suffrage and a ministerial system of government were established. Full independence for Antigua and Barbuda was achieved in November, 1981.

Today tourism is the mainstay of Antigua's economy and employs about one sixth of the work force to provide more than 300,000 American, Canadian, British, and European visitors with memorable, pleasure-filled vacations annually. High quality duty free shops abound in the capital St. John's; attractive shops, boutiques, and casinos are found in some of the larger hotel/resort complexes; most shops are open from 9:00 A.M. to 4:30 P.M. but close around noon on Thursdays and Saturdays.

Land transportation on Antigua is convenient and efficient, but some parts of some roads are in very bad condition. Excellent bus service connects St. John's with virtually all the villages and points of interest; the one way fare between St. John's and English Harbor/Falmouth is about $1.75 E.C. Taxis and rental cars are readily available with prices that often seem higher than in major cities at home. Drive defensively and DRIVE ON THE LEFT!!!

SAILING DIRECTIONS/APPROACHING ANTIGUA

Sailing to Antigua from the St. Maarten/St. Martin area and from St. Kitts, Nevis, and even Monserrat usually means beating to windward 35 to 80 miles depending on the wind direction and the course. All things being equal, many prefer to sail direct from St. Barts to Antigua to minimize adverse currents; others like to cruise to St. Kitts or Nevis before heading to Antigua; a few sail via Montserrat to break up the windward work even more. From Guadeloupe the sail is normally a great ride with sheets eased; no problem.

But no matter what course you select, it is important to make certain you arrive in port in Antigua well before sundown. Except from OLD ROAD BLUFF on the south coast east and north to GREEN ISLAND on the east coast, Antigua is surrounded by offshore reefs, shoals, and obstructions that make approaching after dark very dangerous. And keep in mind that aids to navigation cannot be counted on.

Yachts approaching Antigua from the northwest and west should take care to avoid DIAMOND BANK and SANDY ISLAND and WEYMOUTH REEF and the hazards between them. They should also avoid the several 9 to 10 foot shoals along the west coast from Hawkes Bill Rock south to Johnson Point and especially the dangerous, unmarked 3 foot shoal about one mile off the point between Ffreys and Picarts Bays. South of Johnson Point Cade and Middle Reefs should be given wide berths.

ENGLISH HARBOR

Experts and old Caribbean hands alike agree that Antigua really means ENGLISH HARBOR to yachtsmen. World famous ocean racer and author Carleton Mitchell

NELSON'S DOCKYARD - 1953 *Eiman photo*

described English Harbor in 1948 in "Islands To Windward," his pioneering book on Caribbean cruising, as " . . . the most perfect anchorage I have ever seen . . . probably the finest surviving example of the age of sail . . . " The surrounding hills topped with ancient fortifications provide shelter from virtually all winds, and today extensive facilities for yachts and the pleasure of their crews are close at hand . . . many housed in carefully restored, attractive buildings built in the 18th century to serve the British fleet.

The history of English Harbor as a maritime center stretches back to the 1670s when British captains used it to repair their ships and to protect them from hurricanes. In an effort to attract warships to protect the sugar industry, construction of the East Careening Wharf began in 1729 where Antigua Slipway now stands. Development of the Royal Dockyard on the west side of the harbor was under way in the 1740s and continued on to the pinnacle of its importance during the French Wars from 1793 to 1815. The Dockyard is formally known as Nelson's Dockyard in tribute to Horatio Nelson, hero of the Battle of Trafalger, who had a tumultuous and unhappy tour of duty there as Captain of the frigate Boreas from 1784 to 1787.

After 1815 English Harbor lost much of its importance and began a long, long decline that resulted from the Battle of Waterloo and the waning profitability of Caribbean sugar as well as the introduction of steamships. The Royal Dockyard was officially closed in 1899, and virtually all activities ceased a few years later leaving the handsome 18th century buildings to weather and decay.

The renaissance of English Harbor as the most celebrated and celebrating yachting center in the Caribbean dates from 1947 with the arrival of Commander and Mrs. V.E.B. Nicholson and sons Desmond and Rodney on their schooner Mollihawk. Although this impressive effort has involved the contributions of countless individuals from near and far, the lion's share of credit for the restoration of English Harbor belongs to the Nicholson family and to the Friends of English Harbor, established in 1951 by Governor Kenneth Blackbourne. In addition the remarkable Nicholson family has also provided much of the leadership, inspiration, and driving spirit that have made English Harbor a mecca for luxurious charter yachts and a captivating port of call for cruising yachts from the U.S., Europe, South America, and the far corners of the world.

The life of English Harbor is tied closely to the charter business. The prime season begins with the arrival of the charter fleet in preparation for the Nicholson Brokers Week in early December and continues through Antigua Race Week in late April/early May. Then the charter fleet and cruising yachts gradually thin out and everything slows down, and the atmosphere becomes more relaxed. Summer is peaceful and calm; many restaurants, hotels, and services cut back operations or close completely. In August and September English Harbor dozes quietly in the tropic sun dreaming of the season ahead.

APPROACHING/ENTERING From well offshore to the south SHIRLEY HEIGHTS is a good landmark for English Harbor; it is 485 feet high, has a distinct flat top, and is close to the eastern end of the high ground along the southern shore of Antigua. Closer in, keep in mind that English Harbor is between two large, obvious bays . . . FALMOUTH HARBOR to the west and WILLOUGHBY BAY to the east.

There are no offshore hazards near English Harbor. Entering is straightforward; simply avoid the reef extending NW from CHARLOTTE POINT (where you may recognize the eroded stone formation, the PILLARS OF HERCULES), and proceed into FREEMAN BAY. Don't be discouraged by the unfortunate new houses on the hillside behind the beach in Freeman Bay; they are rare exceptions in an otherwise attractive area.

REGULATIONS & CHARGES Yachts entering Antigua at English Harbor should first anchor in Freeman Bay and take care of clearance formalities. Hoist a yellow Q flag and call Customs & Immigration for instructions. If officials do not come to your boat, the Skipper should go to the Customs office at the north end of the Officers Quarters building to clear in. Ship's papers, passports, and clearance from the last port are required.

Customs is open from 7:00 A.M. to 5:00 P.M. every day; entry fees and Cruising Permit charges are as shown in the Introduction above. A Port Authority official in

Customs will collect the following Harbor Dues and fees in advance:

Anchorage (applies to English Harbor & **Stern To**
            Falmouth Harbor)

$ .03US per foot per day	$ .25US per foot per day
$ .15US per foot per week	$1.50US per foot per week
$ .50US per foot per month	$5.00US per foot per month
$2.50US per foot per season	

These payments include use of the Port Authority showers and toilets in English and Falmouth Harbors and the laundry tubs in English Harbor.

Dockyard Entry - One time charge of   **Surcharge** - $.15US per foot for
$5.00EC for each person on board   vessels over 100' LOA or 20' beam

Electricity and water at the Dockyard are charged for amounts used with $20.00 minimums per boat.

Immigration business can sometimes be handled in the Customs office. Otherwise it must be done at the Police Station just outside the Dockyard.

Harbor Regulations covering both English Harbor and Falmouth Harbor specify a 4 knot speed limit and require dinghies to display a light after sunset. Water skiing and jet skiing are prohibited near anchored yachts. Flares, rockets, fireworks, barbecues, and open fires of any type are also prohibited in the Harbors. Garbage and old oil and fuel must be discarded in the containers provided.

ANCHORING/DOCKING The most popular anchorage is in FREEMAN BAY where the holding is good in the sandy bottom. You can also anchor in ORDINANCE BAY or TANK BAY where the bottom is somewhat muddy and where there is less breeze. Be sure to avoid the heavy 'hurricane' chains shown on our sketch chart; if you do become seriously hooked, call DOCKYARD DIVERS on VHF Ch. 68 for help. You can dock stern to at the Dockyard and at Antigua Slipway where water and electricity are available. If you go stern to at the Dockyard, drop your anchor as far out as possible; the holding in a trough in mid-channel can be poor. It is a good idea to lock your boat

PAYMASTER'S OFFICE - 1953   *Eiman photo*

whenever you leave it unattended and to protect your dinghy and outboard with security wires and locks.

SERVICES In English Harbor and within one mile of it there is an extensive concentration of marine facilities and services; all are easy to reach by land or by water; virtually all monitor VHF Ch. 68. Many suppliers will assist qualified buyers with the paperwork and processing required to avoid the hefty Antigua import duties that can increase the cost of imported parts and equipment dramatically.

Antigua Slipway is a full service yard that can haul yachts up to 120 ft. LOA and 125 tons displacement; the staff can repair and maintain wooden, fiberglass, aluminum, or steel yachts and all their mechanical equipment; it has a chandlery and a fuel dock complete with water and ice. At the Paymaster's Office in the Dockyard SIGNAL LOCKER has been selling and repairing all kinds of electronic and electrical equipment for over 20 years; it also sells and services refrigeration and air conditioning equipment and watermakers. In the same building the legendary Jol Byerley operates

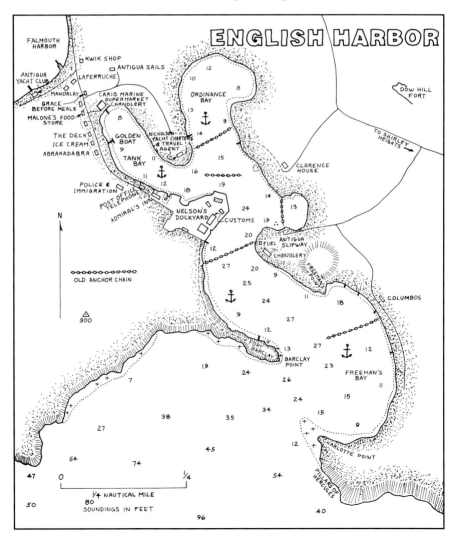

CARIB MARINE
ENGLISH HARBOUR, ANTIGUA

For over 25 years......
Chandlers to the Yachting Industry......

We Stock the Finest......
• MEATS • SEAFOOD • GROCERIES •
• FRESH PRODUCE • HEALTH FOODS •

We Also Carry......
• HARDWARE • PAINTS • CANVAS •
• CORDAGE • DIVING & FISHING •

We Offer......
• PROVISIONING SERVICES •
5% Cash Discount on Cash Purchases over $500

**MOBILE: 464-8196/TEL: 460-1521
FAX/TEL: 809-460-1532**

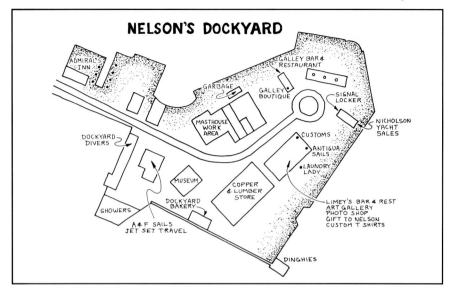

NICHOLSON CARIBBEAN YACHT SALES specializing in fine luxury yachts; he is known as a yacht broker par excellence, a top notch racing skipper, a raconteur, an author, and an expert weatherman whose daily 9:00 AM broadcasts on VHF Ch. 6 start everybody off on the right foot with a smile; Jol also sells Yamaha outboards, North sails, and nautical books.

A & F SAILS and ANTIGUA SAILS in the Dockyard will build new sails to your order and will repair and patch up your old rags in a jiffy; they also do all types of canvas work . . . i.e. awnings, Biminis, covers, etc. TEND ALOFT RIGGING nearby will solve any problems you have with standing or running rigging . . . fabrication, repairs, custom fittings, spares, roller furling gear, etc. as well as lifelines; around the clock emergency service and boat calls are available.

DOCKYARD DIVERS offers SCUBA gear, PADI certification, and twice-a-day dive trips in season and will clean your bottom and, as mentioned, free your hook from entangling alliances. Neighboring JET SET TRAVEL provides efficient airline reservations and tickets, tour arrangements, and day charters.

The heart of English Harbor is NICHOLSON YACHT CHARTER & TRAVEL AGENCY in the olde Powder Magazine between Ordinance Bay and Tank Bay. For over forty years the Nicholsons have pioneered and nurtured Caribbean chartering that forms the foundation of the survival, prosperity, and reputation of English Harbor. The Nicholsons provide comprehensive travel and communications services in addition to their renowned charter operations; as noted, they monitor SSB (08294.0) daily from 8:30 A.M. to 4:30 P.M. and broadcast weather at 9:00 A.M. The Powder Magazine also houses ANTIGUA COMPUTER SYSTEMS that supplies marine computers, computer systems, and a variety of computer training courses.

PROVISIONING In the Dockyard proper the DOCKYARD BAKERY back of the Museum has mouthwatering fresh bread, cakes, and pastries, and local ladies sell a few fresh fruits and vegetables. At the far end of Tank Bay is CARIB MARINE, an excellent supermarket with its own dinghy dock and chandlery, that stocks everything from meat, seafood, groceries, wines and liquor to deli items, health foods, and ice. Just across the road MALONE'S FOOD STORE has fresh produce, meat, poultry, and groceries plus free delivery. A mile away in Falmouth BAILEY'S SUPERMARKET provides a wide selection of groceries, housewares, wine, liquor, and flowers at reasonable prices; free delivery service is available.

For the widest selection of fine provisions and superb quality specialties in Antigua, ISLAND PROVISIONS on Airport Road over towards St. John's is in class by itself and well worth the trip for major provisioning. They supply many of the best hotels and restaurants on the island and will fill your orders with care. With advance notice they will provide Beluga caviar, selected vintage wines, and delectable cheeses, etc.

In downtown St. John's DEW'S SUPERMARKET on Long Street has a wonderful selection of English and American brands together with meat and fresh produce. QUIN FARARA'S LIQUOR STORE in Heritage Quay stocks duty free wines and spirits as well as Havana cigars. THE GRAPE ESCAPE carries a very impressive selection of French, Italian, German, Spanish, American and other fine wines.

ASHORE Since we first called in English Harbor forty years ago our most pleasant experiences have been crowned by leisurely breakfasts and delightful dinners at Admirals Inn and impressive trips to Fort Shirley on Shirley Heights. Their magical charm and timeless beauty will highlight any visit . . . and are guaranteed to recharge your batteries!

Currently, the musical Sunday afternoons and evenings at SHIRLEY HEIGHTS LOOKOUT now attract crowds from all parts of Antigua. From 3:00 to 6:00 P.M. the steel band is relatively laid back and relaxed. From 6:00 to 9:00 P.M. a reggae band takes over with its 8' x 10' banks of speakers that blast the music all the way to the Dockyard and excite the happy gathering of 1,000 or more friendly afficianados in a wild, WILD scene!! Either or both sessions will blow your mind.

ENGLISH HARBOR   *Derek Little photo*

214

SHIRLEY HEIGHTS LOOKOUT BAR & RESTAURANT *Eiman photo*

Partying may be topped by the Sunday jump ups at Shirley Heights, but it rarely stops at sea level. Bonding, liaisons, fun and games get rolling on various days at happy hours starting between 5:00 & 6:00 P.M. at the Galley Bar & Restaurant, the Pub at the Copper & Lumber Store, Admiral's Inn, The Deck, and G & T Pizza at the Antigua Yacht Club. Festivities continue into the evening with steel and reggae bands and discos at various restaurants on different nights of the week; the schedule changes over time, but typically Colombo's Restaurant (Italian, seafood) features a reggae band Wednesdays,

Admiral's Inn (International, West Indian) has a steel band on Saturdays and live music one or two other evenings, Abracadabra (Italian, seafood) cranks up live music Tuesdays, Fridays, and Saturdays, The Galley Bar & Restaurant sponsors a jump up on Thursdays and live entertainment on Saturdays, and the Deck (West Indian, seafood) spins a disco Fridays, Saturdays, and Sundays. Depending on your appetite, tolerance, and endurance, it is easy to play whoopee every night.

All this is in sharp contrast to the situation in the Dockyard in the 18th Century when, according to Carleton Mitchell, the Regulations for the Gate Porter specified "No Porter, Beer, Wine or Spirits of any sort whatsoever is to be brought into the Yard . . . No Foreigner, Stranger or Woman to be Admitted . . . and No Person to be suffered to smoke Tobacco in the Yard . . . "

In the Dockyard The Pub at the Copper and Lumber Store is a popular spot with pub food and, on Tuesdays and Fridays, happy hours that run until 8:00 P. M. Limey's in the Officers Quarters has rotis, snacks, and light West Indian fare at lunch and dinner. Our favorite modest Creole/West Indian restaurant is the Kwik Stop across from the Port Authority at Falmouth Harbor. We have had good reports on Le Cap Horn (seafood, steaks, seafood, and great desserts), La Perruche (French and pricey), and the Inn at English Harbor (Caribbean flavor cuisine & lovely candle light dining).

The shed at the Dockyard entrance and the alley beside the Admiral's Inn are T shirt heaven where the colorful variety is overwhelming, but if you can't find just what you want, head for A C Screen Printing in the Officers Quarters where you can have your own design printed. For interesting material on English Harbor (including English Harbor-An Historical and Archeological Sketch and A Visitor's Guide to English

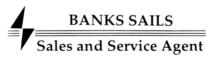

Harbor by Desmond Nicholson), a nice selection of local crafts, post cards, maps, etc. visit the gift shop adjacent to the Museum in the Admiral's House. The heart of Dockyard shopping is the GALLEY BOUTIQUE in the olde Cookhouse where owner Janie Easton has been delighting customers since 1969 with her lovely array of gifts and her beautiful clothing made in the shop to her eclectic designs. SUN YACHTS at the Copper and Lumber Store has top notch bareboat yachts for charter.

If you are pleased by the lovely old buildings in the Dockyard, you will have a field day visiting other historic sites close by. Fort Barclay (or Berkeley) at the entrance to English Harbor can be reached by a foot path from the Dockyard or by the dinghy dock inside the point. Clarence House is just across the water from the Dockyard; it can be approached from the road up to Shirley Heights or from a path leading up from a small dock on the eastern shore of Ordinance Bay. Stout hearted hikers can huff and puff up the road from the Slipway or from Colombo's to the Royal Artillery Quarters and the impressive fortifications on Shirley Heights; the rest of us will be much happier taking a taxi; call JB TAXI on VHF Ch.68 or phone 460-1497 for dependable service.

FALMOUTH HARBOR

FALMOUTH HARBOR provides a large, lovely, well protected anchorage for yachts anxious for more breathing space and less congestion than they can find in nearby English Harbor without sacrificing convenient access to facilities, yacht services, restaurants, entertainment, etc.

ENTERING/ANCHORING/DOCKING The range markers shown on our sketch chart are quite permanent and lead past all hazards on approximately 42° Magnetic across the Harbor to the Catamaran Club on the north shore. The buoys in Falmouth Harbor were all orange or white private markers at the time of our survey; we can't say whether or not they will be in place when you arrive. In any event, don't be thrown off by racing buoys that are placed around the Harbor. Fortunately, Bishop Shoal and the shoals in the northern half of Falmouth Harbor are all easy to see in good light.

If you are heading for the popular anchorage off the Yacht Club and Port Authority in the southeast corner, leave BISHOP SHOAL to starboard and then promptly alter your course to starboard to pass between ST. ANNE POINT and the 5 foot shoal near

FALMOUTH HARBOR   *Derek Little photo*

the range. There is good water 100 yards or so off the shore between St. Anne's Point and the Yacht Club. Anchor where you like; the holding is good. Dinghies can be left at the Port Authority dock, but be sure to lock them securely.

The Antigua Yacht Club Marina is a commercial operation open to the public; if you want to go stern to there make arrangements on VHF Ch 68. There are two dozen slips with 220 & 110 volt electricity, water, and cable TV connections.

To reach Hugh Bailey's Catamaran Club just ride the range past Bishop Shoal on over. The Club has about 30 slips for yachts; fuel, water, and ice are available along with 220/110 volt electricity. Again, make arrangements on VHF Ch 68.

If you want to get away from it all and have more peace and quiet, consider anchoring off the north shore of Falmouth Harbor to the east of the Catamaran Club. The water is good and the surroundings are lovely; just feel your way along cautiously in good light to avoid the obvious shoals. Even better and more peaceful is the small cove tucked behind BLAKE ISLAND to the northwest.

SERVICES Just back of the Catamaran Club is Seagull Services that repairs diesels, outboards, hydraulics, watermakers, and inflatables and does all sorts of metal fabrication; they represent a variety of major suppliers from Avon to Westerbeke. They . . . like virtually all service suppliers in the English Harbor-Falmouth Harbor area . . . monitor VHF Ch 68. Right next door Marionics will repair or order all sorts of electronics gear.

In the northeast corner of Falmouth Harbor MARINE POWER SERVICES has set up a new shop for their comprehensive engineering, supply, and repair operation that

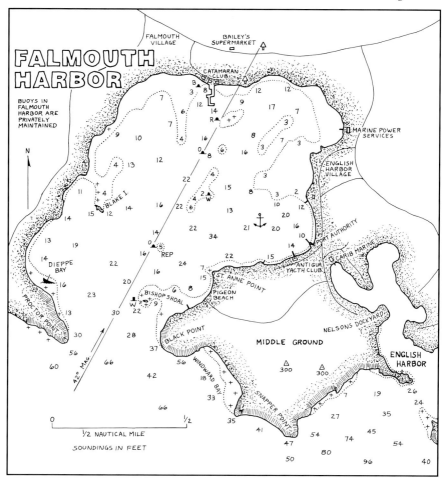

handles any and all problems with generators, diesel engines, watermakers, hydraulics, outboards, refrigeration, and inflatables. They fabricate steel, stainless, and aluminum and are agents for many leading manufacturers. It is no problem to work your way through the shoals and anchor off their dinghy dock. Or just call them on VHF Ch 68; they will come out to your boat to check it out.

Pumps and Power near the Port Authority does virtually every kind of mechanical and electrical repair work and provides a parts ordering service; they supply gas and diesel and will fill propane tanks. Next door The Chandlery stocks a wide variety of marine supplies and equipment and arranges duty free prices for qualified buyers.

Fuel and water are available at the Port Authority dock; showers and toilets are on the site. Sam & Dave's Laundry is further along the road towards Falmouth.

PROVISIONING/ASHORE Please see the comments above for English Harbor regarding provisioning and shore activities. BAILEY'S SUPERMARKET is most convenient for anyone anchored near the Catamaran Club at the head of the Harbor.

Pigeon Beach near the entrance to Falmouth Harbor is the most popular . . . and only topless . . . beach in the area. From the road past the Yacht Club a path climbs over

INDIAN CREEK   *Derek Little photo*

the hill and down to the beach, but it is much easier and cooler to go around in your dinghy. If you go in your 'big boat,' avoid the shoal at St. Anne Point and the shallow water towards the SW end of the beach.

EAST COAST - ENGLISH HARBOR TO NONSUCH BAY

If you relish driving to windward, you will usually have a great time beating up to NONSUCH BAY and GREEN ISLAND. The normal breeze is exhilarating, the coast is fascinating, and except for the entrance to MAMORA BAY and WILLOUGHBY BAY, a good quarter mile offshore clears all hazards. The rugged cliffs, the bays and beaches,

MAMORA BAY   *Derek Little photo*

the caves, and the rolling country will boggle your mind.

INDIAN CREEK is a cozy, secluded rendezvous about two miles east of English Harbor. The entrance is guarded by SUNKEN ROCK that usually breaks the surface (see the photo). The anchorage is completely protected by the high hills and is a good place to ride out stormy weather.

The water is good all around Sunken Rock, but it is best to leave it to starboard when entering. The bottom shoals gradually from 25 feet at the entrance to 12 feet in mid-channel off the dock you will see directly ahead as you get into the creek proper; you can proceed in carefully west of the dock and anchor in 7 to 10 feet in mud. There is only room for a few boats to anchor, but that isn't normally a problem; chances you'll have it all to yourself. The creek shoals rapidly as it swings north again; if you want to explore further, it is best done in a dinghy.

MAMORA BAY just over the hill from Indian Creek is the home of the St. James Club that has made vast improvements since it took over a few years ago from the Holiday Inn. The entrance is in a northwesterly direction straight up midway between the high ground to port and the reef, small island, and point of land to starboard. We found a least depth of 21 feet in the entrance but only one red marker on the starboard side of the channel. We found 15 feet of water inside the Bay over to the red and green markers in the middle. Shoaling has been reported, so check with the St. James Club on VHF Ch 68 to avoid trouble.

Facilities ashore . . . including the docks . . . are for members only, but temporary membership for all on board is granted upon payment of a modest daily mooring or dockage fee. Fuel, water, ice, and 220/110 volt electricity are available at the dock. There are swimming pools, tennis courts, a gymnasium, a deli, a few shops, a casino, and several restaurants (jackets are required in Rainbow and Piccolo Mondo); Rainbow is by far the most upscale; Dockside is more informal and serves lighter fare. The palm fringed beach is smashing, and the snorkeling on the reefs outside the Bay can be great in calm weather. Divers can contact Aquanaut on VHF Ch 68 about dive trips, equipment rentals, tank fills, etc.

WILLOUGHBY BAY should be avoided by everyone except reef pilots who know it well. Its entrance is filled with reefs that are pierced by one narrow channel that is hard to spot even in ideal conditions. Stand well off and sail on by.

Landmarks to the northeast of Willoughby Bay include the lovely HALF MOON BAY and Hotel and, further along FRIARS HEAD marked by a conspicuous white house with a cupola that looks very much like a lighthouse. Next you will see YORK ISLAND that juts up 127 feet out of the sea; do NOT attempt to go between it and Antigua. Beyond York I. NECK O LAND along the coast and GREEN ISLAND, extending out to the east, dominate the scene as you approach NONSUCH BAY.

FORT BARKLEY   *Eiman photo*

NONSUCH BAY

Nonsuch Bay is a great favorite of salty Antigua veterans and newcomers alike because its convenient location, its cool and protected anchorages, its gunkholing and snorkeling, and its lovely, peaceful, and largely unspoiled surroundings. Its mouth, which stretches about one and a half miles from DANA POINT on the north to GREEN ISLAND on the south, is filled with solid barrier reefs that protect it from the open sea without blocking the cooling breezes.

APPROACHING From the south once past Willoughby Bay there are no offshore hazards as you pass Half Moon Bay, Exchange Bay, and Friars Head. Leave YORK ISLAND, NECK O LAND, and SUBMARINE ROCK to port as you head for the entrance between GREEN ISLAND and CORK POINT but take care to avoid the reefs extending south from Green Island. There is plenty of water in midchannel all the way in.

From the north stand well of the northeast coast of Antigua as you head for Green Island, the easternmost point along the coast. Sail past Green Island leaving it to starboard before heading west towards the land. Avoid the reefs off the south shore of Green Island and then proceed as noted above.

GREEN ISLAND is leased by the Mill Reef Club, which owns much of the land on Antigua behind the shore from Exchange Bay to Cork Point, and its members frequently use the beaches in RICKETTS HARBOR and TENPOUND BAY. Visitors can use the beaches (all beaches in Antigua are public property) but are not allowed inland. There is a small anchorage in Tenpound Bay, but we do not recommend it for strangers; the entrance is narrow and can be rough; it is surrounded by reefs and has very little room

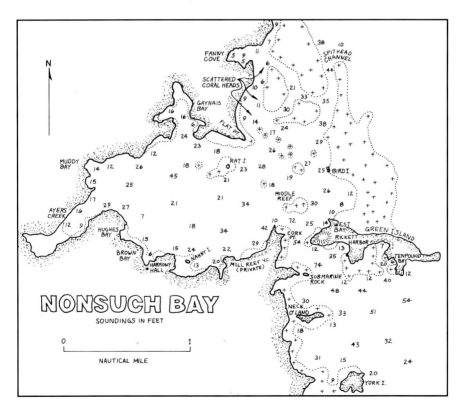

GREEN ISL. - RICKETTS HARBOR *Derek Little photo*

for maneuvering. But we do recommend RICKETTS HARBOR . . . a lovely cove with a straightforward entrance from the southwest. There is room for two or three boats off a beautiful small beach; the bottom is covered with grass, so make sure your anchor digs in properly. Good snorkeling can be found along the reef to the south that normally protects the anchorage from swells.

ENTERING/ANCHORING-NONSUCH There is plenty of clear water in mid-channel between the western end of Green Island and the 'mainland' . . . 30 to 50 feet and more . . . but reefs extend out from both shores. When past the western tip of Green Island, proceed along off its coast to avoid coming to grief on MIDDLE REEF. There is an excellent protected anchorage in WEST BAY with good water over the sand bottom up close to the beach. For a bit more breeze and a more expansive view anchor anywhere behind the protective reef between Green Island and BIRD ISLAND; just pick your spot and anchor as close to the reef as your draft permits. Swimming in the crystal clear water is superb, and there is a great beach on the north shore of Green Island that shouldn't be missed. We found a good deal of dead coral along the reef up to Bird Island, but good snorkeling has been reported north of Bird especially in the area of SPITHEAD CHANNEL.

GUNKHOLING Nonsuch Bay offers wonderful opportunities to explore to your heart's content. The southern shore from Cork Point to AYERS CREEK is full of attractive nooks and crannies; the only unexpected danger to avoid is the 7-foot shoal off HUGHES BAY. Harmony Hall in BROWN'S BAY is an art gallery/restaurant/bar and a delightful place for lunch or light snacks (closed Mondays); the view from atop the old sugar mill is beautiful, and the art gallery and craft shop are impressive. At the extreme southwest end of Nonsuch Bay, AYERS CREEK is a secluded and protected anchorage with few signs of civilization to spoil the wonderful, wild atmosphere; you may have the anchorage all to yourself.

The western shore from Ayers Creek to GAYNIS COVE (a.k.a. Ledcoff Cove and Clover Leaf Bay) is a nice sail-or-motor-by stretch with vacation homes under

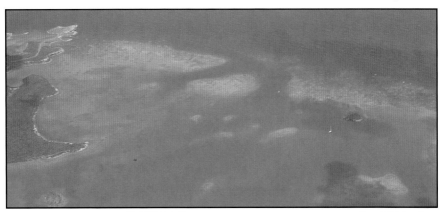

NONSUCH BAY - NORTHEAST PART   *Derek Little photo*

construction along the shore; the MUDDY BAY to GUARD POINT area is a nice place for a lunch stop especially when the wind is a bit north of east.

Alas poor GAYNIS COVE; we knew it well . . . Long regarded as the best hurricane hole in Antigua, it was utterly peaceful, quiet, and lovely. Now progress has dropped a VERY conspicuous pink palace on a hilltop to oversee development rumored to include such wonders as a marina, apartments, restaurants, cafes, and a luxury hotel. We liked it the way it was, but it will still be pretty nice . . . for a while.

RAT ISLAND and nearby reefs are good to explore with mask and fins, but don't hit the shallow reef to the west. There is ample water in mid-channel for most boats to pass between Rat Island and the mainland over to FLAT POINT.

The northeastern part of Nonsuch Bay, as shown in our photo, is out of this world. As you can see, many of the reefs and shoals are quite obvious in clear weather and good light. Gunkholing in SPITHEAD CHANNEL and the channel to the west from its midpoint can be great sport for adventuresome . . . and alert . . . reef pilots; the water is deep, and as mentioned, snorkeling there is reported to be very good. It is possible to anchor at the end of the western channel and take your dinghy to explore over to FANNY COVE and beyond.

The area close to the shore between Flat Cap Point and Fanny Cove is best for dinghies and very shallow draft boats. Although we found 9 feet of water within 100 to 200 yards of the shore, the entire area is full of uncharted coral heads and shoals that can spoil the fun. Local experts may be able to pick their way along without trouble, but dinghies are best for all the rest of us.

LEAVING Virtually everyone leaves Nonsuch Bay to the south between Cork Point and the western tip of Green Island. Those heading north may want to consider leaving through SPITHEAD CHANNEL; with good light, settled conditions, and a dependable engine you should have no problems but do not turn east until you are well past the reefs and shoal to starboard.

NE & N COASTS - GREEN ISLAND TO DIAMOND BANK

One look at the chart should convince all but the most experienced Antigua reef experts to stand well off to avoid the many dangers along the coast between Green

Opposite: NONSUCH BAY; *Derek Little photo*

Island and Diamond Bank. Hazards lie up to four miles of the coast; there are very few obvious landmarks, and there are no buoys marking the reefs. Passages in this area should be made only in settled conditions with good visibility and good light. Allow plenty time to reach your next anchorage while you can still see the underwater dangers.

The reefs and shoals marked by the old tower on DIAMOND BANK extend more than a half mile in an east-west direction with the tower about in the middle. Coming from the north you can pass on either side of Diamond Bank, but give it a wide berth.

NORTHERN COAST - BOON CHANNEL TO NORTH SOUND

BOON CHANNEL is a cruiser friendly passage that lies inside the series of offshore reefs stretching five miles from HORSESHOE REEF on the east to DIAMOND BANK on the west; it is the approach of choice to PARHAM SOUND and NORTH SOUND for everyone except seasoned local experts.

The reefs provide not only welcome protection from the open ocean so there is rarely any more than a modest chop inside but also some of the best snorkeling in Antigua. Tony Fincham of DOCKYARD DIVERS says snorkeling is especially good on Diamond Bank, Salt Fish Tail, and Horseshoe Reef, but obviously, settled conditions are essential.

Working to windward in the protected waters of Boon Channel in good light can be a joy. The passage is about a mile wide in most parts; BOON POINT with its prominent sugar mill and PRICKLY PEAR ISLAND at the eastern end are helpful landmarks. Keep a sharp eye out so you don't crunch into the offshore reefs and be especially careful to avoid the reefs surrounding Boon Point, those that fill most of HODGES BAY, and the extensive ones to the north, northwest, west, and south of Prickly Pear.

The best water around Prickly Pear is well off to the north, but there is a good 10 feet or more to the south between it and BEGGARS POINT. Small boats take vacationers to Prickly Pear for a day of beach work and snorkeling, so don't be surprised by the beach chairs and bodies on the beach and the swarms of people out on the reef. There is a flashing white light on Prickly Pear; it was working when last we passed by, but don't count on it.

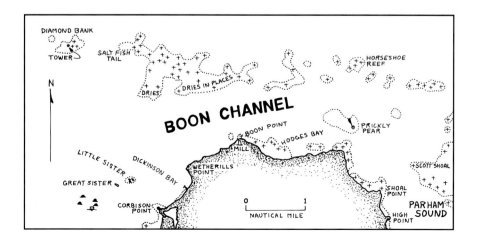

HORSESHOE REEF lies about a mile to the north of Prickly Pear on a bearing of approximately 25° Magnetic. There is a passage out to sea just east of Horseshoe, but we don't recommend it unless you have a competent local reef pilot on board and plenty of insurance.

PRICKLY PEAR TO CRABBS MARINA

A course of 150° Magnetic from Prickly Pear Island leads past all hazards down into PARHAM SOUND between the radio tower on HIGH POINT and the middle of LONG ISLAND. Proceed from there through the dredged channel west of MAIDEN ISLAND on to CRABBS MARINA. The channel has a least depth of 17 feet; its direction changes slightly off the middle of Maiden Island. The problem is that its markers have unusual, if not bizarre, colors and seem to disappear or change positions from time to time. Do not put too much faith in them. Proceed cautiously with an eye on your depth sounder, and you should have no trouble.

LONG ISLAND is home to the lovely (and expensive) Jumby Bay Resort that has attractive buildings with red tile roofs all over the island. The anchorage in JUMBY BAY itself is well protected and utterly beautiful with a long, long dazzling, palm fringed beach. A clear approach runs from just north of the yellow and black cardinal marker north of Maiden Island in towards the small pier in the southern part of the beach. The Bay is shallow with about 7 feet of water some 200 to 300 yards off the beach; the holding is good in sand. Facilities ashore are reserved for guests, but yachtsmen are welcome for luncheon or dinner; advance reservations are required, and gentlemen must wear long trousers and shirts; call Jumby Bay on VHF Ch 17.

Davis Bay on the south side of Long Island is a secure anchorage, but the workshops, generators, and other support facilities for the island are there making the surroundings noisy and less than attractive.

MAIDEN ISLAND is an uninhabited bird watching and shelling island with an anchorage off the southern end of the beach on the west side. Anchor well out of the channel in 8 feet of water, but you may bump on 6 or 7 foot spots on the way in.

CRABBS MARINA consists of a marina and a full service boat yard with a staff that can

LONG ISLAND   *Derek Little photo*

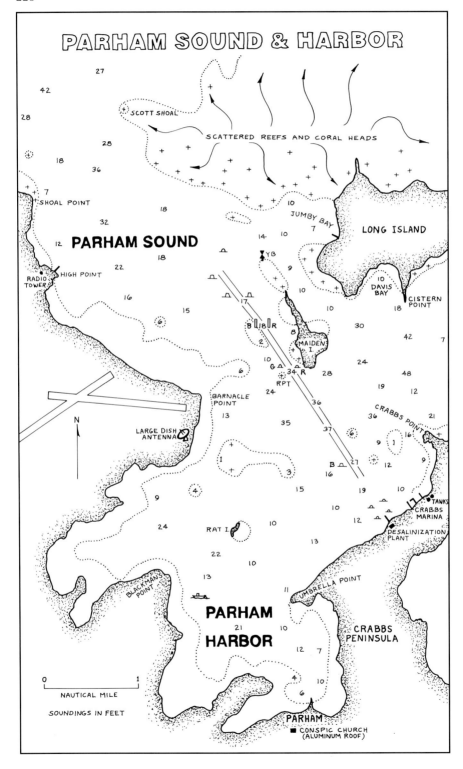

PARHAM SOUND & HARBOR

27

42

28

SCOTT SHOAL

28

SCATTERED REEFS AND CORAL HEADS

18

36

7
SHOAL POINT

18

JUMBY BAY

10

LONG ISLAND

32

PARHAM SOUND

14   10

7

12   HIGH POINT

18

RADIO
TOWER

22

16

DAVIS
BAY

CISTERN
POINT

15

17

9

10

18

6

10

30

42   7

B   B R

8

2

MAIDEN
I.

24

48

10

G

19   12

N

6

34 R

RPT

28

24

36

BARNACLE
POINT

13

35

37   6

CRABBS POINT

21

LARGE DISH
ANTENNA

36

9   16

1

27   12

9

B

1

3

16

9

15

19   10

4

10

10   TANKS
CRABBS
MARINA

9

12

DESALINIZATION
PLANT

24

RAT I.

10

13

22

10

13

BLACKMANS
POINT

11   UMBRELLA POINT

PARHAM

21

10

**CRABBS
PENINSULA**

HARBOR

12   7

0   1

4   10

NAUTICAL MILE

6

SOUNDINGS IN FEET

PARHAM
CONSPIC CHURCH
(ALUMINUM ROOF)

SUNDOWNER AND THE DISH *Eiman photo*

take care of any and all problems a boat may have; alternately, owners can arrange to do their own work. The atmosphere is friendly and informal, and many and many owners dry store their yachts there and/or have them Awlgripped. The facilities include a 50 ton lift, a fuel dock, modest commissary, chandlery, toilets and showers, taxi service, restaurant and bar, and a Customs and Immigration office. For heavy provisioning call helpful taximan Curtis Thomas on VHF Ch 68 or phone him at 463-2168 for a cab to ISLAND PROVISIONS nearby on Airport Road or DEW'S SUPER-MARKET and THE GRAPE ESCAPE in St. John's.

For expert information and advice on cruising around Antigua, talk to William Thomas, a veteran of the local charter business, who runs things in the bar and restaurant at Crabbs. He knows all the best gunkholes and all the worst pitfalls and problems; he will give you friendly, reliable, helpful information. William can also provide terrific Pina Coladas and wonderful seafood or West Indian meals at modest prices.

230

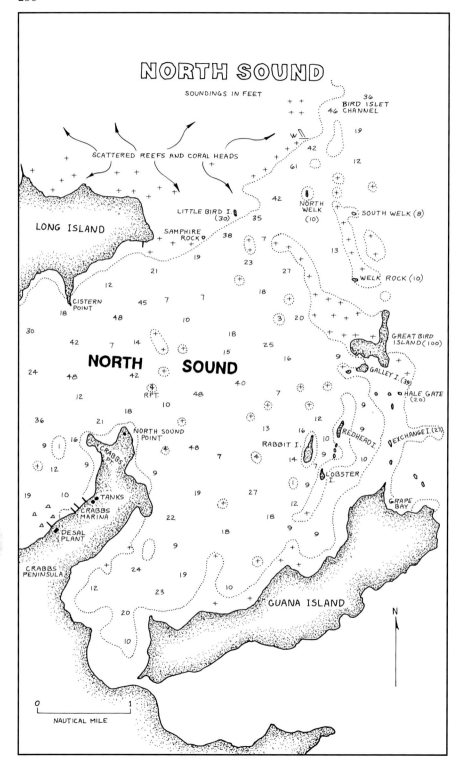

NORTH SOUND

SOUNDINGS IN FEET

BIRD ISLET CHANNEL   36
46
19
42
12
61

SCATTERED REEFS AND CORAL HEADS

42
NORTH WELK (10)
SOUTH WELK (8)
LITTLE BIRD I. (30)   35
LONG ISLAND
SAMPHIRE ROCK   38
13
WELK ROCK (10)
19
23
27
21
12
18
CISTERN POINT   45   7   7
3   20
18   48   10
30
42   7   14   18
GREAT BIRD ISLAND (100)
24   48   15   25   16   9   GALLEY I. (39)
42   40   HALE GATE (20)
4 RPT.   48   7   9
12   10   9
18
36   21   12   9
16   NORTH SOUND POINT   13   16   REDHEAD I.   EXCHANGE I. (27)
9   1   RABBIT I.   10   9
CRABBS PT.   48   7   4   14   10
12   9   LOBSTER I.   9
19   10   9   GRAPE BAY
TANKS   9   27   12
CRABBS MARINA   22   18
DESAL PLANT   18   9
9
CRABBS PENINSULA   24   19   10
12   23   GUANA ISLAND
20
10   N

NORTH SOUND

0   1
NAUTICAL MILE

PARHAM

Parham is a small, quiet village about two miles west and south from Crabbs Marina where a number of yachts are attracted either by the great protection of Crabbs Peninsula or by Mike Fiore's Parham Marine service. The town has a mini market, Jamy's Supermarket, in a brilliant lime green building overlooking the town square, and the modest Billows Court restaurant that features lobster, snapper, and other seafood for dinner.

The approach to Parham is down the coast from Crabbs Marina and around UMBRELLA POINT; it is dominated by views of the large dish antenna at the airport, a small freighter that seems permanently anchored . . . or stranded . . . south of BLACKMAN'S POINT, and the huge bright aluminum roof of a church in the town. Just next to Crabbs is a big industrial type building that houses Antigua's desalinization plant; it is of special interested because we understand that half or more of its daily output of fresh, potable water is dumped into the sea even though much of the island does not have enough water and has no water for days at a time during droughts!!!! The reason, we are told, is a mind-blower: The government has built only enough pipelines to distribute about half the water produced; fantastic!

After rounding Umbrella Point, stay well over to the east towards Crabbs Peninsula to avoid the 4 foot spot off the town. Anchor in close to the west of the town dock in 6 to 8 feet of water.

Parham Marine has a very impressive shop; it does all kinds of mechanical and refrigeration work and specializes in restoring lovely old yachts.

NORTH SOUND

NORTH SOUND is protected from the Atlantic Ocean by a string of reefs and islands along its eastern side that provide a wonderful array of opportunities to explore, snorkel, unwind, and enjoy nature at its very best. If you like getting away from it all and enjoy life without discos and jump ups, a few days in North Sound can be the high point of your cruise. Good light is necessary to help you spot the reefs and shoals.

The most popular and convenient anchorage is in the lee of GREAT BIRD ISLAND. From Long Island the course from CISTERN POINT direct to the western point of Great

GREAT BIRD ISLAND   *Derek Little photo*

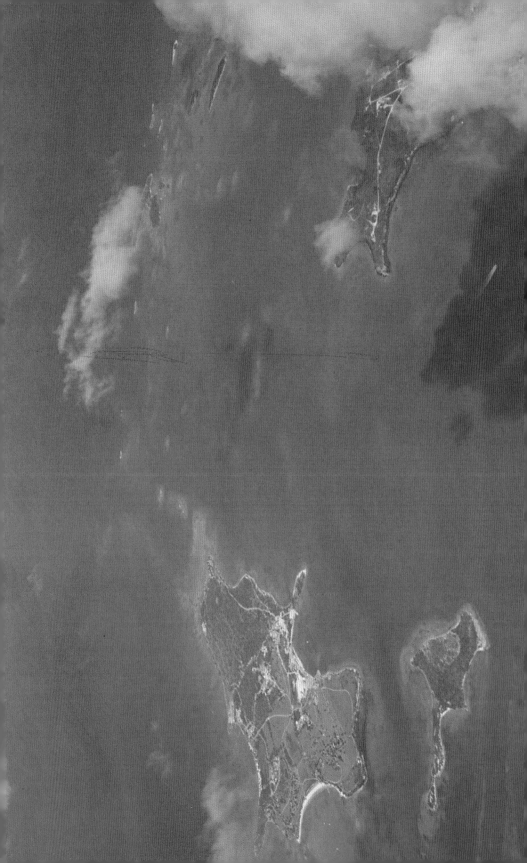

GREAT BIRD ISLAND TO GUANA ISLAND   *Derek Little photo*

Bird passes over one 10-foot spot just east of a large shoal on your starboard. From Crabbs Marina be sure to avoid the 1-foot shoal west of CRABBS POINT; there is good water in midchannel between the two. From NORTH SOUND POINT head directly for the western point of Great Bird; there is one 10-foot spot northeast of North Sound Point, but otherwise the water is good until you are close to Great Bird. We have found the reefs and shoals in the approaches to Great Bird to be very easy to see in good light, but proceed cautiously in case there are some that are not apparent.

Anchor between Great Bird and the two cays just south of its western point; there is 9 feet of water and good holding in the sandy bottom. There are two lovely beaches on Great Bird with good snorkeling on the adjacent reefs. A steep, rocky path leads to the top of the island where the view is breathtaking. It is best to enjoy Great Bird in the morning or late afternoon to avoid the day-trippers who often arrive at noon on big catamarans for lunch, a hike on the island, and snorkeling. They can turn the place into a circus, but fortunately, they depart in mid-afternoon, and peace and quiet return.

GUNKHOLING In settled conditions exploring the reefs and islands on the eastern end of North Sound is without equal this side of the Tobago Cays. You can leave your boat at Great Bird and cover the entire area in your dinghy, or you can motor part of the way, anchor, and go from there by dinghy. The opportunities and delights are endless.

To the north there is good water in the lee of the reefs that extend from Great Bird towards LITTLE BIRD ISLAND; you can anchor there quite happily. The water in BIRD ISLET CHANNEL to the northeast of Little Bird is quite deep, but only experienced eyeball navigators should venture beyond NORTH WELK because the area is full of coral patches and reefs.

To the south of Great Bird there is a wonderful, protected anchorage between REDHEAD ISLAND and RABBIT ISLAND that is very convenient to the reefs and cays shown in our aerial photo. In good light getting to the anchorage and back to Great Bird or Crabbs is not difficult. For even more splendid solitude leave Rabbit Island to starboard, proceed around the reefs and shoals extending to the southwest of LOBSTER ISLAND, and anchor between Lobster and GUANA ISLAND.

Opposite: NORTH SOUND; *Derek Little photo*

WEST COAST

Even the crabbiest olde salts rave about the sailing along this 10 mile stretch of coast between DICKINSON BAY and JOHNSON POINT because the water is generally flat, the breeze is usually great, and they can slide along with eased sheets nonchalantly dodging the rocks, reefs, shoals, and other hazards along the way. Looks great; feels great; is great!

Perhaps most stunning of all are the 10 miles of dazzling white beaches that still

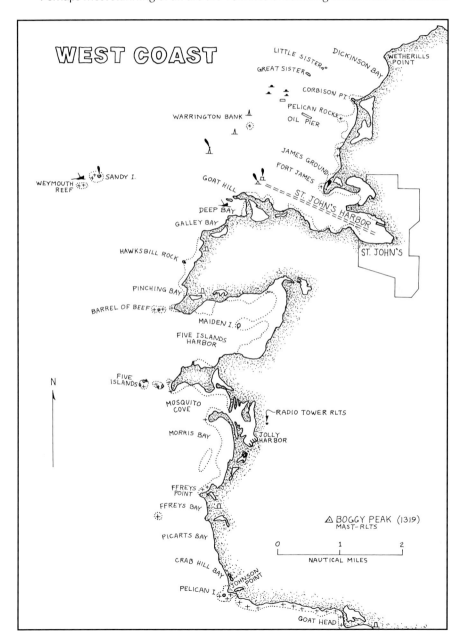

DICKINSON BAY *Derek Little photo*

seem unspoiled even though 30-odd hotels and condo complexes, 3 casinos, and countless restaurants, bars, boutiques, and T shirt vendors operate on or just behind the sand. Along some beaches there are few, if any, signs of 'civilization.'

The water off most of the west coast beaches and anchorages is 10 to 25 feet in depth, but within a few hundred yards of the coast 6 to 10 feet are encountered quite frequently; check your depth sounder continuously or proceed cautiously when you are in close. All the numerous obstructions and hazards are shown on the government and Imray charts, and WARRINGTON BANK and SANDY ISLAND are actually marked. One important danger that is unmarked is the isolated 3 foot shoal/reef about one mile off the point between FFREYS BAY and PICARTS BAY and the nearby sugar mill; we understand a local Coast Guard vessel crashed into it recently, so strangers should be extremely careful when sailing near it.

All anchorages on the west coast, except those in ST. JOHN'S, DEEP BAY, the northern part of FIVE ISLANDS HARBOR, and MOSQUITO COVE are rolly to uncomfortable when occasional northern swells roll in during the winter months.

DICKINSON BAY is known locally as the site of some of the most spirited and fun-filled public parties during Antigua Race Week and has the greatest concentration of beachfront hotels, bars, restaurants, etc. on the island. If you lust for night life, this is the place for you.

The approaches to Dickinson Bay are straightforward, but yachts from the south that are not happy in 10 feet of water are advised to leave GREAT SISTER and LITTLE SISTER to starboard before heading into the shallow Bay. The preferred anchorage is a bit north of the beach under the high ground on WETHERILLS POINT, but even that is very rolly in northern swells.

Halcon Cove Hotel is probably the major operation ashore; its Warrie Pier is a restaurant by day and a watering hole with entertainment by night, and its Clouds restaurant up on the high ground features a cuisine and sunsets that are impressive; and for the high rollers its casino is close at hand.

Millers at Shorty's beachfront bar and restaurant is a lively, entertaining spot that is popular with landlubbers and sailors alike. The choices beyond that include Coconut Grove, The Satay Hut, Spinnakers, Buccaneer Cove, The Lobster Pot, etc.;let your eyes and ears be your guides, and don't call me before ten!

DICKINSON BAY TO ST. JOHNS Beautiful stretches of beach with much less activity than in Dickinson Bay. A nice area for a lunch stop with good snorkeling around PELICAN ROCKS, but anchor well off as there is only 8 to 9 feet of water 200 yards or more off the shore.

ST. JOHNS

St. Johns is the capital of Antigua, the largest town on the island, an official Port of Entry, the center for cruise ships and duty free shops, and a great place for serious provisioning. Yachtsmen who scoffed a few years ago at the thought of calling in St. Johns are having second thoughts now because of recent improvements in the harbor and the town.

ENTERING Most yachts from the north should enter the dredged channel off GOAT HILL to avoid the shallow water in JAMES GROUND, but those coming from the south can round Goat Hill and proceed into the channel at their leisure as the water south of the channel has a least depth of 15 feet well up into the harbor. The channel to the harbor was dredged to 35 feet years ago; we found a few spots west of the Customs dock where the depth was only 30 feet. Off the end of the cruise ship dock we found 24 feet, and towards the new marina at Redcliffe Quay there is 12 feet. The bottom up in the inner harbor is muddy, and the water is murky.

REGULATIONS All clearance and port formalities can be handled at Customs and Immigration behind the first pier to port as you enter. The office is open 8:00 A.M. to Noon and from 1:00 P.M. to 4:00 P.M. weekdays but closes at 3:00 P.M. on Fridays. St. John's is really not set up to clear yachts in and out, but it can be done. The Customs dock is normally full of commercial shipping, but there is a pier to the west where is possible to scramble ashore. Be sure to display your yellow Q flag.

ANCHORING/DOCKING The most convenient and protected anchorage is up in the inner harbor just off the town, but you can also anchor between Customs and Fort James or in BALLAST BAY. The marina at Redcliffe Quay is to be in operation by December, 1992 with slips, water, fuel, ice, etc. and promises to be a great addition.

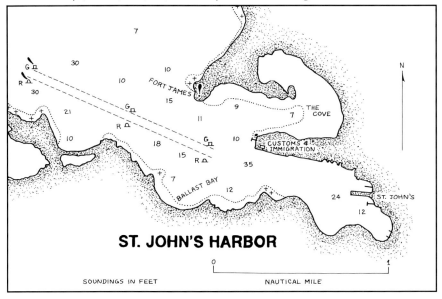

ST. JOHN'S HARBOR

SOUNDINGS IN FEET   NAUTICAL MILE

Welcome Aboard

English Harbour Rum

Distilled, blended and bottled by The Antigua Distillery Ltd. St. Johns, Antigua, West Indies

238

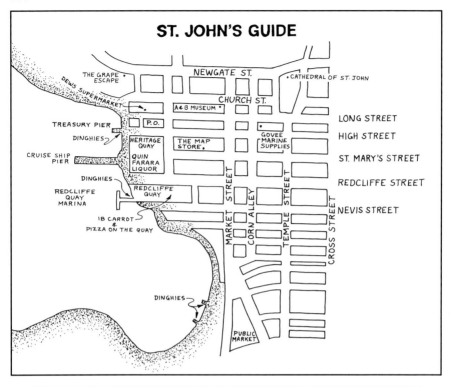

ST. JOHN'S GUIDE

NEWGATE ST.

THE GRAPE ESCAPE

DEWS SUPERMARKET

CATHEDRAL OF ST. JOHN

CHURCH ST.

A & B MUSEUM

TREASURY PIER

P.O.

DINGHIES

CRUISE SHIP PIER

HERITAGE QUAY

THE MAP STORE

QUIN FARARA LIQUOR

GOVEE MARINE SUPPLIES

DINGHIES

REDCLIFFE QUAY MARINA

REDCLIFFE QUAY

IB CARROT & PIZZA ON THE QUAY

DINGHIES

PUBLIC MARKET

LONG STREET

HIGH STREET

ST. MARY'S STREET

REDCLIFFE STREET

NEVIS STREET

MARKET STREET

CORN ALLEY

TEMPLE STREET

CROSS STREET

ENTERING ST. JOHN'S HARBOR *Eiman photo*

ASHORE The Public Market towards the south end of town is a good place for vegetables, fruit and local products like clay charcoal burners and pots, etc. DEW'S SUPERMARKET on Long Street is one of the oldest and best places for serious provisioning on the island; it has virtually everything you might want including liquor. QUIN FARARA LIQUOR STORE in Heritage Quay has a very extensive selection of liquor including ENGLISH HARBOR ANTIGUA RUM, and THE GRAPE ESCAPE on lower Newgate Street has an outstanding cellar of excellent wines from around the world. If you want wine AND roses, be sure to visit THE FLOWER BASKET on Nevis Street for lovely blooms and blossoms for your main salon. GOVEES MARINE SUPPLIES on High Street has a good stock of chandlery items including ropes, chain, hardware, paints, and varnish, etc. The Map Shop on St. Mary's Street stocks a full selection of Caribbean charts, including British Admiralty charts, and cruising guides.

Two major shopping complexes vie for visitors' dollars: Heritage Quay at the cruise ship pier is very contemporary, while Redcliffe Quay nearby on the site of a former slave compound is a charming restoration of many lovely, old buildings. Both are chock full of duty free shops and restaurants; if you like to shop until you drop, you will definitely enjoy the Quays.

When you do drop or want to catch your breath and cool off a bit, visit the 18 Carrot or Pizza on The Quay for a relaxed light lunch and a rum cooler in pleasant

240

DEEP BAY   *Derek Little photo*

surroundings. We have not tried Hemingway's 2nd floor restaurant, but it is a very popular luncheon spot.

The Museum of Antigua and Barbuda in the lovely, old Court House at Long and Market Streets presents a fascinating view of Antigua's history that has an interactive computerized history quiz, artifacts of all types, and exhibits of the island's culture and architecture. Desmond Nicholson has been one of the moving figures behind this gem. The Cathedral of St. John the Divine is the most impressive and most beautiful building in town; the history revealed in the brass plaques inside and the tombstones is most interesting.

ST. JOHN'S TO MOSQUITO COVE/JOLLY HARBOR

DEEP BAY has been a favorite for decades; it is a lovely, cool anchorage that is protected even when northern swells are rolling about. The wreck of the three-masted barque Andes lies at the entrance just north of mid-channel; it is marked with a buoy and breaks the water in several spots. You can go around either side; there is 15 feet of water or more the south of the wreck and at lest 9 feet to the north. Anchor off the northern end of the beautiful beach for the greatest peace and quiet; the depth is about 10 feet some 200 yards off, and the holding is good.

Snorkeling on the Andes is top notch; the eerie hull is clearly visible, and reef fish are plentiful and colorful. For beautiful views above the sea hike up 170 feet to Fort Barrington on the north side of the anchorage via a path that starts behind the beach or enjoy great sunsets, cocktails, dining and dancing at Jaws, a new restaurant up the hill behind the Ramada Renaissance Royal Antiguan Resort . . . the modern high rise hotel tucked unobtrusively behind the southern end of the beach. The Ramada has three restaurants for your dining pleasure . . . Andes, Lagoon Cafe, and Chinese.

Coasting from **DEEP BAY TO FIVE ISLANDS HARBOR** is a pure delight . . . sliding along in beautiful, protected water past one sparkling beach after another with opportunities for lunch stops anywhere your draft will permit. Stay off a few hundred yards, and be sure to pass outside HAWKSBILL ROCK; if you do head into the beach, proceed cautiously to avoid occasional coral and rock along the shore. Tony Fincham of DOCKYARD DIVERS says the snorkeling around SANDY ISLAND and WEYMOUTH REEF is excellent; it would be a super side trip in settled weather, but approach with care because the charts cannot show all the coral in close. Just north of Five Islands Harbor PINCHING BAY is especially inviting with its long sweep of deserted beach under the watchful eye of an old sugar mill.

BARREL OF BEEF (PELICAN ISLAND on some charts) off the point at the northern end of Five Islands Harbor has reefs extending out 100 yards or so on both its east and west sides, and there is a reef coming out from the point. It is possible to pass inside Barrel of Beef in mid-channel between the reefs where there is 11 feet of water; just to the north of this narrow passage there is 9 feet of water. It is more prudent for most to pass west around Barrel of Beef giving is a berth of 300 yards or more.

FIVE ISLANDS HARBOR

Five Islands Harbor could also be called Five Beaches Harbor or Five Hills Harbor or Splendid Solitude Harbor; each is equally appropriate, and you can enjoy them all. There are just a few houses on the surrounding hills; the most obvious inhabitants are the herons, egrets, terns, doves, and pelicans that can be seen from time to time on or around MAIDEN ISLAND. For beautiful, unspoiled, natural surroundings, Five Islands Harbor is hard to beat. The beaches are lovely, and there isn't a T-shirt stand or jewelry salesman in sight!

Be careful of Barrel of Beef if approaching from the north (see comments just above) and of FIVE ISLANDS if coming from the south. In good light both the inner

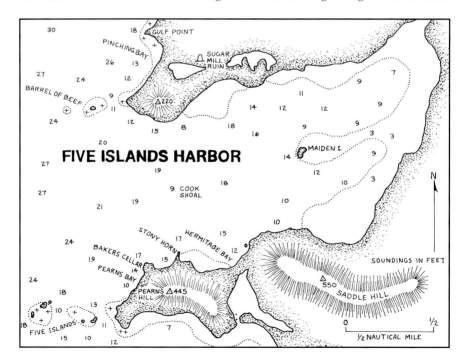

FIVE ISLANDS HARBOR *Derek Little photo*

(eastern) and outer (western) passages at Five Islands can accommodate yachts requiring under 10 feet of water; stay in the middle of the good water and keep a sharp eye out for the reefs on all sides. The outer (western) passage the better of the two, but the best of all is sailing westaround all Five Islands giving them a good berth.

The Imray chart shows an obstruction/danger on a line between the points on either side of Five Islands Harbor. We have not been able to find it, but it may be there. We did find the isolated 9 foot spot known as COOKS SHOAL further in. Generally, bottom shoals gradually to the eastern shore, and there are shallow areas as indicated on our sketch chart. Take care when poking into the shallows; the water is a bit murky, so you'll have to rely on your depth sounder.

Although you can anchor anywhere your draft will permit, most people anchor in the lee of Maiden Island in 14 feet of water; the area further east can be buggy at times. The anchorages in HERMITAGE BAY and between STONY HORN and BAKERS CELLAR are terrific for lunch stops in settled conditions but iffy for overnight because northern swells can make them quite uncomfortable or worse.

MOSQUITO COVE/JOLLY HARBOR/MORRIS BAY

Mosquito Cove provides shoal draft yachts with a pleasant and spectacular anchorage where the water is peaceful even when occasional northern swells come along and where the mosquitoes are not a problem. An additional plus is its proximity to the quiet pleasures of Five Islands Harbor and the bright lights and action of the Jolly Beach Hotel in MORRIS BAY.

The situation has changed dramatically with the development of JOLLY HARBOR in what used to be salt ponds at the head of the Cove. Jolly Harbor, described as the largest marine oriented development in the Eastern Caribbean, is an ambitious expansion of the Jolly Beach operation that will ultimately include 1,500 waterfront condominiums, two shopping centers, a 150 slip marina, a full service boatyard, a golf course, squash and tennis courts, and swimming pools on its 500 acre site. Great care has been devoted to creating a small town atmosphere by developing a number of villages throughout the Harbor.

JOLLY HARBOR BEFORE COMPLETION

APPROACHING/ENTERING Yachts approaching directly from the west should note the IRISH BANK has depths of 9 to 10 feet some two miles off Jolly Harbor. Those coming down the coast from the north must avoid Barrel of Beef and Five Islands as indicated above. Anyone approaching along the coast from the south should take special care to avoid at all costs the 3 foot shoal (as yet unmarked) that lies about one mile to the west of the point that separates FFREYS BAY and PICARTS BAY; it is a real hazard. The radio tower behind Jolly harbor is an excellent land mark.

The water in MORRIS BAY and in Mosquito Cove is relatively shallow, so proceed cautiously as you approach the dredged channel into Jolly Harbor. The channel is well marked (red-right-returning) and has a least depth of 13 feet reported in June, 1992 all the way into the marina at the southern extremity of Jolly Harbor.

REGULATIONS If you have to clear in or out of Antigua and are coming from or proceeding to the west, Jolly Harbor is the most convenient place to handle the formalities. The Customs and Immigration office at the marina are to open in

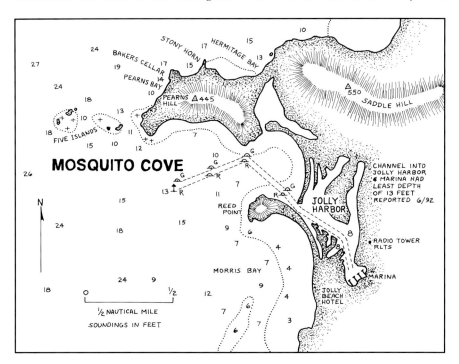

MORRIS BAY & JOLLY HARBOR BEFORE COMPLETION *Derek Little photo*

December, 1992; presumably hours will be weekdays from 8:00 A.M. to Noon and 1:00 P.M. to 5:00 P.M. at a minimum.

ANCHORING/DOCKING The shallow water forces most yachts to anchor quite far off in Morris Bay, but it is possible to get in a bit closer in Mosquito Cove where there is the best protection from the once-in-a-while northern swells. In Mosquito Cove it is not considered cricket to anchor in the channel into Jolly Harbor, and anchoring inside Jolly Harbor proper is not permitted.

Jolly Harbor Marina will have 150 slips that will accommodate yachts up to 200' in length; most are equipped with electricity, water, TV and telephone service. Nearby

are a boatyard with 70 ton lift and mechanical and woodworking shops, a chandlery, showers, and laundry and dry cleaning services. Yacht repairs and support services are available from firms in English Harbor/Falmouth for the '92-'93 season; after that many are expected to be on site in Jolly Harbor.

ASHORE The facilities of Jolly Harbor and Jolly Beach Hotel run the gamut from a casino and a discotheque to a variety of bars and restaurants and selection of boutiques and shops. The marina shopping complex alone will have some 35 shops including The Harbor Supermarket & Deli, THE FLOWER BASKET, and QUIN FARARAS LIQUOR STORE.

The management is intent on making Jolly Harbor a major yachting center where residents and visitors alike will be able to pursue their interests and appetites in convenient, attractive surroundings; they are off to a good start.

MORRIS BAY TO JOHNSON POINT

The coast from FFREY'S POINT to JOHNSON POINT has three spectacular beaches separated by two headlands; the water is crystal clear, and 10 feet can be carried quite close in without problems. The only hazard is the dangerous, unmarked 3 foot spot about a mile off the point between Ffrey's Bay and Picarts Bay. There are no buildings on the beach at Ffreys Bay and only one modest bar/restaurant in Picarts Bay. Crab Hill Village and two small hotels are just behind the beach in Crab Hill Bay.

This is an altogether delightful stretch of coast that is perfect for a lunch stop in good conditions. Few yachts anchor here overnight presumably because it is exposed, and northern swells could be troublesome. But when there are no swells running, overnighting could be wonderful in normal trade wind conditions.

SOUTHERN COAST - JOHNSON POINT
TO FALMOUTH/ENGLISH HARBOR

Falmouth and English Harbor lie some seven miles to windward of JOHNSON POINT; the coast in between has a good deal of shore coral and rocks, but 300 yards off will clear all except for GRANDY ROCK in RENDEZVOUS BAY. There are some fish/lobster trap buoys along the coast that you will want to dodge if you are motoring. The major hazards are CADE REEF and MIDDLE REEF that are 1/2 to 1 mile offshore between JOHNSON POINT and GOAT HEAD. Cade Reef is easy to see; the sea breaks on it, and it currently includes a number of small islands that are about 5 feet above the

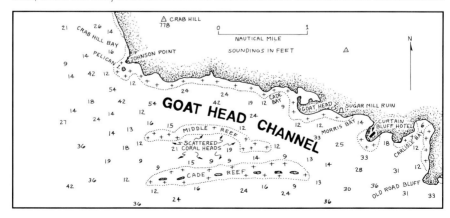

water. Middle Reef is more difficult to spot even when visibility is good because it does not break the surface and normally doesn't make waves. And, of course, neither is marked! SCUBA divers and snorkelers do anchor in between the two in settled weather; if you try it, proceed carefully to avoid the scattered coral heads.

GOAT HEAD CHANNEL is wide enough for tacking, but take special care not to crash into Middle Reef. The deep Channel is well protected by Cade Reef and has a number of possible anchorages that include CADE BAY, MORRIS BAY, and CARLISLE BAY. They are all inclined to be rolly at times, and hotels surround the latter two. The conspicuous Curtain Bluff Hotel has been regarded as one of Antigua's finest for many years; visiting yachtsmen are welcome at luncheon and dinner; gentlemen must wear jackets and ties at dinner; reservations are advised. Participants in Antigua Race Week rave about the impressive parties put on for them by Curtain Bluff Hotel.

ANTIGUA MARINE DIRECTORY

		Telephone
BOATYARDS		
Antigua Slipway	Dockyard	460-1056
Crabbs Marine	Parham	463-2113
Jolly Harbor	Mosquito Cove	462-7595
CHANDLERIES		
Antigua Slipway	Dockyard	460-1056
Carib Marine	Dockyard	460-1521
Gomees	St. John's	462-1224
Jolly Harbor	Mosquito Cove	462-7595
The Chandlery	Falmouth	460-1227
CRUISING GUIDES & CHARTS		
Carib Marine	Dockyard	460-1521
Nicholson Caribbean Yacht Sales	Dockyard	463-1093
The Map Shop	St. John's	462-3993

GOAT HEAD CHANNEL   *Derek Little photo*

ELECTRICAL SUPPLIES & REPAIRS

Marionics	Falmouth	460-1780
Pumps & Power	Falmouth	463-1242
Signal Locker	Dockyard	460-1528
Windward Engineering	Falmouth	469-1791

ELECTRONIC EQUIPMENT & REPAIRS

Electromarine	English Harbor	460-1246
Marionics	Falmouth	460-1780
Signal Locker	Dockyard	460-1528

MACHINE SHOPS/METAL FABRICATING

Antigua Slipway	Dockyard	463-1056
Marine Power Services	Falmouth	460-1851
Pumps & Power	English Harbor	463-1242

MARINAS

Antigua Yacht Club Marina	Falmouth Harbor	460-1444
Catamaran Club	Falmouth Harbor	460-1503
Crabbs Marina	Parham	463-2113
Jolly Harbor	Mosquito Cove	462-7595
Nelson's Dockyard		
Redcliffe Quay	St. John's	462-1847
St. James Club	Mamora Bay	460-1430

MARINE ENGINES & REPAIRS

Antigua Slipway	Dockyard	463-1056
Marine Power Services	Falmouth	460-1851
Pumps & Power	English Harbor	463-1242
Seagull Services	Falmouth	460-3050
Windward Engineers	Falmouth	460-1791

OUTBOARD ENGINE SALES/SERVICE

C.P.R. Equipment Sales	St. John's	462-3345
Island Motors	St. John's	462-2199
Northcoast Marine	St. John's	463-3169
Pumps & Power	English Harbor	463-1242
Seagull Services	Falmouth	460-3050
Windward Engineering	Falmouth	460-1791

PROVISIONS

Bailey's Supermarket	Falmouth	460-1142
Carib Marine	English Harbor	460-1521
Dew's Supermarket	St. John's	462-1210
Dockyard Bakery	Dockyard	460-1474
Island Provisions	Airport Road	460-4289
Malone's Food Store	English Harbor	460-1570

RIGGING

Tend A Loft Rigging	Dockyard	460-1151

SAILS/SAIL REPAIR

A & F Sails	Dockyard	460-1522
Antigua Sails	Dockyard	460-1527
Nicholson's Caribbean Yacht Sales	Dockyard	463-1524

TRAVEL AGENCIES/COMMUNICATION SERVICES

Jet Set Travel	Dockyard	460-1722
Nicholson's Travel Agency	Dockyard	460-1530

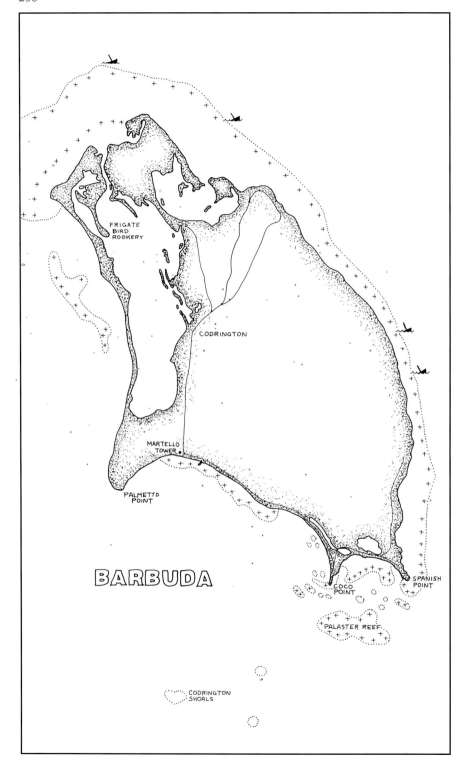

FRIGATE
BIRD
ROOKERY

CODRINGTON

MARTELLO
TOWER

PALMETTO
POINT

BARBUDA

COCO
POINT

SPANISH
POINT

PALASTER REEF

CODRINGTON
SHOALS

BARBUDA

CHARTS: U.S. DMA 25550, 25570, 25608

British 245, 955

Imray Iolaire A3, A26

Barbuda lies 23 (nautical) miles north of Antigua but in many ways is in a different world; the commercialism and tourism that dominate Antigua are unknown in Barbuda which has the honor of being the least developed major island between Puerto Rico and Trinidad. The friendly and self reliant Barbudians, who eeek out their existence largely by fishing, lobstering, subsistence farming, and occasional construction work, like their island the way it is and most resist plans and schemes that threaten their traditional way of life. There are no casinos, no 100-room hotels, no duty free shops, and no discos on Barbuda but lots of peace and quiet in glorious, unspoiled surroundings. The island is flat as the proverbial pancake; its highest point is a mere 147 feet above the sea.

Barbuda is paradise for explorers, nature lovers, and all who enjoy getting off the beaten track. Its miles and miles of fabulous beaches are virtually deserted for days on end; snorkeling off its south coast is mind boggling; and its extensive frigate bird rookery at the northwest point is truly remarkable.

The island was first settled in 1638 by colonists from St. Kitts. Under a grant from King William III in 1690, General Codrington and his family ran the island as a fief for over two centuries; for much of the time slaves were bred there for the market and for the Codrington sugar estates in Antigua. In addition, the Cordringtons stocked the island with deer and other game and used it as a hunting preserve.

When Antigua gained independence in 1983, the English required reluctant Barbuda to join Antigua much the way they forced Anguilla under the control of St. Kitts. Barbudians face constant battles with the government in Antigua to protect their island and their interests, but with their independent nature, they seem to be doing a pretty fair job of it.

Barbuda is surrounded by shoals and dangerous reefs that are not charted in detail or with great accuracy. Cruising there requires experience, expertise in piloting and eyeball navigation, and self reliance; it is not for neophytes. It is best to visit in the spring or later when the possibility of northern swells is minimal and then only in settled conditions with good visibility.

APPROACHING You must obtain a Cruising Permit in Antigua before sailing to Barbuda. The best and safest approach is from Diamond Bank towards PALMETTO POINT; this route clears all offshore hazards between Antigua and Barbuda. Your first sight of Barbuda will be the white buildings of Coco Point Lodge and the adjacent K Club. Huge piles of sand at BOAT HARBOR, the old Martello Tower, and the small hotels and water tower on Palmetto Point will be visible next. Continue on towards Palmetto Point until Coco Point Lodge bears 100° magnetic or more to clear CODRINGTON SHOALS to the west; at that point alter your course, as necessary, for the anchorage you have selected.

From the east coast of Antigua the most direct route is to SPANISH POINT. Check your position as you go and stay east of the rhumb line; the current tends to set you to the west. The white buildings of Coco Point Lodge will be your first sight of Barbuda. Continue on standing east of Spanish Point; when Coco Point Lodge bears about 298° magnetic, turn towards it and continue on cautiously with the breaking reef extending

SPANISH POINT   *Derek Little photo*

south from Spanish Point close aboard to starboard. Follow the reef around to starboard and anchor in 8 to 10 feet behind Spanish Point. We do not recommend this approach for first timers.

If you sail from the east coast of Antigua and elect to take the western approach to Barbuda, it is best to work over to the west soon after clearing Antigua and the reefs north of it to take advantage of the deeper water and to avoid the shoals and banks south of Barbuda and the rough water they can kick up.

Be sure to plan your passage so you will arrive in Barbuda when there is still plenty

COCO POINT   *Derek Little photo*

of good light for eyeball navigation. You will definitely need it when approaching your anchorage. If you sail to Spanish Point, you should arrive by mid day; the afternoon sun can blind you as you head west around the reefs that extend to the south of Spanish Point.

SOUTH COAST

The south coast of Barbuda between COCO POINT and SPANISH POINT is very popular not only because it is most convenient to Antigua and has the best anchorages but also because it has outstanding snorkeling. The Customs and Immigration office is at Boat Harbor in the western part of the coast.

We must say again that the charts of Barbuda should not be relied upon for accuracy or detail. To cruise safely around Barbuda you have to rely on eyeball navigation; you must, for example, be able to distinguish between a dark spot on the water caused by a cloud, a grassy spot with ten feet of water over it, and coral with only six feet of water on it. In good light you should be able to stay out of trouble if you can read the reefs and if you proceed with care.

SPANISH POINT The anchorage just west of Spanish Point is open to the southwest but otherwise is protected by the island and coral reefs. There is 10 feet of water in the entrance and inside as well; holding is good in sand and grass.

The approach from the east is described above. From the west once around Coco Point we motored across GRAVENOR BAY on line between Coco Point and Spanish Point (about 100° magnetic) and had no trouble dodging the obvious isolated coral patches until we were more than half way to Spanish Point. After that we had to swing slightly to the south to go around a series of reefs to port before heading up into the anchorage. No sweat.

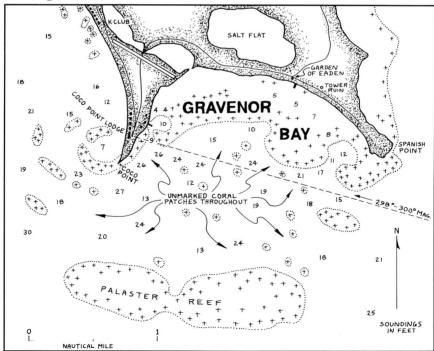

There is a nice little beach with a palm frond umbrella on Spanish Point where you can land to look around; there is a sign for GARDEN OF EADEN DEVELOPMENT COMPANY (watersports, land tours, etc.). A short walk across Spanish Point reveals a breathtaking view up the east coast where a few of the 100+ wrecks Barbuda has claimed can still be seen in the wild surf. The road/path behind the beach leads around to Garden of Eaden and to a road/path up the east coast that provides plenty of opportunity to explore the shore.

Garden of Eaden is George Jeffrey's watersports/tour/fish and lobster operation catering to yachtsmen; it is located near the old dock about half way along the beach in Gravenor Bay a short dinghy ride from Spanish Point; try contacting via VHF Ch 68 before 9:00 A.M. or after 1:30 P.M. George is THE answer to major problems that have plagued visiting sailors for years: Transportation to Codrington and an outboard and guide for the trip to the fantastic frigate bird rookery. He is eager to help and makes it all easy.

The snorkeling behind the reefs in Gravenor Bay is varied and colorful with all sorts of interesting fish and coral. Leave your boat behind Spanish Point and explore the whole area in your dinghy. Nearby PALASTER REEF offers endless opportunities for snorkeling; it is National Park where fishing and spear fishing are prohibited. There are openings in the coral there where a yacht can anchor safely; in calm conditions it is possible to buzz out in your dinghy. Better still, have George Jeffrey take you out and guide you to the best spots.

COCO POINT is owned by Coco Point Lodge that has operated its small, expensive, and very private hotel there for thirty years; it seems politely paranoid about protecting the privacy of its international clientele during the season from mid-November through April. Visiting yachtsmen are not welcome at Coco Point Lodge and cannot use its facilities; the Lodge discourages yachts from anchoring off its buildings when guests are in residence.

There is a small, well-protected anchorage on the east side of Coco Point just east of the Lodge dock. Approach cautiously from Spanish Point or around Coco Point by eyeballing your way through the reefs and coral in good light. You will find 11 feet of water in the narrow entrance between reefs and in the anchorage itself where there is room for a only a few boats. You have easy access to the wonderful snorkeling behind the reefs, but you will definitely be discouraged from landing on the Lodge property.

The popular anchorage off the west coast of Coco Point north of the Lodge buildings is protected and calm except when northern/western swells roll in during the winter making it uncomfortable to untenable. The water off the spectacular beach is beautifully clear, and the area is relatively free of coral north of the Lodge for about half a mile. Further north off the new K Club there are numerous patches of coral that must be avoided; a few buoys have marked a passage through the reefs, but they may not be there when you arrive.

The K Club is also a seasonal operation and is reported to be the most expensive hotel in the Caribbean. Call on VHF Ch 10 to arrange for luncheon or dinner; haute cuisine and prices to match. You may be able to call a taxi from K Club for a visit to town and the frigate bird rookery.

BOAT HARBOR is a scruffy little rolly basin to the west near the old Martello Tower where huge piles of sand await shipment abroad. There is a Customs office where yachts leaving Antigua/Barbuda can clear out. The channel is marked with a few buoys, and the depth inside to reported to be about 8 feet.

WEST COAST

Most of the water within two miles of the west coast of Barbuda is less than 25 feet deep; when swells from the North Atlantic reach these shoals, they can build up to dangerous heights before breaking with tremendous force. Thus, yachts should avoid this entire area in winter when northern swells are most likely to come in. The time to enjoy cruising along the spectacular 9 mile, deserted beach and the snorkeling on TUSON REEF and the reefs north of it is in April and later when conditions are more settled. Even then be very careful; the water is often murky, and charts cannot be counted on to identify every reef and coral head precisely.

In the past old hands used to visit Codrington by anchoring off the west coast at the southern end of the Lagoon, dragging their dinghies over the sand, and rowing into town! Today it is much simpler to get a cab and ride in.

The construction company that built the luxurious K Club has its own more modest, attractive, and reasonable Palmetto Hotel on PALMETTO POINT; its square water tower is easy to spot. Yachtsmen are welcome at its restaurants and bar, and Management advises they will help get cabs.

CODRINGTON

Codrington is a small, peaceful, sunbaked village of modest houses and shops. It has a Post Office and a Cable and Wireless office and is the site of Barbuda's commercial airport. Tucked in among the narrow, winding streets are a few markets that stock canned good, groceries, meat, poultry, and sodas; liquor can be purchased at a combination bar/liquor store. The bakery has wonderful fresh bread, rolls, and a few pastries. Lobster, fish, and fresh local vegetables are available sometimes; you just have to ask around. Fresh lobsters are most readily available when the fishermen collect them at the town pier for sale in the commercial market.

Codrington is the place to engage boat and a guide to the fabulous rookery where the sky is filled with thousands of frigate birds and acres of bushes are covered with their nests. A visit is an incredible experience, especially in the spring when the young are still in their nests, and the parents fly in again and again to feed them.

PALMETTO POINT & WEST COAST *Derek Little photo*

BLEAR EYE *Priacanthus arenatus*

E̲II̲R

ANGUILLA 5c

E̲II̲R Anguilla

Sterna dougalli
ROSEATE TERN $1·35

NEVIS

Bougainvillea 30c

GRUNT *Haemulon sciurus* 25c

E̲II̲R

ANGUILLA

E̲II̲R Anguilla

Pelecanus occidentalis
BROWN PELICAN 5c

NEVIS

Yellow Bell 5c

RED HIND *Epinephelus guttatus*

E̲II̲R

ANGUILLA 35c

E̲II̲R Anguilla

Zenaida macroura
TURTLE DOVE 10c

NEVIS

Coral Hibiscus $5

1796-1797 30c

BATTALION COMPANY OFFICER 45TH REGT OF FOOT

ST. KITTS

1790 55c

BATTALION COMPANY OFFICER 9TH REGT OF FOOT

ST. KITTS

125c

INFROU

NEDERLANDSE
ANTILLEN

Hawk-wing Conch 15c

NEVIS

NEVIS

Blue Petrea $3

ST KITTS

Lesser Antillean
Bullfinch $1

ST KITTS

Yellow-
crowned
Night-Heron 10c

ANTIGUA BARBUDA

SILVER SPOT *Dione Juno*
20c

ANTIGUA BARBUDA

PYGMY SK PIPER *Oarisma Nanus*
$10

ANTIGUA BARBUDA

ORBED SULPHUR *Aphrissa Orbis*
50c

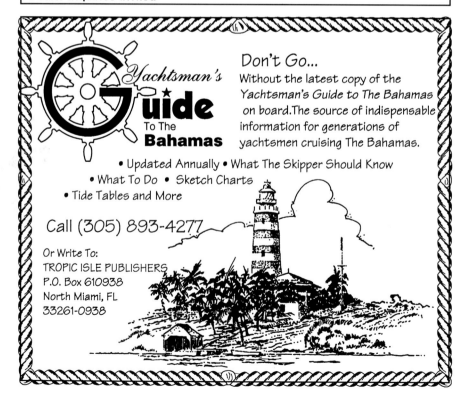

Index of Advertisers

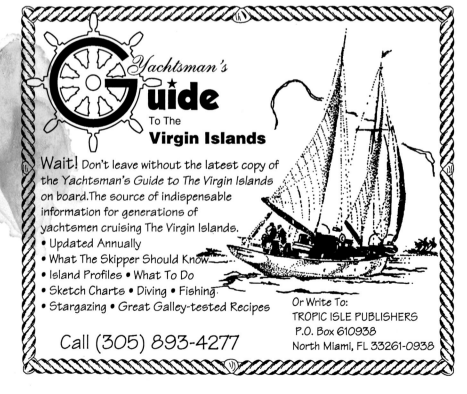